THE SHREWSBURY TO CREWE LINE

A Detailed History

by

Bob Yate

Copyright Book Law Publications. — First published in the United Kingdom in 2014.

ISBN 978-1-909625-33-4

ACKNOWLEDGEMENTS

Primary documentation has been accessed at the following locations:

National Archives, Kew - Rail 410/292, 294, 295, 303, 304, 305, 306, 349, 814, 816. MT6

House of Lords Record Office – Parliamentary Acts

National Railway Museum, York – Working Timetables

Shropshire Archives, Shrewsbury – Shrewsbury Chronicle, OS maps and archive plans

Cheshire Archives, Chester - Chester Chronicle, Chester Courant, OS maps

Whitchurch Library - Whitchurch Chronicle, archive material

Author's collection - Photographs, maps, public timetables, working timetables and sectional appendices

The following secondary sources of information were consulted :

"Locomotive and Train Working in the Latter Part of the Nineteenth Century", E.L.Ahrons (W.Heffer & Sons, 1952)

"Encyclopaedia of British Railway Companies", C.Awdry (Guild Publishing, 1990)

"Intruders at Crewe", A.C.Baker ("British Railway Illustrated", Vol.10, December 2000)

"Transport in the Whitchurch Area, Part II – Canal and Railways", D.B.Barnard (Whitchurch Area Archaeological Group, 1985)

"A Milennium History of Whitchurch", J. Barton (Whitchurch Historical & Archaeological Group, 2000)

"A Regional History of the Railways of Great Britain, Vol.11 – North and Mid Wales", P.E. Baughan (David St. John Thomas, 1980, reprinted 1991)

"Down the Line", R.M.Bevan (C.C.Publishing, 2007)

"Industrial Locomotives of Cheshire, Shropshire & Herefordshire", A.J.Bridges (Industrial Railway Society, 1977)

"Directory of Railway Stations", R.V.J. Butt (Patrick Stephens, 1995)

"A Regional History of the Railways of Great Britain, Vol. 7 – The West Midlands", R. Christiansen (David & Charles, 1983)

"Rail Centres – Crewe", R.Christiansen (Ian Allan, 1993)

"LNWR Chronology", C.R. Clinker (David & Charles, 1961)

"Clinker's Register of Closed Passenger Stations and Goods Depots in England, Scotland and Wales 1830-1977", C.R.Clinker (Avon-Anglia Publications, 1978)

"Contractors Locomotives – Part VI", D.Cole & F.D.Smith (Union Publications, 1982)

"Willaston", J.Collins (Cheshire County Council, 1972)

"140 Years – Crewe to Shrewsbury Line – A History and Guide", J. Cresswell (booklet by Crewe & Shrewsbury Passengers' Association, 1998)

"LNWR Mile and Gradient Posts", R.Foster ("The LNWR Society Journal", Vol.7, No.1, June 2012)

"Milepost 158 – the Story of Crewe and its Railways (Part 6)", I.J.Glover ("The LNWR Society Journal", Vol.6, No.12, March 2012)

 "The Locomotives built by Manning Wardle & Company – Volume 3 – Broad Gauge & Works List", F. W. Harman (Century Locoprints)

"LMS Engine Sheds – Volume One – The LNWR", C.Hawkins & G. Reeve (Wild Swan, 1981)

"The Life and Labours of Thomas Brassey", Sir Arthur Helps (1894, reprinted Nonsuch Publishing, 2008)

"The North and West Route – Volume Two, Shrewsbury and Hereford", J. Hodge (Wild Swan Publications, 2008)

"The Manchester and Milford Railway", J.S. Holden (Oakwood Press, 2007)

"The Cambrian Railways – A New History", P. Johnson (Oxford Publishing Company, 2013)

"The Cambrian Railways", R.W.Kidner (Oakwood Press, revised 1992)

"Wrenbury and Marbury", F.A.Latham (Whitchurch Historical & Archaeological Group, 1999)

"The Battle of Shrewsbury 1403", P.J.Morgan

"Rail Centres - Shrewsbury", R.K.Morriss (Ian Allen, 1986) "Railway Reminiscences", G.P, Neele (McCorquodale & Co.Ltd., 1904 – reprinted E.P.Publishing, 1974)

"A Gazeteer of the Railway Contractors and Engineers of Central England, 1860 – 1914", L. Popplewell (Melledgen Press,1986)

"Crewe – Station, traffic and Footplate Working in the 1950s", W. Phelps (Ian Allan, 1999)

"Chester to Whitchurch", A. Robinson ("LNWR Society Journal", Vol.4, No.6,September 2004)

"Chester to Whitchurch – A Forgotten LNWR Byway"", A. Robinson ("Back Track", Vol.21, No.3, March 2007)

"British Railways Layout Plans of the 1950s – Volume 11 : LNW Lines in the West Midlands" (Signalling Record Society)

"The Jellicoe Trains", E. Talbot ("Railway Archive No.23", Lightmoor Press, 2009)

"The Story of Wem", I.Woodward (Wem Town Council, 1952, enlarged 1976)

"By Great Western to Crewe", Bob Yate (Oakwood Press, 2005)

"Shropshire Union Railway", Bob Yate (Oakwood Press, 2003)

RCTS Acts files

Contemporary reports from various issues of the following periodicals : Railway Magazine, Trains Illustrated, Modern Railways, Railway Observer, Steam Railway, Freightliner.

Websites – Shropshire History, Disused Stations, Old Maps, Hadnall & District History Group, Shropshire Railway Society CD, Network Rail, Arriva.

I am also indebted to the following individuals for contributing a great deal of personal and detailed archival information :

Tony Collins at Hadnall Local History Group.

Huw Edwards, London – for the 1865 detailed Line Plans.

Maude Gould at Whitchurch Historical & Archaeological Group.

John Bentley, Norman Lee, Don Rowland and Ted Talbot – LNWR Society.

Roger West, Prees Lower Heath – local historian.

Industrial Railway Society incorporating research by Brian Janes in the REC records, Kew and Paul Teather.

Mention should also be made of the staffs at Crewe, Nantwich and Wem libraries used to accumulate information and to provide local contacts.

Every effort has been made to ensure that photographs used in this work are credited to the appropriate photographer and / or copyright holder. Sincere thanks go to the photographers so credited for permission to reproduce their images. In some cases the author has not been able to determine the individuals concerned, and apologies are offered to anyone omitted or incorrectly attributed.

Printed and bound by the Amadeus Press, Cleckheaton, West Yorkshire.

Published by Book Law Publication, 382 Carlton Hill, Nottingham, NG4 1JA

CONTENTS

INTRODUCTION

The Crewe to Shrewsbury line was conceived in 1853 by the LNWR as a link for its traffic from the North West of England to South Wales, which would link with the independent Shrewsbury and Hereford Railway. In addition, there was much agricultural produce from the rich Shropshire countryside to be carried to the hungry towns and cities in Lancashire and further afield. Furthermore, this would enhance the LNWR presence in Shrewsbury, which at that time only comprised the Shropshire Union line from Stafford, opened in 1849. All this could be achieved without treading on the toes of the rival Great Western, whose ambitions in this area were only realised in the following year. However, the LNWR were slow to construct the line, and after some negotiations concerning the final approach into the Shropshire county town, only began in 1856, with completion two years later.

The line soon proved its worth, with the LNWR Central Wales line opening in 1867, and giving a further southwards route, this time to Swansea. In 1886, the opening of the Severn Tunnel gave yet another route southwards, this time to Bristol, enabling the company to rival the Midland Railway who had hitherto monopolised the route from the North West to the West Country.

In the meantime, the Oswestry, Ellesmere & Whitchurch Railway opened its eponymous route in 1862 (in which year it also became part of the Cambrian Railways), and so traffic from West Wales was added to the line at Whitchurch. With the completion of the Wellington & Market Drayton Railway in 1867, the Great Western joined the line at Nantwich, and was permitted running powers to Manchester (but only ever exercised these as far as Crewe). This was to see substantial freight traffic between the Home Counties and West Midlands to Manchester over the years.

The final development came five years later with the opening of the Tattenhall Branch, to give a through route for LNWR trains between Shrewsbury and Chester, by-passing Crewe. This was important for the company's coal traffic from South Wales to Birkenhead.

The scene was set for the next 80 years, during which time the line played a vital role in both World Wars. The proximity of Crewe Works enabled the line to attract a varied selection of motive power. However, by the 1960s there was an almost inevitable decline in both passenger and freight traffic, both nationally and on this line and its junction routes. Closure of the Tattenhall Branch to passenger traffic had already occurred (in 1957), and the 1960s saw withdrawal of freight traffic too, with the Cambrian line to Oswestry and the former GWR line to Market Drayton and Wellington also closing completely. Fortunately, the strategic importance of this line was recognised, and after a period of relative decline, efforts were made to attract new traffic. The investment in infrastructure and rolling stock has proved worthwhile, showing significant increases in both passengers and goods, to the extent that the future appears assured.

ABBREVIATIONS

The following abbreviations are used throughout the text :

BR	British Railways (later British Rail)	OEWR	Oswestry, Ellesmere & Whitchurch Railway
DMU	Diesel multiple unit	PJR	Potteries Junction Railway
GCR	Great Central Railway	PWWEC	Permanent Way, Works & Estate Committee (of LNWR)
GWR	Great Western Railway		
LMR	London Midland Region (of BR)	SURCC	Shropshire Union Railways & Canal Company
LMSR	London Midland & Scottish Railway	TPO	Travelling Post Office
LNWR	London & North Western Railway		
MR	Midland Railway	WD	War Department
NMD	Nantwich & Market Drayton Railway	WDR	Wellington & Drayton Railway
NSR	North Staffordshire Railway	WMCQR	Wrexham, Mold & Connah's Quay Railway

DEFINITIONS

To avoid repetition in the text, the following descriptors are used to refer to frequently occurring buildings, structures or operating procedures:

Second class stations

These comprised the red brick main building incorporating the stationmaster's house, with its gabled roof positioned parallel to the running line. Three elegant tall chimneys protruded through the tiled roof and staff offices were incorporated on the ground floor. Abutting this building was a single storey extension towards the platform that contained the booking hall, waiting rooms, toilets and entrance from the station forecourt. This was fully glazed on the platform side and a small canopy forming an extension of the flat roof was cantilevered outwards for the protection of passengers. A further two rather shorter chimneys led from this extension. The brickwork for the entire station ensemble was relieved by pale stone quoins around the edges of the building, beneath the gable ends, around the doors and windows, and on the chimney surrounds. This enlivened what would otherwise have been a very plain red brick construction. A similar style, which we have seen was built by Daniel Climie, was also used by this contractor for stations on the Coalport branch built immediately afterwards.

This standardised construction was used at Hadnall, Yorton, Prees, Wrenbury and Willaston.

Traditional level crossings

Level crossings operated from an adjacent signal box, by means of a large diameter wheel to open and close the crossing gates. The gates were mainly constructed of wood, painted white, with substantial iron bracing. A red circle was affixed in the centre of each gate to warn oncoming traffic that the gates were closed against them.

All level crossings were initially protected by this arrangement, with those at the more remote (and so less frequently used) locations being operated by a local crossing keeper, who was housed in a nearby cottage. His operating mechanisms were usually contained in a small hut, along with levers for signals (all subsequently interlocked) to warn oncoming trains when the gates were set against them.

Half barrier level crossings

The first updated version for level crossings began to appear during the 1970s, whereby the manually operated gates at the busier locations were replaced by power operated half barriers. These lifted vertically to 90 degrees from the road surface to permit road traffic to pass through, rather than across the track as previously.

User operated level crossings

The lesser used crossings became unmanned from the 1980s, when plain metal gates were installed, that opened outwards (i.e. not across the track). In most locations, two gates were provided : a wide one for vehicular traffic, and a smaller one for pedestrian traffic. A telephone is situated nearby for the operators of vehicular traffic to inform the respective signalman when the larger gates are being used. Pedestrians are expected to exercise caution when crossing the line, at their own risk.

LOCATION MAP

Showing opening dates of routes and 1922 ownership

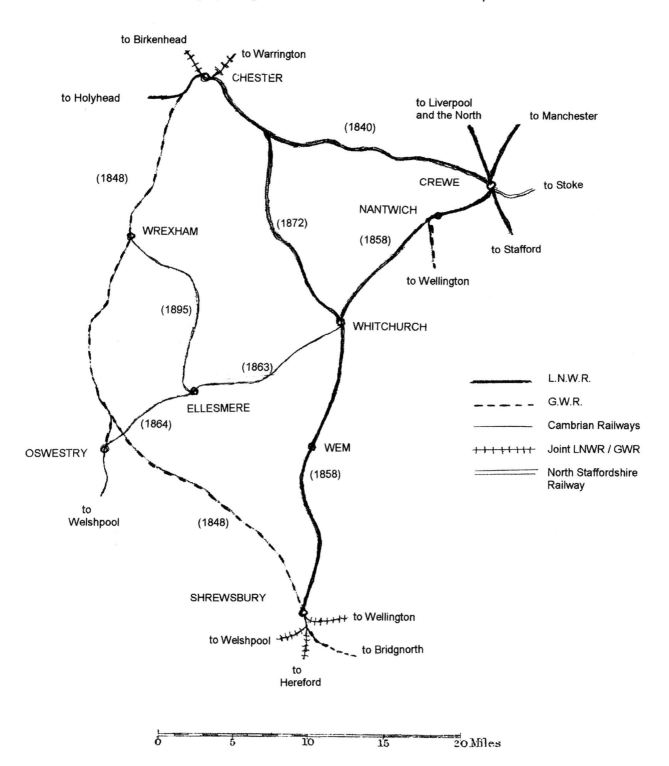

CHAPTER ONE

THE BEGINNINGS

In order to appreciate the reasons for the construction of the Shrewsbury to Crewe line, it is necessary to consider firstly the development of earlier railways and proposed lines in the area.

Background

Crewe was first served by the Grand Junction Railway, opening from Warrington to Birmingham on 4 July 1837. The Chester and Crewe Railway opened on 1 October 1840, but had already been absorbed by the Grand Junction Railway on 1 July of that year. Next, the Manchester and Birmingham Railway opened from Manchester (London Road) to Crewe on 10 August 1842. These railways were amalgamated into the London and North Western Railway (LNWR) as from 16 July 1846. Subsequently, the importance of the Chester line as a direct link to Ireland was underlined when an independent concern, the Chester and Holyhead Railway opened their line on 1 August 1848. However, the Britannia Bridge was incomplete at this time, and so through working was only implemented on 18 March 1850. The LNWR worked this line from the outset, but it was not until 1 January 1859 that it absorbed the Chester and Holyhead Railway Company.

Turning to developments at the other end of our line, plans for a line from Chester to Shrewsbury via Oswestry were deposited on 29 November 1845 by the Shrewsbury, Oswestry and Chester Junction Railway. This company was promoted by the North Wales Mineral Railway with whom it amalgamated on 27 July 1846 and was renamed the Shrewsbury and Chester Junction Railway Company. Their line from Ruabon to Saltney (just west of Chester), where it joined the Chester and Holyhead Railway, opened on 4th November of that year. Eventually the line southwards, actually avoiding Oswestry, opened to a temporary station at Shrewsbury on 16 October 1848.

However, into the hectic activity of railway building in the area during the 1840s a further independent line, the Worcester, Shrewsbury and Crewe Union Railway, was promoted in 1846. This had hoped to provide a link from the planned London Worcester and South Staffordshire Railway at Stourport on the River Severn, which would follow northwards via Broseley, and Coalbrookedale to the eastern side of Shrewsbury. This proposed line would have crossed the Severn four times in the final 10 miles towards Shrewsbury ! No connection appears to have been planned with the Shrewsbury and Chester Railway, under construction at the time. It would then continue northwest to the east of Shawbury, slightly west of Market Drayton, then through Audlem and Stapeley to Crewe. So although connecting Shrewsbury and Crewe, this line would have run more to the east of the LNWR line as eventually built, and would not have passed through Whitchurch. The engineers were Sir John Rennie and Francis Giles, and the prospectus stated that a capital of £1.5 million would be required, made up of 300,000 shares of £50 each, with £2-10s-0d to be deposited on application. The Company attracted considerable interest, and the provisional committee comprised 42 members, with the Committee of Management being represented by the following :

Sir Thomas Winnington, Grosvenor Square, London and Stanford Court, Worcestershire
William Gabbett Beare, Porchester Place, Connaught Square, London
Henry Dann, 46 Duke Street, St. James, London
Capt. Thomas Fothergill, 37 Bedford Square London and Kingthorpe, Yorkshire
Capt. James Grignon, Charles Street, St. James, London
John Knill, Thames Street, London
Anthony Morris Storer, 5 Upper Hyde Park Street, London and Purley Park, Berkshire

The Company claimed to provide the shortest route from the North of England to the South West and South Wales for the movement of coal, iron and manufactured goods. That may well have been true at the time, but with the formation of the LNWR during that same year, and the expansion plans of the GWR, its application for an enabling Act was lost and the railway was never built. However, it is interesting that the route from Worcester to Shrewsbury was later used, at least in part, by the Shropshire Union Railways and Canal Company for its proposed line also in 1846 (again never built), and for the eventual Severn Valley Railway which opened in 1862 and passed to the GWR in 1872.

At this time the line into Shrewsbury from Wellington, built jointly by the Shrewsbury and Birmingham Railway and the Shropshire Union Railways and Canal Company was under construction, and opened on 1 June 1849 into the new General station, which had opened on that day. By the time of opening, the Shropshire Union company had already been leased to the LNWR.

A further three years elapsed before the Shrewsbury and Hereford Railway opened to goods traffic on 30 July 1852, and to passengers from 6 December 1853 at which time their trains also began to use the General station at Shrewsbury. With effectively four companies using the General station, it was necessary for this important hub to be administered by a joint committee, comprising representatives of the subject companies.

Inevitably, further amalgamations and absorptions of the initial companies occurred, so that the lines became the properties of the GWR and LNWR as follows :

Chester - GWR, 1 September 1854
Hereford – Joint LNWR and GWR, 1 July 1862
Wellington Joint - Shropshire Union leased to LNWR, June 1847
- Shrewsbury & Birmingham Railway acquired by GWR, 1 September 1854

So it can be seen that the lines radiating from Shrewsbury had become the properties of either the LNWR or the GWR mostly by 1854 and entirely by 1862. Upon Grouping in 1923,the LNWR lines passed to the LMSR, and the joint lines remained in the joint ownership of the LMSR and GWR.

Returning to 1850, a line from Shrewsbury to Crewe remained an obvious link for the LNWR to exploit as time and finances permitted.

An early print of the façade of Shrewsbury station, as opened in 1849, and consisting of just two storeys. The original architecture can be seen to have been beautifully balanced. Compare this view with the one on p101 when an extension to the left and the third storey was added.
[Shropshire Records & Research]

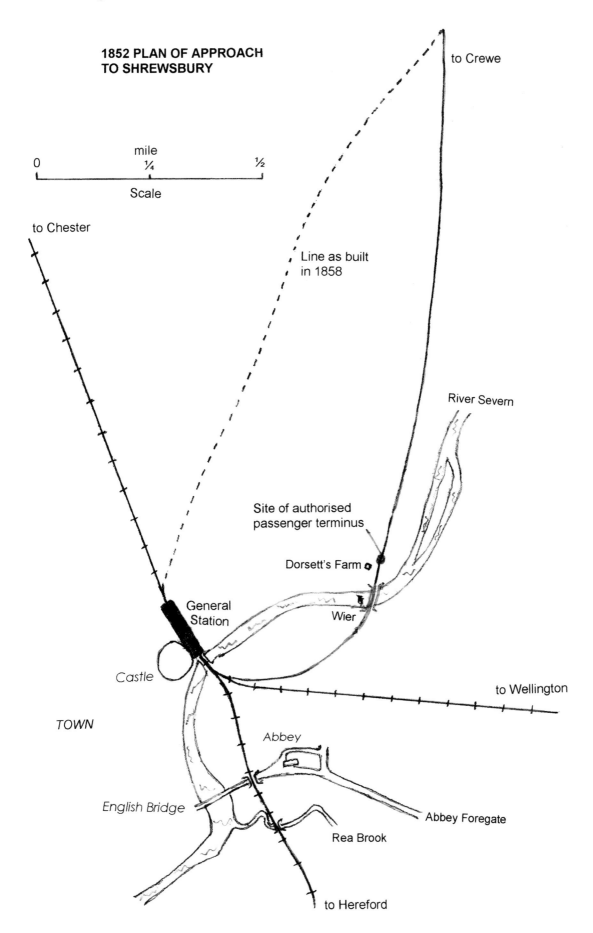

**1852 PLAN OF APPROACH
TO SHREWSBURY**

mile
¼
0   ½

Scale

to Chester

to Crewe

Line as built
in 1858

River Severn

Site of authorised
passenger terminus

Dorsett's Farm

Wier

General
Station

Castle

to Wellington

TOWN

Abbey

English Bridge

Abbey Foregate

Rea Brook

to Hereford

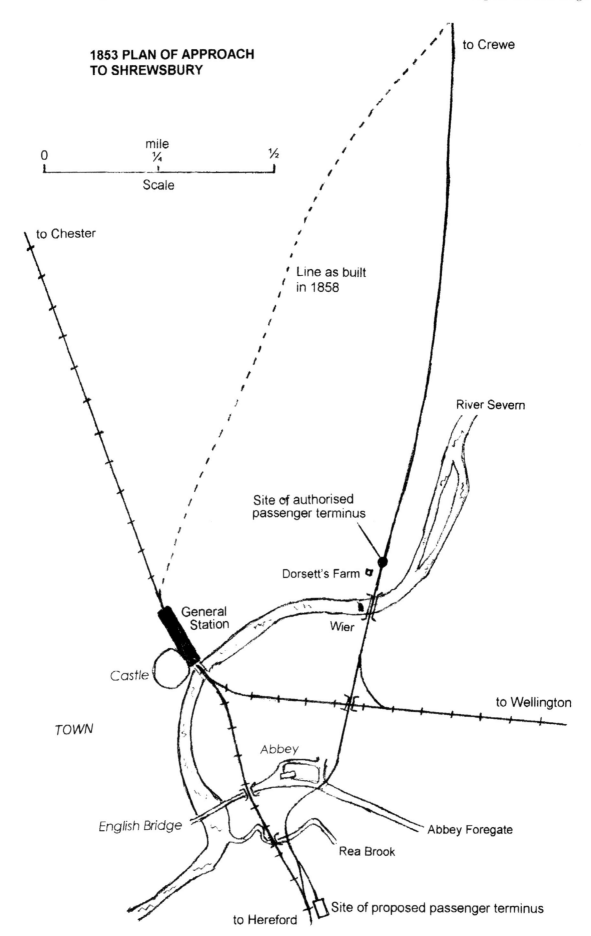

**1853 PLAN OF APPROACH
TO SHREWSBURY**

mile
0 ¼ ½
Scale

to Crewe

to Chester

Line as built
in 1858

River Severn

Site of authorised
passenger terminus

Dorsett's Farm

General
Station

Wier

Castle

to Wellington

TOWN

Abbey

English Bridge

Abbey Foregate

Rea Brook

Site of proposed passenger terminus

to Hereford

Planning and Authorisation

Access to the Shropshire county town of Shrewsbury via the SURCC line from Stafford and the joint line from Wellington was important to the LNWR, as it provided a source of traffic from the rich farming community in this large county. However, one major drawback by 1850 was that this line faced south at Stafford, so that any goods or passenger traffic faced a change of trains or remarshalling if required to travel north. With the opening of the line to Hereford in 1852, further traffic was available at Shrewsbury and so the LNWR sought ways of tapping into this source of revenue. The LNWR Board were also well aware of the desire to maintain good relations with its neighbours and competitors, particularly where joint lines were involved. So the LNWR Chairman, Lord Anson is reported to have commented that "we have no intention whatever of interfering with the Chester and Birkenhead line, or of losing any ties of friendship which now bind the two companies together". So rather than duplicate any route directly northwards, it was decided to link Shrewsbury to the hub of the LNWR at Crewe. Plans were prepared, and first deposited at Shrewsbury County Court on 30 November 1852.

An enabling Act was drafted and presented to Parliament, which was passed on 20 August 1853 as the "London and North-Western (Crewe and Shrewsbury Extension &c) Act, 1853" (Vict. 16 & 17, chapter 216). Section 3 of the Act provided for a railway "from junction at Crewe with main line of Company to Shrewsbury in enclosure No.2 on plans in the parish of Holy Cross and St. Giles". Section 32 authorised five years for the construction. However, the Act did not proceed without difficulty, for the House of Lords did not permit the intended route into the town at Shrewsbury. The original plans intended that the line southwards from Hadnall would run to the east side of the town, cross the River Severn on an 11 arch bridge, each span measuring 20 feet, and connect at a west facing junction with the joint line from Wellington only about 30 yards from the bridge over the Severn near to the station. The House of Lords were concerned that there would be too much congestion in Shrewsbury General station, and so amended the plans so that the line would terminate in fields on the north side of the river, near to Dorsett's Barn (close to the Severn Weir). This was some distance from the town, and as there would be no direct connection to the railways in the area, this was obviously not to the liking of the LNWR, who then stepped back to consider their options, during which time no work began on the line.

The next plans were deposited on 30 November 1853, with the line running across the River Severn as in the previous year's plans, but amending the river bridge to be of 14 spans of 20 feet. However, the section further south was totally revised. Now the line ran directly southwards, crossing the Wellington line on a 100 yard viaduct, stated to built as 10 arches of 30 feet span and 15 feet height clearance – which allowing for the piers does not exactly add up. Continuing south, the line crossed Abbey Foregate and then the Rea Brook, but the plans do not mention the bridge construction required at these locations. It then curved to the southwest, then directly southward again, to make a connection with the Hereford line at a south facing junction at Coleford, more or less on the site of the later locomotive depot. Interestingly, the plans show a "New Engine Shed" of two roads facing south, just north of this junction, which was presumably a proposed site for the Shrewsbury & Hereford's locomotive shed, as this was not eventually built until 1856, was of five roads, and on a site a little further south, facing in the opposite direction. A short distance before making this junction, a spur ran into what would have been a terminus station for the LNWR, alongside the S&HR, on the later site of the Coleham locomotive shed.

Between the crossings of the River Severn and the Wellington line, a chord was indicated to run southeastwards from a north facing junction, to join the Wellington line at an east facing junction, just west of the SUR and SBR locomotive sheds at Underdale Road. These 1853 plans were not submitted in any new Bill before Parliament, so it can only be assumed that the LNWR took soundings as whether it was likely to be approved. As the response to the earlier Act had been to limit the approach to the northern side of the river, it would appear that this view still prevailed, and these ambitious plans were dropped. It has to be said that the site for the terminus station at Coleham was as inconvenient for the town centre as the one at Dorsett's Barn.

Whereas the population along the intended route had supported its construction, this gradually turned to frustration as time passed and there was no sign of any progress. The *"Shrewsbury Chronicle"* reported that a meeting of local townsmen at Wem on 24 January, 1856 had heard that *"not a single spade has been put into the ground"*, even though 2½ years had elapsed since the passing of the Act. The same newspaper reported soon after, on 8 February, that a meeting had been held at Whitchurch Town Hall during which it was stated that although almost all the land in the area had been acquired for the railway, there had been no progress on the ground. Mr William Smith, who owned a local foundry, contributed £100 towards a 'fighting fund' to urge the LNWR into action. A meeting on the following day at the Crown Hotel, Nantwich heard the interested parties of that town complain of a similar lack of action.

It is perhaps surprising at first glance that the LNWR had not proceeded with construction on the northern end of the line, whilst continuing with the debate concerning the approach to Shrewsbury. But considering the wider implications, the circumstances of the time were not wholly conducive to the outlay of expense. Firstly, the Crimean War (October 1853 to February 1856) had proved to suppress the country's economy, and had also had an effect on the number of able bodied men available for new construction works. Also, the LNWR had been concentrating on the modernisation and expansion of its works at Crewe.

But with these events behind them, the LNWR was spurred into action, possibly assisted by pressure from these local groups. New plans were prepared and a further Act, the "London and North Western Railway Act, 1856" (Vict.19 & 20, chapter 123) was passed on 21 July, 1856. Section 3 of the Act provided for a railway "from Shrewsbury in enclosure No.7 on plans for the London and North-Western (Crewe and Shrewsbury Extension &c) Act, 1853 in the parish of Middle to junction in General Station at Shrewsbury at north end thereof with railways at that station". Section 15 extended the period for construction to 20 December 1858 and Section 17 gave powers for the use of Shrewsbury General station. The new route involved a sharp curve (600 feet radius) at the north end of the station, just north of the junction with the Chester line. Whilst this has proved to be an operating restriction (and the site of the 1907 disaster!), the new route at least provided a through route for trains from the North West to the South. The earlier route would have entailed either a reversal in the station, or complete avoidance of the station altogether. So, perhaps the House of Lords had a point after all.

Another problem for construction was that this new section at Shrewsbury now had to cross the original course of the River Severn near Ditherington. This was known to be of a particularly boggy nature, and may well have been the reason for selecting the original unacceptable route.

Construction

The LNWR estimated that the completed railway would cost £350,000 or £10,600 per mile. The project continued with Joseph Locke as the Principal Engineer, John E. Errington as his Chief Engineer, and Donald Campbell as Resident Engineer. Daniel Tyson was the architect for lineside buildings and bridges. The railway was to be constructed with earthworks to permit a double track to be laid, but only a single track (with passing places) to be laid in the first instance. The contract for construction was awarded to Thomas Brassey, although it is not known if any other bids were tendered. The contract for the Crewe to Wem section was signed by Brassey on 7 August 1856 for the sum of £65,500, giving Thomas Dixon and William Wardell (both of Chester) as his guarantors. W. Clarke was appointed as "Engineer to the Contractors". Brassey himself provided a bond to cover the extent of the work on 1 October 1856. The contract specified that a penalty of £500 per day would be payable for exceeding the contracted dates. Ten level crossings and 26 occupation crossings were to be provided, along with bridges over the Shropshire Union Canal and the River Weaver near Nantwich, the latter to be approached by an embankment 14 feet high.

1857 PLAN OF AUTHORISED GOODS RELIEF LINE

The good and patient people at Whitchurch were able to celebrate the coming of the railway (at last) when a foundation stone was laid at the site of Whitchurch station on 23 March 1857. A report in the "*Shrewsbury Chronicle*" three days later recounted that the peals of St. Alkmund's Church were ringing, and that the ceremony was "*witnessed by the assembled folk of all ages. George Kirkpatrick, Esq. performed the task at 4 p.m. using the trowel and mallet most artistically*". After speeches the party repaired to the Victoria Hotel and partook "*of every comfort that man could wish.*"

Thomas Brassey was well known as a manager of men, with sufficient expertise to motivate his employees without coercion, and to encourage loyalty. Looking after his men generated productivity, and by selecting the right subordinates he achieved enviable results. Labourers were paid between 2s 9d and 3s 0d per day, at a time when agricultural labourers were generally paid just 1s 0d per day, although this latter did increase somewhat during harvest time. His agent for the 32½ mile line was Mr. Miles Day, who was able to report rapid progress, particularly as most of the land had already been acquired. By August 1857, Errington reported to the Board that the first section, from Crewe to Nantwich was well advanced with track already laid, and that half of the earthworks for the reminder were complete. However, some of the property in Shrewsbury had still not been acquired, although negotiations were continuing.

At this time, further thought had been given by the LNWR to the approaches to Shrewsbury, and plans were deposited at Shrewsbury County Court at 1 o'clock on 30 November 1857 for a goods line that would avoid the junction north of the station. This was to depart from the main line just south of Ditherington Mill, passing to the east of St. Michael's Church, crossing St Michael's Street (later A519), the SURCC Shrewsbury Canal and Wharf, burrowing under Howard Street and finally joining the up relief line at the east side of the General station at a south facing junction. The powers for this line were included in the "London and North Western Railway (Additional Powers) Act, 1858" (Vict. 21 & 22, chapter 131) which was passed on 23 July 1858. Three years were allowed for completion. However, this line would have entailed considerable works, involving a major road crossing, diverting a section of the Shrewsbury Canal and associate basins and the demolition of several properties. In the end, only the southern end of the line from the canal wharf to the station was constructed, with the area alongside the wharf being redeveloped as the Howard Street Goods Depot. As all the necessary land had already been acquired, the new goods depot opened later in 1858,and the remaining powers were allowed to lapse. Perhaps it was just as well that the through line was not introduced, as the rather sharp curve under Howard Street and adjacent to the station would not have suited through goods working.

Nonetheless, considerable work was necessary at the junction with the Chester line, as the bridge over Cross Street need to be widened, which was achieved by inserting a girder extension on its west side. This consisted of a cast iron span of 34 feet, approached from the Crewe direction on an embankment and a masonry viaduct of three arches of 25 feet each.

Returning to the pace of construction, the LNWR Permanent Way, Works and Estate Committee (PWWEC) reported on 9 July 1857 that in their estimated steel rail requirements for the year 1857, 2,625 tons of rail would be required for the Crewe to Shrewsbury line, with a further 1,475 tons in the following year. This was ostensibly to be supplied by Crewe's steel mill, but was eventually supplied by the Ebbw Steel Works at £9-7s-6d per ton.

On 21 February 1858, Daniel Climie of Trinity Terrace, Shrewsbury was awarded the contract for station buildings, waiting sheds, platforms and goods sheds as follows :

Nantwich	£2,901-15s-11d
Whitchurch	£2,562-11s-11d
Wem	£2,490- 3s – 9d
Extras	£27– 0s – 0d
TOTAL	£7,981-11s- 7d

It is worthy of note that shortly after, in August 1858, Daniel Climie obtained the contract to build the first 2¼ miles of the LNWR Coalport branch, from Hadley Junction to near Wombridge.

On 8 April 1858 the PWWEC noted that further stations would be required at Willaston, Wrenbury (described as Lord Combermere's station), Prees (Lord Hill's station), Yorton (Mr. Garner's station), Hadnall and Tilstock – although for this latter, the committee noted that this would not be necessary if the LNWR had to pay for the land, which at that time had been given without charge. These comments suggest that apart from the stations being built to serve the needs of the local populace, they were also included as part of the negotiations for acquisition of the lands, and thus to serve the former owners of the land, who obviously wanted access to the railway.

The following month the PWWEC ordered that the tender from Francis Berry & Company for a 20,000 gallon water tank to be installed at Whitchurch at a cost of £400 was accepted. An engine to pump water into the tank was to be made at Crewe by Mr. Ramsbottom at an estimated cost of £130. The stations at Willaston, Wrenbury, Prees and Yorton were approved, subject to a third bedroom to be provided in each of the buildings. Those for Tilstock and Hadnall were deferred for further consideration. On 28 May, Messrs. Errington, Norris (LNWR Northern Division Operating Superintendent) and Ramsbottom (LNWR Northern Division Locomotive Superintendent) reported on the required engine turntables, sidings, crossings, cranes and other equipment that would be necessary before opening of the line. However, details of these requirements were not recorded in the minutes.

The "*Shrewsbury Chronicle*" of 24 May, 1858 reported as follows :

LOCAL INTELLIGENCE - WHITCHURCH

Shrewsbury and Crewe Extension Railway

Our railway station here is fast approaching completion, and although small, it will be a very neat and pretty place of architecture, added to which its out-offices, engine house, tank, spacious goods shed, &c., reflect great credit to the Resident Engineer, Donald Campbell, Esq., C.E., and the architect (sic) and contractor Mr. Daniel Climie.

On 10 June 1858 the committee heard that one station would be sufficient for the company between Wem and Shrewsbury, and if so, the site at Merry Lane would best suit the Grinshill stone quarries. This would also be ideally situated as midway between the two towns. However, if the company had to have a station at Hadnall, then the distance could be divided into thirds, and so one at Yorton would be better suited than at Merry Lane. Just two weeks later the committee ordered that a station must be erected at Hadnall, and so Yorton rather than Merry Lane was also fixed. Mr. Errington also reported that the portion of the line required by the Act to be opened on 20 August would be completed in time. Interestingly, the committee also ordered that a tender from Messrs. Joyce of Whitchurch for clocks, required by the Board of Trade at each station, should be referred to the Stores Committee. On the subject of level crossings, sheds of brick and slate construction and 9 feet square were to be erected at Nantwich and Wem for the accommodation of crossing keepers.

However, despite the lack of really challenging engineering works, all did not always proceed without difficulty or mishap, as the "*Shrewsbury Chronicle*" reported on 11 June, 1858 :

"*LOCAL INTELLIGENCE – WEM*

SHREWSBURY AND CREWE EXTENSION RAILWAY – It cannot but be gratifying to every intelligent observer to remark, if not admire, the energy and rapidity displayed within these few weeks past, in forwarding the operations of this undertaking. A body of men, numbering upwards of fifty, who are believed to be the most powerful and efficient that ever visited the north of Shropshire, are now within a mile of the town, completing, in their progress from Crewe to this place, the laying down and fixing of the permanent rails, and who are expected to reach the river Roden, at Wem, by the termination of the current week. But at this spot a difficulty presents itself, which cannot be but deeply regretted : the foundations on which the bridge – or rather viaduct of three arches, across the river Roden – is founded appears to have been too deceptive for the eagle eye of the chief surveyor, for on removal of the temporary supports the abutments immediately indicated the insufficiency of their foundation, and on being slightly tested, one of the arches completely broke down, the other two presenting a very dilapidated appearance. Active operations are now going on to clear away the ballast and materials of the broken down arch, and it is much to be feared that a reconstruction of the whole bridge will be necessary. The permanent rails, from this point to within a very limited distance of Shrewsbury, have been completed ; and it is hoped that this unforeseen difficulty in the engineering department may not in any way retard the opening of the line, as a temporary erection could easily be raised to enable passengers to pass from one train of carriages to another on the opposite side of the river. While on this subject it would be improper to pass by without noticing both the taste of the engineer in selecting the ground for the Wem station, and the ability and energy displayed by Mr. D. Climie, the contractor. The ground selected lies on the east side and close to the town. The roads to Drayton, Lee-bridge, &c., pass on one level crossing at the north end of the station. The front of the building commands a full view of Hawkstone-park, the residence of Viscount Hill, the pleasure grounds of which are, by the liberality of that nobleman, open to the public. The beauty and antiquarian associations connected with this magnificent park are supposed to be equal, if not superior, to any nobleman's residence in England. The architecture of the station is understood to be from the designs of the engineer, and equally reflect credit on both his taste and scientific acquirements. To the intelligent contractor, Mr. Climie, the town owes lasting gratitude. Only a few months ago a case was brought by the town surveyor before the justice court, craving warrant to break up part of a field some distance off, in order to search for road metal, which could not anywhere in the neighbourhood be found. This warrant, contrary to the wishes of the occupant, was granted ; but, after a lengthened search, the attempt proved abortive. On the spot allocated for the station, close to the town, Mr. Climie had produced many thousands of tons of excellent road metal, and shown where many thousands of tons more can be got. He has also, by the assistance of his able and efficient coadjutors, brought his contract near to a close : and the station bids fair to be an honour to him and an ornament to the town."

In fact, this account is in error in designating Daniel Climie as the contractor – he was responsible for the various buildings along the line : the contractor for the line was Thomas Brassey. Stage payments given in the minutes of the LNWR committees confirm this arrangement, although it is possible that Brassey subcontracted some work to Climie, such as the bridge over the River Roden. The newspaper would also, I fear, not be very popular with the Board of Trade for suggesting that the travelling public should (or even be prepared) to take one train from Shrewsbury, then walk over a temporary structure to another to complete their onward journey

Further mishaps occurred during 1858, with the construction of an embankment to become known as 'Crewe Bank' over the original River Severn bed in Shrewsbury. The unstable nature of the ground in this area conspired to cause a collapse, but this was soon rectified. North of Whitchurch further a further collapse occurred where the line passed Blackmere (or Blakemere).

Mr. Errington explained on 8 July that progress was still satisfactory, with no doubt that the line would open on time. Electric telegraph had been ordered. The committee heard that an engine turntable would be required at Wem, but its exact location could not be determined until the new works were completed. (It subsequently transpired that no such turntable was ever provided at Wem.)

The junction with the Chester line at Shrewsbury was not finally agreed upon until 23 July 1858, just one month before the line was due to open. This would seem to be cutting things a bit fine, but by 24 August the junctions at Shrewsbury had been completed by the GWR. On this date, it was also decided to provide goods offices at Nantwich, Wem and Whitchurch at an estimated cost of £60 each. Daniel Climie was further instructed to build a retaining wall of 80 feet long at Whitchurch for the coal wharf. It is presumed that this wall was the one that separated the station platform from the coal yard (and later formed the boundary wall of the down side bay platform) thus preventing coal dust from blowing towards waiting passengers.

In the meantime, the LNWR had served its First Notice of Intention to open the line to the Board of Trade on 13 July, 1858, and a Second Notice on 5 August. Consequently, Colonel Yolland was instructed on the following day to inspect the line and report on its suitability for passenger traffic. He accomplished this on 17 August, and submitted his report the next day.

Of interest in the report are that the rails were double headed, of 83 lbs per yard and in lengths of 21 feet. In general his report was favourable, although he does mention that the rail joints for about 13 miles of the railway are 'fished', whereas for the remainder the joints are made using 'joint chairs'. Curiously, he does not then mention this in his list of matters requiring attention, as neither method was considered as unacceptable – it just seems that he would have preferred one method of making the joints, rather than two.

His report then goes on to list matters requiring attention :

> *"With the exceptions to which I shall shortly advert the Line is well finished off and in very good order.*
> *In making my inspection, I noticed the following :*
>
> 1. *There is an unauthorised Level Crossing established at 14 m 70 chains – the road at which it occurs appears to have very little Traffic on it, and it is said to have been constructed in error and from only looking to the Plans deposited before Parliament.*
>
> 2. *Distant Signals in both directions on the Main Line at the Crewe Junction remain to be established and the arrangements for working the Points from the Signal Box are still incomplete.*
>
> 3. *The station Buildings and Platforms are unfinished at Wrenbury, Prees, Yorton and Hadnall.*
>
> 4. *The Handles of the Levers for working the distant Signals to be brought together at Willaston, Nantwich and Wrenbury.*
>
> 5. *The Signal arrangements at the Shrewsbury Junction are incomplete – so as to place the whole control in the hands of one man.*
>
> 6. *There is a short portion of fencing on the same Level as the soil in the field close to it – near Wrenbury – at present it is not a safe fence against Cattle.*
>
> 7. *Two Temporary Water Tanks and some of the contractors' sheds require to be removed.*
>
> 8. *The Platform of an Under Bridge near Yorton is only laid in a temporary manner – and the joints along that portion of the Line which is not fished, require to be carefully gone over, as the compressed oak keys do not fit the rails in all cases and when that is the case they leave bad joints.*
>
> 9. *The Mile Posts though mostly put up are not marked and no gradient boards have been put up.*
>
> *I have not received any undertaking showing the manner in which it is proposed to work this Single Line – and I am of opinion that by reason of the incompleteness of the works, the Crewe and Shrewsbury Branch of the London and North Western Railway cannot be opened for Traffic, without danger to the Public using the same."*

The 'unauthorised level crossing' would be that at Heath Lane, and as this remained in situ, there was presumably no other objection to it, especially as no other correspondence on this matter has been traced. Items 2 to 9 are really relatively minor points, but his final conclusion regarding the lack of an operating system is more serious. The Railway Department of the Board of Trade in its Minute No.3599 dated 18 August concluded "Opening postponed for one month". Therefore, it is all the more surprising to find that the line did open for passenger traffic just 2½ weeks later. Again, no further correspondence has been found to suggest that matters were resolved to the satisfaction of the Board of Trade. So presumably the LNWR were somehow able to convince these authorities as to the safety of the line – or they simply went ahead with the opening anyway.

Opening of the line

A lengthy report was carried in the "*Shrewsbury Chronicle*" of 3 September, 1858, and is reproduced in its entirety, as not only does it record details of the opening, but also gives a unique description of the line at the time, and in a most readable prose :

"OPENING OF THE CREWE AND SHREWSBURY RAILWAY

On Wednesday last (1st September) this line of railway, through its entire length, was opened for traffic. There were none of the usual demonstrations to mark this which in many respects nevertheless is an important event….The length of the line is 32¼ miles, and the works have generally been of a light nature. Between Wem and Shrewsbury they have been the heaviest, the cuttings being all in either heavy stiff clay or rock. From Wem to Whitchurch the works are more than usually light. Between Whitchurch and Crewe the cuttings have been through a light red sand, which has been used for a considerable distance as ballast, and however agreeable it may appear to the eye, it is extremely unpleasant to the traveller, as the fine particles, gathered up by the velocity of the train, enter through the crevices of the carriages, and form a most disagreeable covering to the clothing. The number of bridges is beyond the average; they are generally faced with best blue Staffordshire bricks, except those nearer to Shrewsbury, which are built of Grinshill stone. At Battlefield there has been the heaviest cutting….At present there is only a single line of rails, but the bridges, embankments, &c., are made for two, which will be laid as soon as possible….Mr. Donald Campbell is the resident engineer for the company, and Mr. W. Clarke the engineer for the contractors…Mr. Miles Day is the agent for the contractors at the Crewe end of the line…The first class stations are built of blue bricks, and the second of red and white…Mr. Norris, the superintendent of the northern section of the London and North Western lines, will have management of this branch.

There are five trains each way on week days, and one on Sundays. On Wednesday morning the first train left Shrewsbury at 6.50., and Crewe at six.

At the general station, in this town, considerable alterations and re-arrangement of the roads had been necessary, and in doing so very considerable improvements effected. The junction with the Crewe line is formed by a double road, the one up and the other down. The trains in and out ran from the platform as to and from Chester. The ticket platform is placed about 300 yards from the booking office. Among the alterations close to the station we may mention that the buildings near to the face of Castle foregate-street, and to the Great Western goods yard, have been taken down, the girder bridge spanning Cross-street has been widened, and a strip taken off the Great Western yard. The curve out of the station, caused by the peculiar nature of the position in which it has been built, is very sharp, being 280 yards long, with a radius of 8 ½ chains. The line passes out of the general station over the present girder bridge across Castle foregate, on to an embankment, secured by retaining walls, over a viaduct of three arches, which forms the principal entrance to the Great Western yard and premises. Passing onwards is another embankment, and then a girder bridge, which will form another way to the Great Western property, and may constitute the entrance to the goods yard which will be here made, should the loop line from near St. Michael's Church to the Shropshire Union wharf not be constructed. We have now reached as far as the thread manufactory of Messrs. Marshall, at the back of which the line passes upon an embankment, and here considerable difficulty was experienced in the construction, in consequence of the boggy nature of the ground, which is believed to be a portion of the old bed of the river Severn. Upon one occasion the ground sunk at least 20 feet, thereby causing much loss of time and great expense. The line then curves to the right, through an average cutting of 18 feet, crossing the Old Heath road, from Castle-foregate to Cross-hill, by a girder bridge, the road being diverted under the railway. Still forward to the right, through another cutting, crossing, upon the level, the road from Harlescott to Hadnal (sic). From thence there is a steepish gradient along a lengthy heavy embankment through Battlefield, leaving the old church (built to commemorate the battle of Shrewsbury), about 240 yards to the left. At this point there is a splendid prospect of Shrewsbury obtained, backed as it is by the vast amphitheatre of Shropshire and Welsh mountains in the far distance. On the right is the picturesque hill of Haughmond, beneath which lies Sundorne Castle. Once beyond Battlefield Church the line dips into a long shallow cutting of 1500 yards, and follows the course of the Whitchurch road for about a mile, when it diverges and crosses the road from Hadnall to Harmer-hill where Hadnal (sic) station is built. At this place considerable crowds was evinced to see the trains, and the area of the station was thronged throughout the day. We are now four miles and a half from Shrewsbury. Continuing still to the left, leaving, leaving Hardwicke and Black-birches to the right and left, the Haston road is crossed, and the line passes down to the pools at Sansaw. The cutting here is through a band of rock, of the same strata as Grinshill, which is only a short distance to the right, forming a picturesque and bold feature in the landscape. The next station is Yorton – not Yarton as printed in the time tables, and Yarnton as on the tickets – seven miles from Shrewsbury. Here, even, were numerous sight-seers when the trains arrived. The station will accommodate Yorton, Broughton, Harmer-hill, Grinshill, and Preston Brockhurst. Passing remains of the old church at Broughton, the line swerves to the right, passing into a long cutting, crossing the Wem road at the eighth mile-stone, and at no great distance from Shooter's-hill, the road being diverted and carried over the line by a skew stone bridge. Straight on for the village of Tilley, on a low embankment, the line keeps parallel with the turnpike-road, at an average distance of 160 yards, and crosses the Tilley road on the level, where a lodge is built. Continuing to the right, still on an embankment, where the old road from Shrewsbury to Wem is diverted alongside the line for about 220 yards, where the Wellington road is thrown into the same deviation, and carried under the railway by a girder bridge, the line running into the old road where the toll gate formerly stood. At this point a wooden screen is being erected to cover the line from the sight of horses on the turnpike road. The river Roden is crossed by a massive bridge of three arches of Grinshill stone. Some three months since the bridge fell, owing to a treacherous foundation, but it has since been built on large piles. Immediately past this bridge Wem station ground is reached, the station being built on the left side, close to the convergence of the Hawkstone and Aston roads, which have been diverted and carried across the railway by a level crossing. We are now ten and a half miles from Shrewsbury. The arrival of the first train on Wednesday morning was looked forward to with much interest, and large numbers of people assembled to witness it, and this was the case throughout the day. Several flags were hoisted from various points, and the station was tastefully decorated with flowers, banners, &c. Ample accommodation is here afforded, in wharfs, sidings, &c., so as to ensure the easy conducting of the traffic. Wem is a little to the left, and the line then passing through a fine agricultural country, the most prominent object in the landscape being the bold and well timbered heights of Hawkstone, four miles from Wem, and to which place we understand the proprietor of the hotel at Hawkstone intends to run an omnibus to convey visitors to the park. A straight run is here made for about five miles, the village of Edstaston being about half a mile to the left. At Walmer-lane the line crosses the road on the level; and here is placed Prees station, the village of that name being nearly a mile and a half distant. It will accommodate Whixall and Coton, and be the nearest station to Hodnet, Morton Say, and Market Drayton. The distance from Shrewsbury is fourteen miles, and Coton-hall and the village of Tilstock are passed to the left. From Wem for about five miles the works are exceedingly light, being merely formings. Here we dip into sand cuttings and embankments, and cross the Whitchurch and Prees road at the eighteenth mile stone, by a *skew bridge, the approaches being considerable easy. Through a deep sand cutting, past Edgeley-hall, Whitchurch station at the Rye-mills is 18¾ miles from Shrewsbury, is gained. The road from Whitchurch to Nantwich is carried by excavated approaches under the railway by a girder bridge. The station is built on the left, and there is plenty of accommodation prepared for traffic. It will be about three quarters of a mile from the centre of the town, and approached by way of Green-road. In this town, as at Wem, there was much anxiety evinced to see the first train, and large crowds were at the station long before the appointed time. A curious story is told of a spirited son of Crispin, who, with his wife, had made up his mind to have the first ticket issued, and to go in the first train to Shrewsbury. He carried out his design so far as the tickets were concerned, but being deeply interested in viewing the wondrous locomotive and the newly-painted carriages, he paid little attention when they moved forward from the opposite platform to where they were standing, merely remarking, in reply to an urgent request that he should take his seat, "Oh, they'll come back for us." In this expectation, as a matter of course, he was disappointed; the train did not come back, and the poor fellow and his better half had to endure many a pointed joke and much hearty laughter. At the station there were no decorations; but a large flag floated from the church tower, and the bells rang during a portion of the day. In the afternoon, the shops were generally closed, in order to afford the tradesmen an opportunity of taking trips by rail, a privilege which large numbers availed themselves of. Proceeding onwards the line curves to the right, still in a cutting, and quickly comes to an embankment close to Yockings-gate farm on one side and Blackmere on the other. Here great difficulty was experienced in the formation of the line owing to the boggy nature of the land upon, which the embankment was being formed. The weight of the superincumbent soil caused the ground on each side to spew out for a considerable distance. The next station to Whitchurch is Wrenbury, 23 ¼ miles from Shrewsbury, previous to gaining which we leave Shropshire. Combermere Abbey is about a mile and a half from the line to the right, and Marbury-hall to the left a mile away. The country about here is quite flat, abounding in woods and fine meadow and pasture land. From Wrenbury, where crowds of sightseers were assembled, the railway passes almost direct to Nantwich, crossing the Birmingham and Liverpool canal, by a long girder bridge, and the river Weaver by an arched girder bridge of 65 feet span – the largest on the line. Just before we reach Nantwich there are two level crossings. The station is on the left of the line, on the confines of the town, and is 28 miles from Shrewsbury. The crowds here were considerable, and lustily cheered as the trains passed from their gaze. The next station is Willaston, 29¾ miles from Shrewsbury. In a few miles Crewe is gained, the junction with the old London and North Western being formed close to the North Stafford line, and runs up the North Western line to the south end of the station, the terminus being behind the present large platform, and opposite the hotel entrance. Ample accommodation will be here afforded for passengers and general traffic."*

Whilst there is no doubt that the ballast used on the southern section of the line was inadequate and quickly ground into a powder, as described above, the ballast used was actually sandstone from the local Grinshill quarry, and not "light red sand". The report makes no mention of any local celebrations at Shrewsbury for the departure of the first train, but then it is unlikely that the local populace would have thronged to watch the spectacle, as they had become used to trains in Shrewsbury for ten years by then.

This report also alludes to the intermediate stations, all of which opened with the line on 1 September 1858, and all of which possessed just one platform. These were sited on the up side at Hadnall, Yorton, Prees and Wrenbury; and on the down side at Willaston. Passing loops were provided with additional platforms, initially only at the 'first class' stations at Wem, Whitchurch and Nantwich.

The report comments on the diversion of two roads in Wem, which if left undisturbed would have required two level crossings within one hundred yards. So the decision was made to change the road layouts so that they met and diverged each side of a single level crossing. This arrangement eased the traffic flow on both road and railway, but was made not without considerable effort. The report also hardly mentions the two bridges at Nantwich, where the line crosses firstly the Birmingham and Liverpool Canal, then the River Weaver. The latter was possibly the largest feat of construction on the line.

Post completion works

On 17 January 1859, the PWWEC was advised that the costs for the line totalled £269,610 comprising land (£55,499), works (£117,995) and other costs (£96,116). Subsequently, the LNWR General Finance Committee was advised in October 1859 that the final estimated cost of the line was to be £324,816 with further anticipated costs of £25,184 which would equal exactly the original estimate. Cost of doubling the line was set at £70,000. However, the eventual costs were advised to this committee in 1860 as being £341,000, although by this time the cost of doubling had risen to £79,000. As both amounts total £420,000 there would appear to have been some judicious use of 'estimates' in the reported figures.

So it is apparent that doubling of the line was uppermost in the minds of the LNWR Board, even so shortly after completion. Further traffic reached Shrewsbury from the Craven Arms to Knighton line, which opened in 1860 and with extensions into Central Wales already in hand, there was an indication of yet further traffic. Meanwhile other works and improvements became necessary, mainly resulting from the local traffic generated along the line. As doubling of the line had commenced in 1861, it is presumed that many of these works would have been carried out at the same time. Almost certainly, some would have become necessary as a result of the layout changes resulting from the doubling.

Lord Chandos, Chairman of the LNWR, responding to criticism that the line was not double tracked, explained that the line was built as a single line initially 'to keep out competitors'. It has been suggested that this comment was simply an excuse for not wishing to spend too much at the time, otherwise why build it to double track formation in the first place? Alternatively, it may be that he was genuinely concerned that other schemes planned or promoted at the time might wish to gain running powers over the line. These could drain the LNWR's own traffic, but as a single line this would not be an attractive option for such promoters. There certainly were such proposals, but in the end those schemes that did come to fruition only served to enhance the LNWR traffic, as we shall see in subsequent chapters.

The LNWR was evidently always on the look out for new passenger traffic. A rather strange entry in the PWWEC minutes dates from 17 January 1859 which records that it agreed "*to provide a private way from the Nantwich lock-up across the Company's land to the railway station for Police and Prisoners only. Rent of one shilling per annum is payable, but the privilege should be withdrawn if the Company find it objectionable.*" There is no record as to how long this agreement lasted.

Tenders were received by the PWWEC on 8 November 1860 for a passenger shed at Wrenbury, as follows :

William Tarrat	£135
W. Jackson	£200
Morrris & Meakin	£285

William Tarrat's tender, being the lowest was accepted, even though it was lower than the Engineer's estimate of £170.

A crossover became necessary at Wrenbury, presumably following the doubling of the line at this location, and so connecting the two running lines and permitting access from the down side to the goods yard which was situated on the up side. This was installed by 7 June 1861.

The PWWEC authorised the platforms at Willaston, Prees and Wrenbury to be lengthened by 20 yards on 5 July 1861. Further minor works were also authorised on this day : alterations to the porters' rooms at Wem and Nantwich, and a fence of iron hurdles to be erected on the platform at Wrenbury. A tender from Gough & Sons for a weighing machine in the goods yard at Hadnall was accepted on 15 April 1862.

Widening was completed in stages, seemingly from the Crewe direction, and as each stage was completed (i.e. from one station to another) the traffic was allowed to use the new running lines. Inevitably, it was not possible to leave the existing single line entirely in place. While the track alongside the up platforms could remain undisturbed, some realignment was required where the existing track passed alongside the down platforms. This work was finally completed in 1862, although as we shall see later, there was no immediate increase in passenger services.

These works were reflected in Shrewsbury, where further changes were necessary to cope with the anticipated additional traffic, as well as increased volumes from the other lines. Between 1861 and 1863, a new platform was added on the eastern side, adjacent to Howard Street, for the use of local services, and this required an additional roof span. The existing platforms were lengthened by some 400 feet, which required extension of the existing roof spans. Whilst the arrangement of existing platforms was otherwise unaltered, the new platform meant that the old arrivals platform then became an island platform. The use of the original 'arrivals' and 'departures' platforms was changed so that they became used by through main line services passing in each direction, which was a much more logical use of the available track space as well as for passenger convenience. A new Joint Committee comprising solely representatives from the LNWR and GWR was formed in 1864, resulting from the absorption of the earlier independent companies. This obviously made for a more efficient organisation to administer the busy station. Eventually, in 1872, a new subway was constructed to link the platforms.

Much later, the cattle pens were rearranged at Wem (cost £33) by order of the PWWEC on 21 September 1871. On 16 May 1872 this committee authorised the offices at Whitchurch to be altered, and further goods sidings to be provided at an estimated cost of £6,810. In addition, a goods warehouse was to be erected at Prees, along with a 30cwt crane and a crossover for the goods sidings at a cost of £357. On the 20 August 1872, the PWWC authorised the expenditure of £1,460 for further coal sidings at Whitchurch, and for Poole's Siding to be extended at £52. The works at Whitchurch were carried out during the construction of the Tattenhall branch, and indicate that laying of the new junction was taken as an opportunity to improve the handling of goods at this location. As the Cambrian branch from Oswestry had been in operation for some eight years by that time, it is almost inevitable that improvements would have become necessary.

CHAPTER TWO

FURTHER PROPOSED LINES

During the 'Second Railway Mania' of the 1860s, several schemes were proposed for other railways in this area, but were never built. Some because the schemes were simply not realistic, and others because the backers ran out of money either because the schemes could not attract the necessary finance, or because the company had concentrated its resources on other lines. Those that would have linked or crossed the Shrewsbury to Crewe line are given below in chronological order, starting with two earlier proposals. The more outlandish schemes are not included.

Manchester and Milford Railway

Plans were deposited in 1845 for a scheme to link the two towns in the title of this railway, although from the outset it required running powers over the Manchester and Birmingham Railway between Manchester and Crewe. Southwards the line was planned to continue through Whitchurch, Oswestry, Welshpool, Newtown, Llanidloes, Lampeter, Newcastle Emlyn, and Haverfordwest to Milford Haven. A branch was to run from Devil's Bridge to Aberystwyth. It was engineered by Rastrick, and was estimated to cost around £2.6 million.

Like many other schemes of this period, it never received Royal Assent, and the initial plan disappeared, although several portions of its overall route did appear in later railways. Eventually this company's railway was constructed (opening throughout in 1867) but only ran from Aberystwyth to Pencader (south of Lampeter), with an isolated branch from Llanidloes to Llangurig that curiously never opened. Thus the railway never reached anywhere near the two towns in its title. From our point of view, the proposed section from Crewe to Whitchurch is one that was later used by the LNWR, although slightly modified.

Shrewsbury and Chester Junction Railway

In 1846 plans were deposited for a branch line from near Leaton (4 miles northwest of Shrewsbury) from a south facing junction on this company's line to run northeastwards to Wem at a point some 200 yards south of the eventual station. Here it was proposed to link with an authorised line of the SURCC who had obtained powers in their Act of 1845 to convert their canals into railways. This would have necessitated a new line to link with the SURCC's nearest canal, at Prees, some four miles northwards. Authorisation was contained in the Shrewsbury, Oswestry and Chester Junction (Crickheath and Wem Branches) Act, 1846, passed on 27 July of that year, but there was no mention of the link northwards to Prees. Perhaps this 'missing link' caused the project to falter, and so powers to abandon the branch to Wem were applied for, and contained in the Shrewsbury and Chester Railway (Birkenhead Station) Act, 1851. It appears that other than preparing the plans, no other work was ever done on this proposed branch to Wem.

However, the scheme did not go away entirely, as on 29 November, 1853 the company deposited further plans for a line of 4 miles 1 furlong and 50 chains from near Rednal on their Chester line to join the proposed LNWR line at Broughton (just north of Yorton) at a north facing junction. In this case, no Act was obtained and the project seems to have quietly disappeared.

Oswestry, Ellesmere and Whitchurch Railway

During 1861 the OEWR planned to make a line from near Welshampton (two miles east of Ellesmere) southeastwards to join the LNWR Crewe – Shrewsbury line about one mile north of Yorton station. However, this plan was not accepted in Parliamentary Committee, and so it was revised to run instead to join the LNWR at Wem. Authorisation was enacted on 7 August 1862, in the OEWR Act (Vict.25 & 26, chapter 218) for the construction of this branch, to be completed within three years. It was to join the LNWR Crewe – Shrewsbury line at a south facing junction near Creamore Farm, just over a mile north of Wem station, and near to the 20¾ mile post from Crewe. As the OEWR was not enjoying cordial terms with the GWR at this time, it was intended that traffic from the Wrexham area, via a Wrexham to Ellesmere line proposed by the WMCQR, would be able to reach the Midlands more directly, avoiding the GWR routes. However, the OEWR decided against building the Wem branch, and it was formally abandoned in the Cambrian Railways (Additional Powers) Act (Vict.28 &29, chapter 277) of 5 July 1865. Possibly the reason for abandoning these plans lay with the intransigence of the WMCQR, as their proposed branch from Wrexham to Ellesmere was never built. Instead many years passed before an independent concern, the Wrexham & Ellesmere Railway constructed that line, opening in 1895 and worked by the Cambrian.

A further branch had been included in plans deposited on 29 November 1862, leaving the Wem branch near to the hamlet of Waterloo at a north facing junction, and running for 1 ¾ miles to Prees. Here it would join the LNWR line at a north facing junction immediately south of the station level crossing. This was proposed in conjunction with the schemes detailed in the following section, but was never proceeded with.

Drayton Junction Railway
Wrexham, Mold & Connah's Quay Railway

Plans for this line were deposited on 30 November 1861. The Drayton Junction Railway was an independent concern promoting a 10½ mile line from the LNWR Crewe to Stafford main line at Mill Meece, through Market Drayton to a south facing junction with the Crewe to Shrewsbury line at Prees, 3½ miles north of Wem. Not surprisingly, the LNWR objected and the line never achieved its enabling Act. However, the small but ambitious Wrexham, Mold & Connah's Quay Railway (WMCQR) revived the scheme the following year, and on 29 November, 1862 deposited plans for a similar scheme. This time the eastern end of the line ran parallel with the LNWR from near Mill Meece to Stafford, where it formed a junction. At the other end, the railway would have formed a junction with, then crossed the LNWR Crewe – Shrewsbury line at Whitchurch to join a separately promoted WMCQR line running westwards to Wrexham. This too ran into fierce opposition from the LNWR. Undaunted, a further scheme was deposited a year later on 30 November,1863 this time including a triangular junction at Prees, from where the branch of the authorised Oswestry, Ellesmere & Whitchurch Railway (OEWR) mentioned above, would connect. Strong objections by the LNWR prevented the authorisation of this line.

However, the WMCQR was evidently persistent in its objectives, for the following year on 29 November, 1864, it presented further amendments to its plans. This time the line near Whitchurch was rerouted to form a junction with the OEWR near Bettisfield (5 miles south west of Whitchurch) thus connecting with its planned line from Wrexham to Ellesmere. Once again it failed in Parliament, but the following year presented further plans with its Drayton Railway Extensions, deposited on 30 November 1865. This incorporated a revised junction near Stafford to take a further line towards Cannock Chase (and thus tap the newly emerging coalfield there). The LNWR must have breathed a sigh of relief when this plan was rejected by Parliament, and proved to be the last from this particular direction. Benjamin Piercy was given as the engineer for all of these plans, although the final plans also included Francis Croughton Stileman, and John Robinson McClean (who had earlier championed the South Staffordshire Railway).

Potteries Junction Railway
Shrewsbury and Potteries Junction Railway

Plans were deposited by the Potteries Junction Railway on 30 November 1862 for a line from Newcastle-under-Lyme via Market Drayton to a north facing junction with the Shrewsbury to Crewe line at Whitchurch. It then proceeded northwestwards on to Pulford (5 miles south of Chester), where another north facing junction would be made on the Shrewsbury and Chester Railway. The plans were modified in the following year, when the section from Market Drayton to Whitchurch and Pulford were dropped, possibly because of the rival plans of the WMCQR.

In 1864 the company changed its name, and on 30 November, 1864 deposited plans, which whilst similar to those of the PJR, westwards from Market Drayton ran to the LNWR Shrewsbury to Crewe line, but did not make a junction. Instead it ran parallel alongside for ½ mile as far as Battlefield, on the outskirts of Shrewsbury, where it turned south to join the Shrewsbury and Birmingham Railway at a west facing junction. This southern section virtually replicated the original plans of the LNWR in their initial attempt for the Crewe line to enter Shrewsbury, as we have seen in Chapter One. As might be expected the LNWR and GWR objected, and the line never received Parliamentary approval.

Birkenhead, North Wales and Stafford Railway

Plans were deposited at Shrewsbury County Court on 30 November,1872 for this complex series of railways. The first line left the WMCQR at Wrexham, then made a connection with the GWR Shrewsbury to Chester line north of Ruabon, continuing eastwards from Cefn to join the LNWR at Whitchurch, then across to the GWR Wellington and Market Drayton line. It then used running powers over the North Staffordshire Railway line for a short distance before heading south-eastwards to join the Stafford and Uttoxeter Railway at Stafford. The surveyor was given as Charles S. Cheffins and the engineers as W.H.Barlow and T.E.Minshall. In April 1873 several 'influential townsmen' of Market Drayton are said to have supported this proposal. Although the line had been properly surveyed, it faced the combined opposition of the LNWR, GWR and NSR and never received its enabling Act.

Whitchurch, Nantwich and Cheshire Lines Junction Railway

The plans for this proposal were deposited in 1883, and were for two lines. The first was to leave the Cambrian Railways' Ellesmere line southwest of Whitchurch and head north, making a further junction with the LNWR Tattenhall Branch, and then to run further north to join the Winsford Branch of the West Cheshire Railway. The second was to run from the GWR Market Drayton to Nantwich line, just south of Nantwich, cross over the Shrewsbury to Crewe line and join the first line near Brindley Bank (4 miles north of Nantwich). The intention was to give the GWR a route to Manchester, but like its other attempts it never materialised. Although stated to be engineered by Edgar O. Ferguson, no Act was ever authorised for its construction.

CHAPTER THREE

PASSENGER WORKINGS

In this chapter we will look at the frequency of passenger and associated workings over the line from the start in 1858 until 1966. This latter year has been chosen as the starting point of 'modern' workings, mainly because it marked the demise of steam working. However, it also marked a change in the manner of working the line. Train services joining or leaving from the three connecting lines (Market Drayton line, Cambrian line and Tattenhall branch) will be dealt with in later chapters. Consequently, all such traffic is excluded from the data referred to in this chapter ; we shall be dealing purely with that traffic that ran between Shrewsbury and Crewe, and between intermediate points along the route.

Early services : 1858 to 1888

As mentioned briefly in Chapter One, the opening services on 1 September 1858 comprised five trains each way on weekdays and one on Sundays. These ran on weekdays from Shrewsbury at 6.50am, 9.25am, 12.40pm, 5.00pm and 7.40pm, and on Sundays at 3.00pm. From Crewe they were timed to leave at 6.00am, 8.50am, 12 noon, 5.20pm and 7.40pm, with Sundays at 11.30am. The first up, and second and fifth down weekday services, plus both Sunday trains conveyed carriages for 1st, 2nd, and 3rd class passengers. All other trains conveyed only 1st and 2nd class carriages. A copy of the timetable is reproduced opposite, from which it may be assumed that the trains conveying only 1st and 2nd class passengers ran to / from Manchester and / or Liverpool in the north and Hereford in the south. As the line southwards from Shrewsbury to Hereford was still an independent undertaking at this time (the LNWR did not acquire its stake in this line until 1862), there was presumably at least a change of engines at Shrewsbury. However, timetables from these early periods can be notoriously misleading, and any such assumptions must be treated with care. Even in later days, the attaching or detaching of through carriages were sometimes subject to pretty sharp timings, leading the unwary to assume that they were through trains. Conversely, in the days before restaurant cars were available, some trains that were ostensibly two separate workings, lingered for half an hour or more (particularly at Shrewsbury), to enable passengers to visit the refreshment rooms.

The fastest trains in 1858 were the 9.25am and 12.40pm from Shrewsbury, both taking only 1 hour 5 minutes, although the latter made additional stops at Yorton (shown here incorrectly as "Yarton") and Prees. The slowest was the 6.00am up from Crewe, which took a whole two hours, despite stopping only at Nantwich, Whitchurch and Wem. Some of the trains stopping at every station took nearly half an hour less ! Bearing mind that the line was single for much of its length, trains crossed at either Wem or Whitchurch. For the purposes of our study, it is prudent to consider these early services as mostly 'local' in nature.

Less than two years later, in April 1860, the pattern of services was identical, although some of timings had changed. For example, the first three up services then departed Crewe at 8.40am, 10.45am and 3.10pm, whilst the remainder showed little, if any, change. But just four months later, in August of that year one weekday service each way had been added : the 12 noon up was reinstated, and the 12.40pm down was replaced by one at 11.55am and one at 1.55pm. A further down Sunday service left Shrewsbury at 7.00am, and an additional up Sunday train left Crewe at 8.35pm. Using the same criteria as for 1858, it would appear that three weekday trains ran to / from Manchester and / or Liverpool. This overall pattern of six each way on weekdays and two on Sundays remained the same throughout 1861 with only minor time changes. By January 1863 the line had been completed as double track throughout, so an increase in services might be expected. However, there was no change on weekdays, and the Sunday service had actually reverted to one each way.

But the March to June 1867 Working Timetables showed that one further weekday service had been added, although the Sunday service remained at one each way. One hour and five minutes remained the fastest time between Shrewsbury and Crewe.

Five years later, the June 1872 Working Timetable showed a further service each way on weekdays, with still just one on Sundays. At this point, it could reasonably be claimed that one train, the 1.25pm up from Crewe could be considered as an "express" as it stopped only at Whitchurch and achieved an overall time of just 50 minutes.

This brings us to the point at which the "North & West Expresses" can be considered to have begun. The impetus for the introduction of these workings can be said to have been the opening of the Severn Tunnel, on 1 December 1886. It became clear to the LNWR that they could tap the traffic potential of South Western England, which had hitherto been the province of the GWR and the Midland Railway. The only limiting factor was the lack of standard gauge track beyond Exeter, a deficiency not remedied until May 1892. Also, by the judicious use of 'through carriages' they could access parts of South Wales passenger traffic, although a limited through semi-fast service had operated from Shrewsbury to Newport (Mill Street) until 1882 . The only other route to South Wales was, of course, their Central Wales line, which the LNWR had operated since 1867. However, this was never considered as an "express" route due to its meandering nature, and so alternatives had to be sought.

The "North & West Expresses"

This section will examine the development of these "express" services, and for the benefit of clarity, local services between Shrewsbury and Crewe will be dealt with in the following section.

The June 1888 Working Timetable shows that expresses had been introduced between Shrewsbury and Crewe, with 6 up weekday (one less on Mondays), leaving Crewe at 1.20am (MX), 9.30am, 11.30am, 1.12pm, 4.00pm and 4.35pm. The first, third and fifth and Sunday were non stop, but the second and fourth paused at Whitchurch to facilitate Cambrian connections, and the sixth, although described as an express, actually stopped at Nantwich, Whitchurch and Wem. The 1.20am departure was the sole up Sunday express. There were just 3 down weekday expresses, leaving Shrewsbury at 12.40pm, 7.05pm and 10.25pm, all of which were non stop. Sunday did not benefit from any down expresses.

On 1 July 1888 a new service was introduced with the cooperation of the GWR between Crewe and Bristol. The through trains were worked by the LNWR north of Shrewsbury, and the GWR southwards. Through carriages to / from more northerly locations were added or detached at Crewe, in a procedure that was to become something of a hallmark (if not a considerable complication) for the services over the many years to come. Further additions were made at Pontypool Road and Bristol. There were initially three trains in each direction, and in the Summer of 1889 a fourth was added. With the gauge change finally settled in 1892, some of these trains ran through to other destinations in Devon and Cornwall, although in many cases the carriages were added or detached from existing services to the required destinations. By 1900 through carriages from Glasgow, Edinburgh, Manchester, Liverpool, Leeds, Newcastle ran to Bristol, Exeter, Paignton, Kingswear, Newquay, Penzance, Newport and Cardiff. But any intending passenger may well have to change carriage at least once en route, even though remaining in what was essentially the same train. The potential for actually reaching one's intended destination at this time must have bordered on "extremely risky"! The number of such services were obviously greater in Summer, as the increasing number of affluent middle class families could afford to spend holidays at the attractive resort areas of South West England and Wales. However, one of the negatives was that in order to cater for the distance travelled, and the inevitable changeover at resort hotels, many of the workings ran during the night or at least in the early morning hours.

Passenger comfort was being addressed at last, as corridor trains had been introduced on the "North & West" services by 1904, which was much later than on the principal LNWR services elsewhere. The Winter service in February 1908 comprised 4 up weekday and two Sunday expresses, complemented by 6 down weekday and one Sunday. There was little change by April 1910, which saw this increase slightly to 7 up weekday (two less on Mondays), and two on Sundays. The corresponding down workings totalled 7 (one less on Mondays) and two on Sundays. These services were known as the "West of England Express", with the exception of the 9.00am departure from Bristol to be known as the "Scotch Express", as it conveyed through carriages to Glasgow. More impressively, the 12.45pm from Bristol by then had been upgraded with the benefit of a Luncheon Car (to Liverpool), and the 4.10pm departure grandly promised a "Luncheon, Tea and Dining Car" all the way from Plymouth to Liverpool. Similar facilities were offered by a corresponding number of southbound services.

In January, 1912 the LNWR joined many of the other British railway companies in abolishing the use of second class travel, so that in future only 'first' and 'third' classes remained.

Whale "Precursor" Class 4-4-0 no. 515 CHAMPION runs into Whitchurch with an up train in 1923, still carrying its LNW number and livery despite the proliferation of LMS wagons in the yard. From the number of carriages this working is almost certainly a semi-fast service, stopping only at the major stations en route. The road bridge in the background rises over the Tattenhall branch, and the houses appear to be recently built.
[G.Coltas Collection]

The splendid array of semaphore signals at the north end of Shrewsbury station frame two services awaiting departure in 1956. The services are not known, but on the left, Stanier "Jubilee" 4-6-0 No.45644 HOWE is certainly at the head of a West To North express, whilst 'Black Five' no. 45102 is heading a stopping train. At the end of the platform on the left, the right hand skewed running-in board appears to be an LMS example, whilst the left hand board has been replaced by a BR (WR) enamel board. [R.Mulford]

Britain's involvement in the Great War officially began on 5 August, 1914, but there were initially no major changes to the railway timetables – in fact restaurant car facilities were only slowly withdrawn from 1915 onwards, although many were later reinstated as the war progressed. The October 1914 Working Timetable showed a level of service virtually identical to that in 1910, but the number of express services was reduced during the later period of this conflict. Primarily due to the ensuing shortage of manpower, this situation did not really improve to its prewar levels until 1921, when the numbers were 6 up weekdays, one up Sundays, 8 down weekdays and one down Sundays. There was little change in the following year, (5 up weekdays, 2 up Sundays; 7 down weekdays, 2 down Sundays) which was period of great uncertainty, as the Liberal government of the day was considering nationalisation of the railways, but in the end went for a partial solution, which we know as the "Grouping". The LNWR then became part of the LMSR Company as from 1 January 1923.

Interestingly, as a result of the General Strike (4 to 13 May, 1926) the LMS introduced a temporary timetable, running from 31 May until further notice, to cater for stock and locomotives not available, and more seriously, the continuing shortage of coal. The effect on the North to West expresses was to limit these to one up and two down on weekdays, with none on Sundays.

The 1920s and 1930s saw large changes to the aspirations of the 'working classes' arising from their improved pay and working conditions, which was reflected in their ability to take holidays of up to one week away from home. So it is not surprising that the holiday destinations served by the "North & West Expresses" saw this reflected by an increase in frequency. The following table may help to appreciate the changes occurring in this and subsequent periods :

			Number of services						
			Mon	Tues	Wed	Thurs	Fri	Sat	Sun
1931	Summer	Up	6	7	7	7	7	12	3
		Down	7	7	7	7	7	7	3
1939	Summer	Up	8	10	10	10	12	22	4
		Down	7	7	7	7	7	16	4
1939	Emergency	Up	4	4	4	4	4	4	3
	Timetable	Down	4	4	4	4	4	4	1
1944	Summer	Up	10	9	9	9	9	11	5
		Down	11	10	10	10	11	11	6
1952	Summer	Up	8	8	8	8	10	18	5
		Down	10	9	9	9	10	18	7
1958	Summer	Up	8	8	8	8	13	20	5
		Down	9	9	9	9	10	22	9
1962/63	Winter	Up	7	7	7	7	8	13	5
		Down	7	6	6	6	7	15	8
1964	Summer	Up	7	7	7	7	8	10	5
		Down	11	11	11	11	11	10	8
1966	Summer	Up	7	7	7	7	10	18	7
		Down	10	11	11	11	11	22	7

West to North expresses changed engines at Shrewsbury, which made for an interesting spectacle. During the 1950s and 60s, the BR Standard Pacifics allocated to Cardiff's Canton shed were regular performers on the southern leg of these services, and were turned out well by their home shed, as we see here with No.70016 ARIEL, which has just arrived with the 4.10pm Swansea – Manchester on 2 June 1961. [Transport Treasury / J. Harold]

After the removal of No.70016, Stanier 'Black Five' 4-6-0 No. 45298 takes over the Swansea express for the run to Manchester. Interestingly, the engine is paired to a self-weighing tender. On the right, Stanier "Jubilee" 4-6-0 No. 45678 DE ROBECK awaits departure with a northbound stopping train. [Transport Treasury / J. Harold]

At Willaston on 17 April 1954, Stanier ' Black Five' 4-6-0 No. 45134 passes at the head of an up 8-coach express. The station was well decked out with flower beds, although it was to close to passengers within eight months. [H. Townley/ J.M. Bentley Collection]

Rebuilt "Royal Scot" 4-6-0 No. 46131 THE ROYAL WARWICKSHIRE REGIMENT steams through Willaston with an up North to West express in the early 1950s. The LMS 'target' station nameboard has survived on the down platform. [H. Townley/ J.M. Bentley Collection]

On a wet 19th of May in 1952, "Royal Scot" Class 4-6-0 No. 46163 CIVIL SERVICE RIFLEMAN gets under way after a pause in Whitchurch station with a southbound train. The line to Oswestry can be seen curving off to the right, as well as the Cambrian Junction signal box that controlled the junction and the southern end of the station. [P.J.Garland Collection]

Stanier "Princess Coronation" 4-6-2 No. 46251 CITY OF NOTTINGHAM heads southwards out of Willaston with a heavy North and West express on 23 June 1956. The carriages comprise a consistent cream and carmine livery, and appear to be mostly of Western Region origin, reflecting the alternate use of LMR and WR stock on these services. [H. Townley/ J.M. Bentley Collection]

Rebuilt "Royal Scot" 4-6-0 No. 46119 LANCASHIRE FUSILIER speeds into Whitchurch with a southbound North and West express on 27 September 1958. It has just passed beneath the lengthy pedestrian suspension footbridge. [E.R.Morten]

A relief Paignton to Manchester London Road express passes the village of Haston, north of Hadnall on 5 September 1958 behind Stanier "Jubilee" Class 4-6-0 no. 45629 STRAITS SETTLEMENTS. [M.H.C. Baker]

On the same day Shrewsbury shed's BR Standard Class 5 4-6-0 no. 73131 passes the same location at Haston with the 11.30am Swansea to Manchester London Road. Ten sequentially numbered BR Standard Class 5s fitted with Caprotti valve gear (nos. 73125 to 73134) were provided to the Western Region when new, and all initially allocated to Shrewsbury, but eventually all moved away. [M.H.C. Baker]

A work stained Hughes / Fowler 'Crab' 2-6-0 No. 42925 hauls a 12 coach North and West express through Willaston on 23 June 1956. The varied nature of the stock suggests that this was probably a relief service, as such workings tended to comprise whatever passenger stock could be found lurking in a Division's sidings. [H. Townley/ J.M. Bentley Collection]

Passing through Yorton in the mid 1950s, Stanier Pacific No. 46254 CITY OF STOKE-ON-TRENT of Crewe North shed, heads an up North and West express consisting of LMR 'blood and custard' stock. The station nameboard dates from the LMS days. [P.Ward]

Polmadie shed's Stanier Pacific no. 46223 PRINCESS ALICE, in ex-works condition, heads a southbound north and West express out of Wem on 18 October 1956. At least the first two vehicles of this service are Collett former GWR stock. [M.H.C. Baker]

"Patriot" Class 4-6-0 no. 45507 ROYAL TANK CORPS of Crewe North shed, approaches Yorton with the 7.10am Manchester London Road to Paignton and Plymouth, consisting of 10 coaches. The date is 2 September 1958. [M.H.C. Baker]

West of Willaston, Stanier "Jubilee" 4-6-0 No. 45638 ZANZIBAR gets into its stride with an up North and West express comprised of a motley assortment of carriages. The date is 23 June, 1956. [H. Townley/ J.M. Bentley Collection]

Shrewsbury offered the photographer a number of interesting views at the north end, as engines were changed. Here, fresh from overhaul at Crewe Works and bearing its 31B (March) shed plate B.R. Standard 4-6-2 No. 70009 ALFRED THE GREAT is taking water, preparatory to relieving the engine of an incoming West to North express around 1960. The southern footbridge was still in place at this time. Meanwhile, on the right, Collett "Grange" Class 4-6-0 No.6833 CALCOT GRANGE has arrived from the Hereford direction. [P.Ward]

South of Yorton station, Stanier 'Black Five' no. 45189 of Crewe North shed heads a lengthy West to North express on 13 September 1961. [M.H.C. Baker]

About two miles north of Whitchurch, red liveried Stanier Pacific No. 46228 DUCHESS OF RUTLAND with an up seven coach North and West express on 30 August 1962. [Lens of Sutton Association – R.G.Nelson]

Stanier Pacific No. 46248 CITY OF LEEDS in lined out red livery makes a fine sight as it heads southwards around 1964 with a surprisingly short six coach load of equally well turned out maroon passenger stock. It has just left Wem and is about to cross the Tilley Road level crossing. [P.Ward]

As we have seen in earlier photographs, some of the North and West expresses were reduced to just six coaches at various times. One such example is seen here, with B.R. Standard 4-6-2 No.70051 FIRTH OF FORTH steaming through Hadnall around 1964. Although the station had been closed for about four years by this time, it was evidently still kept in good order. [P.Ward]

The increase in services in the 1930s is not surprising, and the number of starting points once again increased. This meant that trains were often remarshalled several times along their intended route. Conversely, some through carriages developed into through trains in their own right. The 1939 Emergency Timetable is included to illustrate those measures that were considered necessary on the outbreak of World War II. However, these restrictions were not to last, as can be seen from the frequencies shown for 1944. The movement of troops during this war would have of course, greatly increased the traffic over this (and almost all other) lines, but data relating to such movements is simply not available. The remainder of the services during the 1950s show a steady growth, particularly at weekends, and in order to ensure reasonably comparative data, most of the periods illustrated here relate to the Summer months. The exception is for 1962/63 Winter which is shown to illustrate the level to which the "North & West Expresses" fell during these months. The next consideration is that of the increased use of the motor car during the early 1960s. Perhaps the most surprising aspect here is that these express services did not diminish as much as might have been expected - for the general level was still higher than in the 1950s, and overall by 1966 was easily comparable. A further factor at work at this time was the electrification of the West Coast main line during the early to mid 1960s, which caused a change in the pattern of some through services, particularly those from the West Midlands to the North West, some of which were rerouted via Shrewsbury and Crewe. As an example, the "Pines Express" which was routed this way, then via Wellington to Wolverhampton from September 1963 until 1967, as mentioned in Chapter 7. Another change that was to be introduced gradually, was the inclusion of a stop for some through "North & West Expresses" at Whitchurch. This began shortly after nationalisation, and by the mid 1950s two or three daily trains would make a stop here, but by the 1960s there were five or six such stops made in each direction. On occasions, stops were also inserted at Nantwich and Wem, presumably for the benefit of those locals travelling on holiday, although they would almost certainly need to make further changes of train at some later stage in their journey.

Local stopping services

Starting again in 1888, when there was a clear separation of through expresses from local stopping trains, we can examine the frequency of services over the period up to the outbreak of the Second World War :

Overall it must be said that there was no great change in the level of local services between 1888 and 1939. Obviously, timings changed periodically, but not radically. However, there were some interesting workings : firstly, the 'alternate Mondays' working from Crewe at 1.45pm to Wrenbury in 1910 was intended for the benefit of cattle auctions at Wrenbury on these days, and ran from around 1900 until after the outbreak of the Great War. There was no return working shown, so presumably persons attending the auction returned by normal schedule services, at whatever times were convenient. It is easy to imagine that when the auctions were over, many people would refresh themselves until whatever time the local pubs shut. Curiously, the SO working from Crewe to Nantwich ran in the same path with the 1.45pm departure time.

Amid the peasant countryside that typifies this line, LNWR Bowen – Cooke "Prince of Wales" Class 4-6-0 No. 2275 EDITH CAVELL makes easy work of a northbound stopping train around 1920, possibly approaching Willaston. This engine was completed at Crewe in November 1915, renumbered by the LMSR as 25647, and withdrawn in January 1935. [J.M. Bentley Collection]

Bowen – Cooke "Prince of Wales" Class 4-6-0 LMS No. 5672 CONDOR arrives at the old Platform 4 of Shrewsbury station with an up stopping train at 12.44pm on 17 August 1933. This locomotive was built at Crewe as LNWR No.867 in January 1916, rebuilt with outside Walschaerts valve gear in 1923 (as shown here), and was withdrawn in December, 1936. It is recorded as having its name removed in July 1933, but the date of this photograph belies that assertion. A G.W.R. vehicle is occupying the bay platform in the background. [E.R.Morten]

In 1910, of the 8 Crewe to Shrewsbury workings, two continued to Hereford and one to Pontypool Road. In the down direction, of the 8 Shrewsbury to Crewe timings, two originated from Hereford. In 1914 there were four through Hereford workings each way included in the 9 Shrewsbury – Crewe services each way on weekdays. Sundays saw one up and two down services (one of the latter from Hereford), plus one each way between Whitchurch and Crewe. By 1921 only one such weekday working in each direction continued to / from Hereford.

	1888 Up	1888 Down	1910 Up	1910 Down	1921 Up	1921 Down	1931 Up	1931 Down	1939 Up	1939 Down
WEEKDAYS										
Between Crewe and :										
Nantwich	2 +1SO	2 +1SO	1 +1 SO	1 +1 SO	1 +1SO	1 +1SO	1 +1SO	1 +1SO	1 SO	1 SO
Wrenbury			1MO*		1	+1 SX				
Whitchurch	2	2	3	3	2	3	2	2 +1SO	4	4 +1SO
Shrewsbury	6	10	8	8	8 +1MO	8	7	9 +2SO	7 +1SO	9
Between Whitchurch and S'bury			1	1			1	1	1	1
Wem and Shrewsbury									1 WSO	
* note : runs on alternate Mondays										
SUNDAYS										
Between Crewe and :										
Whitchurch			1		1	1	2	2	3	2
Shrewsbury	2	1	2	2	1	2	1	2	3	6

During the early 1910s the LNWR experimented with the use of steam propelled railmotors. These were tried on the stopping services from Crewe to Nantwich, after the opening of the halts at Nantwich Newcastle Crossing and Gresty (adjacent to Gresty Green) on 1st January, 1911. In 1914 there were four weekday workings in each direction and one more

Stanier Pacifics often performed 'fill-in' turns, such as No.46254 CITY OF STOKE-ON-TRENT with this local stopping train from Crewe to Shrewsbury, seen here at Willaston on 28 September 1952. The driver is returning to the cab, possibly as he has stopped across the level crossing. The footbridge gave access to both platforms, but also gave pedestrians access across the line whilst the gates were closed. [H. Townley/ J.M. Bentley Collection]

One evening in 1953, Stanier "Jubilee" 4-6-0 No.45595 SOUTHERN RHODESIA (of Crewe North shed) rolls into Whitchurch with a northbound stopping train from Shrewsbury. Locomotives of all types were used on the local stopping trains, not just for running in after overhaul at Crewe Works, but for a whole host of other operating reasons. It has just passed the Whitchurch Cambrian Junction signal box. [Whitchurch Archeological & History Group]

The large LMS running-in board dominates this scene, proclaiming the many available at Whitchurch, as Stanier Class 5 4-6-0 No.45308 (of Carlisle Upperby shed) arrives with a Crewe to Shrewsbury stopping train in the mid 1950s.[B.K.B. Green]

Fowler "Patriot" Class 4-6-0 no.45515 CAERNARVON leaves Yorton with the 12.15pm all stations service, comprising four non-corridor coaches, from Shrewsbury to Crewe on 11 September 1959.The station can be seen in the distance. [M.H.C. Baker]

on Saturdays. The up trains departed from Crewe at 11.15am, 1.45pm SX, 2.00pm SO, 6.14pm, 8.35pm and 11.05pm. These stopped at Gresty, Willaston, Newcastle Crossing and terminated at Nantwich just 14 minutes after leaving Crewe. Return workings from Nantwich were at 12.05pm, 2.10pm SX, 2.25pm SO, 7.15pm, 9.30pm, and 11.35pm SO. The lack of early morning services makes it questionable as to whether this may have been of benefit to workers in Crewe. Nonetheless, the interruption caused by the Great War is likely to have caused some operating inconvenience, and as these halts were closed on 1 April, 1918 it is believed that this service ceased at the same time.

The temporary timetable introduced as from 31 May, 1926 was mentioned earlier. The effect was to limit the services to 6 up and 5 down weekday stopping trains between Crewe and Shrewsbury. The Crewe – Whitchurch service of one up and two down was not changed, nor the Crewe – Nantwich Saturdays only one return trip, and so also the Mail trains. Sunday trains between Crewe and Shrewsbury were one up and two down, with just the one Mail train in each direction to complete the line service.

In 1931 the Sundays Only 11.05am from Crewe to Shrewsbury was booked as a passenger service only as far as Whitchurch, from where it continued to Shrewsbury purely as a parcels train.

	1949 Up	1949 Down	1952 Up	1952 Down	1956/7 Up	1956/7 Down	1962/3 Up	1962/3 Down	1965/6 Up	1965/6 Down
WEEKDAYS										
Between Crewe										
and : Whitchurch		1SX	1	2	1	1	1		1FSX	1FSX
Shrewsbury	8	7	7	8	7	7	10	11 +1SO	6	9
Between										
Wem and										
Shrewsbury		1WSO		1SO		1SO				
SUNDAYS										
Between										
Crewe *and :* Shrewsbury	3	3	3	3	3	5	3	3	0	0

Once more the overall level of services had changed little in the immediate post nationalisation period. The WSO working was a late evening service for the benefit of Wem inhabitants returning from Shrewsbury at 10.52pm and Wem, but this Wednesday working had been discontinued by 1952 when only the Saturday working remained. Evidently the good people of Wem no longer felt it necessary to have a late night out in the county town on a Wednesday as well as a Saturday. This SO service was still timetabled in 1958, but had disappeared by 1962. The return working was as empty stock at 11.25pm back to Shrewsbury.

Just one train ran through from Hereford to Crewe by 1949 and this continued until 1957. Incidentally, in March 1957 it was noticed that the 5.45pm stopping service from Shrewsbury to Crewe was being worked by a WR "Hall" class 4-6-0 rather than an LMR engine, and that this returned on the 11.00pm parcels working to Pontypool Road. However long this lasted, it was relatively short lived, as DMUs were introduced on to the local stopping services from June, 1958. This introduction resulted in the increase in service levels seen above for 1962. In 1963 the BR regional boundaries were changed so that the LMR Chester Division took over all lines from Craven Arms northwards. This caused a change of policy resulting in an increased number of 'expresses' making stops at Nantwich, Whitchurch and / or Wem, so that the number of purely stopping services was correspondingly reduced. This is apparent in the levels shown for 1965/6, especially in the complete withdrawal of them on Sundays. This enabled the intermediate stations to be closed, with a consequent saving in staff costs.

In 1965/6, a curious working was the 17.55 FSX from Crewe to Whitchurch and return at 18.40, which was shown as "not advertised", and for which no explanation has been found.

Mails, milk and other traffic

Mail had been required to be transported by rail by the Railways (Conveyance of Mails) Act, 1838 which imposed an obligation on all existing and future lines for this transportation. Our line was always an important route for the transport of mails (or parcels, as sometimes described) because of the nature of its north to west route. Shrewsbury had a major sorting office, the result of it lying at the heart of the other lines arriving from all directions. The first Travelling Post Office (TPO) trains incorporating onboard sorting arrived in Shrewsbury in 1857 from Tamworth, where mail had been transferred from London trains. But the major impact was the introduction in 1891 of a York – Shrewsbury TPO, which was complemented by a sorting carriage attached to a Bristol – Manchester "North & West Express" from 1895. This became so busy that it was soon a train in its own right, leaving Bristol at 7.40pm, for Crewe, and later extended to Normanton. In 1897 it was further extended to Stalybridge. Eventually, in 1902 it was finally extended to York, and the service in both directions became known as the "York Mail". In 1910 the southbound service was run in two parts : Crewe to Cardiff , and York to Shrewsbury. However, this was short lived, as the Cardiff portion was withdrawn in 1922, and the TPO service reverted to the York – Shrewsbury section only. This service continued to operate until the withdrawal of TPOs nationwide as from 9 January, 2004.

That, however, is only one part of the story of the mail trains, as many others without the benefit of TPOs continued running as "mails" or "parcels" over the line. Much of the mails and parcels traffic was carried by ordinary passenger trains, either in the guard's compartment, or in vans attached to the front or rear of passenger trains. However, due to the sheer volume sometimes involved, it was more expedient to run special trains, designated in the various working timetables as "mail trains" or "parcels trains".

Mention must be made of the terrible accident that occurred to the north of Shrewsbury station, during the night of 15 October, 1907. The 2.05pm "Night Mail" from Crewe to Bristol approached the tight curve at the approach to Crewe Junction well in excess of the 10 mph speed restriction, resulting in the derailment of the engine and 14 of the 15 vehicles comprising the train. The guard and two signalmen later testified that the speed of the train was estimated at 50 – 60 mph. The driver, fireman and 16 others were killed in the accident, with most of the leading wooden bodied coaches badly damaged. A further 31 persons were badly injured. The engine, Whale "Experiment" class 4-6-0 no. 2052 STEPHENSON which had only been built some 10 months earlier was also badly damaged, but although its tender was scrapped, the locomotive was rebuilt, carrying on in service until December, 1930. The train had been running to time, and was due to stop in the station. But it is believed that the driver, who knew the road well, had been on duty for four of the preceding five nights and was possibly drowsy as a result. The fireman, also well experienced, should have realised that they were travelling too fast, but because he was getting ready for the station stop, was unaware of their exact position at the time. The guard had tried to operate the vacuum brake, but at that moment the driver had just applied it, so any further application was ineffective. Evidently the driver had realised his mistake too late.

In 1931 the only down parcels train operating was the 12.55pm MX Penzance to Crewe, passing through Shrewsbury at 2.35 / 2.55am the next day, and arriving at Crewe at 3.45am. This train also ran on Sundays. An up parcels from Stockport (1.50am) to Hereford passed through Shrewsbury at 4.28 / 4.55am, but on Mondays only it ran just from Crewe (3.42am) to Shrewsbury.

By 1939 the Stockport to Hereford working had been revised to leave there at 3.50am and to run to Bristol, but continued to terminate at Shrewsbury on Mondays. The Penzance to Crewe working continued as in 1931. In 1944 the Penzance – Crewe then left the Cornish port an hour later at 2.00pm, and the Stockport working reverted to its 1.50am departure time, running to Cardiff rather than Bristol, and there was no working on Mondays at all. Additional workings were at 11.42am from Crewe to Craven Arms on weekdays, and at 10.00am from Crewe to Shrewsbury.

With the return to peacetime, the down workings in 1949 were the 2.00pm MX Penzance to Crewe including Sundays, and a 5.15pm Carmarthen to Crewe, running via the Central Wales line and passing through Shrewsbury at 9.40pm (excluding Sundays). In the up direction, the 2.00am Stockport working reverted to Bristol once more, and the Craven Arms and Shrewsbury workings were discontinued. In their stead, a short working ran from Crewe at 5.35am to Whitchurch (excluding Sundays and Mondays), calling at Nantwich and Wrenbury. A further working was introduced, at 2.35pm MX from Crewe to Pontypool Road.

By 1958 the number of parcels workings had increased considerably. In the down direction these passed through Shrewsbury as follows :

3.12am - MX Penzance (dep.2.00pm) to Crewe (including Sundays)

8.55am - MX Shrewsbury to Crewe, calling at all stations except Yorton

9.58pm - Swansea Victoria (dep.4.25pm) to Crewe

10.48pm - Swansea Victoria (dep.6.30pm) TPO Mails to York

In the up direction there were:

2.10am - Crewe (dep.1.25am) to Cardiff, including Sundays

3.07am - York (dep.9.50pm) to Swansea Victoria TPO Mails – Sundays mails to Shrewsbury only, train ran instead to Hereford.

3.46am - MX Crewe (dep.3.00am) to Pontypool Road

4.48am - MX Stockport (dep.2.00am) to Bristol

8.13am - MX Crewe (dep.6.32am) to Shrewsbury, calling at all stations except Yorton

10.47am - Sundays only Crewe (dep.10.00am) to Newport

3.05pm - Crewe (dep.1.55pm) to Hereford MSX, Pontypool Road SO

7.52pm - SO Crewe (dep.6.50pm), calling at Whitchurch, to Willesden Junction, via Stafford

There was a considerable reduction by September 1962 with the down traffic consisting of only the 8.55am MX Shrewsbury to Crewe, the "York Mail" (now leaving Swansea at 6.25pm) and a 7.35pm Carmarthen to Crewe running SX and 'as required'. In the up direction, the 6.50pm SO Crewe – Willesden Junction was dropped, the 3.00am MX from Crewe was extended to Cardiff and there were a number of minor time changes. The local stopping parcels from Crewe at 6.32am continued to call at Hadnall, even though that station had been closed to passengers since May 1960.

Finally, a review of the June 1965 to April 1966 Working Timetable shows a resurgence in parcels traffic, with the following down workings passing through Shrewsbury :

00.38 / 00.52am MX Cardiff (21.35pm) to Crewe

09.01 MX Shrewsbury to Crewe all stations – now starting from Abbey Foregate station

18.21 / 18.24 SX Pontypool Road (15.52) to Manchester Mayfield empty vans

20.57 / 22.50 Aberystwyth (18.05) to York

23.48 / 00.10 Penzance (11.40) to Crewe

In the up direction the workings were :

02.20 / 02.30 Liverpool (00.15) to Cardiff, mails only as far as Shrewsbury

03.17 / 04.10 York (21.52) to Aberystwyth

03.50 / 04.50 Stockport (01.50) to Pontypool Road

14.09 / 15.25 Crewe (13.12) MX to Pontypool Road

18.27 Crewe to Shrewsbury 'as required', calling at Whitchurch only

23.50 / 00.20 SX Crewe (22.56) to Cardiff

So, despite a number of changes over the years, the basic pattern of origins and destinations remained unchanged, with perhaps the notable exception of the destination for the "York Mail" from Swansea to Aberystwyth. By 1982 this had been abbreviated to terminate at Shrewsbury, and the local 'stopping' parcels service was obviously only destined to linger a little while longer. However, whilst Shrewsbury was still regarded as a hub for the sorting and distribution, the conveyor linking the station to the sorting office was taken out of use around 2008 and removed entirely in 2013. There are proposals for this sorting office to close in 2014, with the alternatives offered of sorting at Wolverhampton and Telford being strongly resisted. The decrease in postal traffic resulting from the expansion of internet usage, and local carriers, makes some changes inevitable, so it will be interesting to see what does eventually transpire.

Milk and other perishable traffic was also designated a 'Class A passenger traffic' for obvious reasons. Milk traffic was not noted as separate workings before the 1920s, so it is assumed that as it was shipped in cans, these were simply added to the guard's vans of local passenger workings during this early period. In 1931 there was one down weekday milk train, which left Whitchurch at 9.37am non stop for Crewe, arriving at 10.00am. An empty milk train from Stafford at 5.25pm then called at all stations to set down empty cans, between Shrewsbury and Whitchurch where it terminated at 9.14pm. The dairy at Dorrington, to the south of Shrewsbury on the Hereford line produced through traffic, for which a Sunday down working passed through Shrewsbury at 9.20pm, Whitchurch at 9.50 / 10.09pm, arriving at Crewe at 10.32pm. In the up direction, weekday empty milk trains ran non stop from Crewe at 1.00am to Shrewsbury (1.48am), at 5.00am MO to Whitchurch (arrive 5.30am), and at 2.15pm (ex- Liverpool 11.24am) all stations to Whitchurch (arrive 3.15pm). This latter working is noted "conveys passengers from Wrenbury alternate Tuesdays", perhaps indicating that although passenger stock was provided it was of a limited nature, as they would only be travelling the 4¾ miles to Whitchurch. There were no up Sunday milk workings.

In 1939 there was a considerable simplification, with just one down working on a Sunday at 10.09pm from Whitchurch to Crewe, which also conveyed the empty stock of the 9.20pm stopping passenger service from Crewe. There was no down weekday or up Sunday milk traffic, and the up weekday traffic consisted solely of a 1.00am departure from Crewe for Dorrington, which was to run 'as required'.

After World War II there were no further milk trains run separately, other than those from the Cambrian branch, which are described in Chapter 6.

Other perishable traffic included fish, and fruit and vegetables, the latter being mainly seasonal in nature. In 1931 just one fish train was worked on weekdays, being the 4.53pm from Myrtle Hill Junction (Carmarthen) to Crewe, passing Shrewsbury at 10.00pm. This working continued in 1939, and a return working of empty fish vans was shown as departing Crewe at 12.30am MSX. However, none were shown in 1944 or 1949, but by 1958 there was a 6.30pm SX departure from Crewe for Bristol with empty fish vans which continued until 1963, but no apparent full train working. It is presumed that such a working must have passed over the MR route from Bristol.

There were almost certainly many other workings for fish and perishable traffic, particularly during the harvest seasons, but these would have been run as 'special workings' under Special Traffic Notices, and so not incorporated into the scheduled Working Timetables.

Excursions

Excursions for local inhabitants to places of interest, and more popularly to seaside resorts became commonplace, as working people became entitled to public holidays and to having only to work for half a day on Saturdays. Usually, such

Hughes – Fowler 'Crab' 2-6-0 no. 42938 leans to the curve on the embankment as it passes Battlefield with an up North and West express on the misty Autumn morning of 12 October 1959. It will shortly reach the urban outskirts of Shrewsbury. [M.H.C. Baker]

An unusual choice for a special working, this Stanier 2-6-4T No. 42575 of Crewe North shed is seen passing through Nantwich station on 6 August 1962. The stock comprises the usual motley collection, in this case a Gresley corridor, a BR standard corridor, and then at least three non-corridor carriages. This may have been a troop train. [B. Brooksbank]

excursions would start from one major town and pick up at the nearby, smaller stations en route. Such events began quite early in the history of railways, and this line was no exception. One such event was recorded in the *"Whitchurch Herald"* of 3 June, 1871 :

> *"WHITSUNTIDE HOLIDAYS. – The London and North-Western Railway, with their usual liberality despatched trains from various stations on the line to places of note, during the Whitsuntide holidays, in order that the working classes might enjoy themselves at a low figure. On Monday an excursion from Whitchurch proceeded to Liverpool, Manchester, Warrington, Chester, and other places, when many availed themselves of the opportunity presented to them. The train, by which the Whitchurch people travelled, on its arrival at Liverpool, contained between 700 and 800 persons. Several other trains were similarly laden with living freight. On Wednesday a day trip to Manchester, for the Belle Vue Gardens festival, was announced. Upon this occasion, too, there were many excursionists."*

Many day excursions traversed the line on their way from starting points particularly in Lancashire to the seaside destinations along the South Wales coast and the Somerset and Devon coasts, travelling the routes of the North & West expresses. Other destinations included the West Wales resorts, especially Aberystwyth, and to avoid the Summer congestion in Shrewsbury would take the Cambrian line at Whitchurch. These will be further commented upon in Chapter Six. The LNWR first promoted these excursions and the tradition was continued by both the LMSR and BR.

Wem carnival was a local celebration, held in the first week of September, that attracted people from some distance. Always hoping for extra revenue, the LMSR introduced special cheap day return tickets to this event in 1935, in which year the carnival was held on 4th September.

CHAPTER FOUR

GOODS WORKINGS

The first available details of goods workings relate to the four month period of March through June, 1861. On weekdays there was just one through working, from Crewe at 2.00am, calling briefly at Whitchurch from 2.45am until 2.55am and reaching Shrewsbury at 3.45am. Two local workings left Crewe at 5.30am and 8.35am, the first calling at all stations, but the second (also noted as conveying coal) not calling at Willaston, Wrenbury and Prees and eventually arriving at Shrewsbury at 8.55 and 11.40am respectively. All of these ran Tuesday to Sunday only. In the down direction, there were corresponding workings, leaving Shrewsbury at 5.20pm (local), 8.30pm (semi-local), and 1.00am (through), arriving in Crewe at 8.45pm, 11.05pm and 3.00am respectively. However, these ran Monday to Saturday and there were no Sunday down goods workings. This marked the end of single line working, and so it can be expected that goods workings increased markedly with the completion of full double line working by 1862.

In 1867 the number of through workings had increased to 5 each way on weekdays (except for 2 down on Mondays). These now ran between Manchester, Liverpool or Crewe and Newport, Hereford and Shrewsbury. The other two were coal trains, running from Abergavenny to Birkenhead, and to Springs Branch (Wigan) and the return empties. There was one local working between Crewe (depart 6.50am) and Whitchurch (arrive 7.35am) and returning at 9.10am. It called at all stations including Poole's Siding, situated between Wrenbury and Whitchurch. This location will be more fully discussed in Chapter 9. A further 'limited stop' local goods ran from Crewe at 11.40am to Shrewsbury as in 1861, with the return working at 4.10pm from Shrewsbury. Again there were no up Sunday workings, but three down workings ran from Shrewsbury at 12.15am (Birkenhead coal train), 1.30am (Newport – Crewe), and 2.30am (Hereford – Manchester).

Just five years later, the number of through weekday workings had grown from 5 to 8 (except for Mondays when there were 3 down). The local workings remained the same. One of the down Sunday workings now ran from Llandovery via the Central Wales line, to Liverpool.

In 1888 there were 10 down and 11 up workings (except for Mondays when there were 7 up). Only one coal train now ran, as those for Birkenhead now passed over the Tattenhall branch and are therefore not included in these figures. This was a down "Loco Coal" from Abergavenny to Crewe, with the corresponding return up empties. Local goods workings were principally the same, but there was one daily working from Crewe (at 6.20am) to Nantwich and return (at 8.50am) which called at Willaston in both directions. Sundays now featured 4 up through workings, and two down, plus a coal train from Abergavenny that terminated at Whitchurch (at 4.05pm).

Moving on to the 'inter-war years' the situation for through workings can be summarised as follows :

	September 1929		September 1936	
	Up	Down	Up	Down
Monday	7	8	7	8
Tuesday	9	16	10	16
Wednesday	9	20	10	20
Thursday	9	15	10	15
Friday	9	17	11	17
Saturday	10	12	13	12
Sunday	2	3	2	3

Local stopping traffic had also increased measurably, with two each way between Crewe and Whitchurch on weekdays in 1929, plus one each between Crewe and Nantwich, Crewe and Shrewsbury, Hadnall and Shrewsbury, and two between Wem and Shrewsbury. This gave another five goods workings on the line each way, each day. Further workings were made between Prees and Whitchurch, and Wem to Crewe in the down direction only. Interestingly, the 10.00am Crewe Basford Hall to Shrewsbury called at Prees Camp Siding from 12.43pm to 1.05pm. This location will again be discussed in detail in Chapter 9. In 1929 Poole's Siding was seemingly extravagantly served (from 6.08am to 6.25am) by the 4.40pm MX Copley Hill (Leeds) express freight to Abergavenny Junction.

The number of local goods workings was similar in 1936, although Prees Camp Siding did not then appear in the timetable. But Poole's Siding was then only served by the 2.05pm Basford Hall to Whitchurch local freight (from 2.45pm until 3.00pm). The one daily Crewe – Nantwich and return working continued through both 1929 and 1936. Almost all through goods

B.R. Standard Class 5 4-6-0 No.73035 of Shrewsbury shed (89A at this time) takes the Crewe line at Shrewsbury station with a down class 'E' express freight around 1962. [P.Ward]

The unusual footbridge at Wem frames B.R. Standard Class 4 2-6-0 No. 76044 working a permanent way train in August 1966. The decorative edging at each end of the truncated section of the footbridge canopy suggests that this may have been the original, somewhat surprising, design. [P.Ward]

Approaching Hadnall with an up express freight on 26 September 1964, one of several B.R. Standard "Britannia" Pacifics allocated to Crewe North at the time, No.70001 LORD HURCOMB was in fine condition. [Transport Treasury / R.F. Smith]

workings in this period called at Crewe Bank, Shrewsbury presumably for a change of engines or crew, although some of those terminating or originating in Shrewsbury did so at Coleford, near to the GWR / LMS engine sheds.

Following World War II, the level of through traffic at first declined, then started to improve :

	October 1946		Sept 1958 - June 1959		June 1961- Sept 1961		June 1965 – March 1966	
	Up	Down	Up	Down	Up	Down	Up	Down
Monday	8	13	4	9	4	6	5	6
Tuesday	8	13	6	9	6	8	7	12
Wednesday	8	14	6	9	6	8	7	10
Thursday	8	13	6	9	6	8	8	11
Friday	8	13	6	9	5	8	7	12
Saturday	7	14	6	9	1	7	5	11
Sunday	3	4	0	1	0	4	1	1

Devoid of nameplates and cabside numberplate, "Manor" Class 4-6-0 No. 7812 ERLESTOKE MANOR shunts the yard at Wem in September 1965. This locomotive is now preserved on the Severn Valley Railway. The tall crane on the left marks the premises of Isherwood's timber merchant, now a housing estate. The bowstring footbridge has since been replaced by a modern steel plate version slightly further north to align with this new housing development.[P.Ward]

After taking water in Whitchurch station, Collett "2251" Class 0-6-0 No. 3214 prepares to leave with a special southbound cattle train on 5 October, 1960. [Lens of Sutton Association – R.G.Nelson]

A thick hoar frost coats the trees in the background, as Collett "Grange" Class 4-6-0 No. 6816 FRANKTON GRANGE pauses in the down loop at the south end of Wem with a northbound freight in September 1965. [P.Ward]

During this period the use of Crewe Bank for engine and crew change purposes was gradually replaced by Harlescott Sidings, as these had been expanded, and offered a larger loop in either direction for the increased capacity of the freight turns.

Local goods turns remained principally the same as prewar, with around two trips each way between Crewe and Whitchurch, and also between Shrewsbury and Whitchurch. In 1958 / 59 the 8.25am from Harlescott to Whitchurch was booked to collect empty water cans from Heath Lane Level Crossing, as the crossing keeper's cottage at this location was not furnished with mains water. These were taken on to Whitchurch, and returned as full on the 12.10pm Whitchurch – Shrewsbury. Incidentally, this working was also unusually scheduled to call at the Wem WD depot from 1.06pm to 1.20pm.

This working was retimed in 1961 to leave Whitchurch at 12.10pm, still calling at Heath Lane Crossing, but only to call at Wem WD depot "as required".

There was some further variation in the other local workings; for example in 1961 there was only one Whitchurch – Shrewsbury, but three Crewe – Whitchurch weekday workings. Meanwhile the solitary weekday Crewe – Nantwich local goods, and return, continued to operate.

In 1965, there were still two local goods working each way. The first left Coleham at 06.40am SX, calling at Crewe Bank,

Fowler "Patriot" Class 4-6-0 No. 45518 BRADSHAW of Liverpool's Edge Hill depot moves out from the up goods loop at Whitchurch in April, 1958 with a southbound Class "E" express freight. [Kidderminster Railway Museum]

Harlescott sidings, Wem, Prees and arrived at Whitchurch at 11.20am. This working now collected the empty water cans from Heath Lane Crossing. The return working was retimed to 12.21pm ex- Whitchurch, with the full water cans, and made the conditional call at Wem WD depot sidings. It called at the same stations as the down working, but terminated at Crewe Bank, at 15.07.

The second local goods was the daily Nantwich goods, which now left from Crewe Sorting Sidings North at 06.35, but no longer called at Willaston as the goods facilities had been withdrawn, and arrived in Nantwich at 06.56SX. On Saturdays it continued on to Whitchurch at 08.03, arriving there at 08.35. The return working was from Nantwich at 07.40 SX to Gresty Lane. On Saturdays this left Whitchurch at 10.25, calling again at Nantwich and arriving in Gresty Lane at 11.28.

The third was the 08.20 from Crewe Sorting Sidings North directly to Whitchurch, arrival at 09.07. This returned at 13.35 from Whitchurch, calling at Wrenbury from 13.52 to 14.10, and arrived at Gresty Lane at 16.25.

Many of the through workings also called at Whitchurch, but not at any of the other yards en route. Origins and destinations for these workings in 1965/66 included yards in Cardiff, Swansea, Llanelly, Milford Haven, Neath, Pontypool Road, Hereford and Shrewsbury to the south, and Manchester, Leeds, Glasgow, Crewe and Middlewich to the north.

Former GWR locos were often found on freight workings from Shrewsbury to Crewe in the closing years of steam, as shown here, with "Hall" Class 4-6-0 No. 6903 BELMONT HALL passing through Wrenbury with an up Class "H" working around 1964. The persons on the signal box steps seem more interested in the photographer. [Kidderminster Railway Museum]

South of Yorton, Stanier class 8F 2-8-0 no.48110 heads a fully fitted freight towards Shrewsbury on 13 September 1961. [M.H.C. Baker]

Local goods workings ceased when the respective depots closed, although in some cases there had been little or no traffic for some time. The individual dates for withdrawal of goods facilities are as follows :

Hadnall - 2 November 1964	Yorton - 6 April 1964
Wem – 5 April 1971	Prees – 6 October 1969
Whitchurch – 1 November 1976	Wrenbury – 6 July 1964
Nantwich – 4 September 1972	Willaston – 2 November 1964

Thus it will be seen that there was no mass withdrawal of goods facilities, rather that local circumstances determined when it was deemed uneconomic to continue with them.

One of the stalwarts of freight operation on former LNWR lines, Bowen-Cooke 0-8-0 No.49243 approaches Willaston with a down freight on 4 July 1953. [H. Townley/ J.M. Bentley Collection]

The level crossing gates at Willaston are closed, with two or three lads on their bicycles waiting for them to reopen, but not until Stanier 8F 2-8-0 No. 48724 has passed with a northbound freight on this unrecorded date. The crossing gate wheel is visible in the new signal box on the left. [H. Townley/ J.M. Bentley Collection]

Fowler "Patriot" Class 4-6-0 No. 45538 GIGGLESWICK makes a sure footed start out of Gresty Lane Up Yard with a northbound express freight on 30 March 1958, almost certainly heading for the independent lines. The Mornflake Oats mill is prominent in the right background. [G.Kaye]

CHAPTER FIVE

OPERATING

Locomotives

There are no definitive records of the types of locomotive operating from the earliest days of the line. During the relatively short period that the route was operated as a mostly single line railway (1858 – 1861) it is fairly safe to say that the locomotives used would have been those cascaded down from main line duties. The latest and therefore more powerful locomotives would have been used on the main lines radiating elsewhere from Crewe. Therefore, it seems likely that some of the GJR locomotives would have been used here, notably the 2-2-2 and 2-4-0 types for passenger work, and the 0-4-2 and 2-4-0 goods engines, built either by outside contractors or, increasingly, at Crewe. Of course, it is also eminently possible that some locomotives from other LNWR constituent companies may have been used, as their duties were taken over by more modern machines.

Folllowing the doubling of the line, it is possible that some of the Shrewsbury and Hereford Railway locomotives, some of which were based at Shrewsbury, were used on duties to Crewe after that concern was absorbed jointly by the LNWR and GWR in 1862. These were mostly built by Peto, Brassey and Betts at their Canada Works in Birkenhead, and comprised the usual 2-2-2, 2-4-0 and 0-4-2 types. Also in 1862, the Northern and Southern Divisions of the LNWR were combined, and although this did result in some movement of engines between the two former areas, this was not widespread. The conclusion is that former Southern Division locomotives, mostly of the Bury type, are not likely to have been used here.

An atmospheric, possibly Edwardian view of a footplate crew aboard LNWR Webb 18" Goods ('Cauliflower') 0-6-0 No.2327 at Whitchurch shed. This engine emerged from Crewe Works in March, 1896, and after becoming LMS No.8414 in June, 1927 was withdrawn in August, 1932. The driver (on the left) is believed to be Joseph Parker Stockton, a local man. [K. Parbutt / Whitchurch Archaeological & History Group]

LNWR Northern Division types more likely to be associated with this line include the several Trevithick designs of 2-2-2 and 2-4-0 for passenger work, and 2-4-0 goods types. John Ramsbottom was appointed as Northern Division Locomotive Superintendent in 1857, taking over the entire system from 1862, and so perpetuating his designs, most of which would have appeared : his well known "Problem" or "Lady of the Lake" 2-2-2s and 'Jumbo' 2-4-0s for passenger work, and particularly his numerous "DX" goods 0-6-0s.

Francis Webb's appointment in 1872 resulted in further developments of Ramsbottom's design of ' Jumbo' 2-4-0s, which were turned out in considerable numbers from 1874. These classes varied in their cylinder dimensions and wheel diameters, but were visually very similar, and intended for passenger work. They were of a rugged design, with the last remaining in use until 1933. We have seen that they became the staple engines for use on the Tattenhall branch for many years, including into LMS days. Webb's somewhat controversial divided drive 2-2-2-0 compounds of five classes ("Experiment", "Dreadnought", "Teutonic", "Greater Britain" and "John Hick") were allocated to Shrewsbury shed at one time or another and certainly found favour on passenger workings southwards to Hereford, so are entirely likely to have regularly worked to Crewe. Interestingly, Ahrons commented on one of the "Dreadnoughts", No.685 HIMALAYA saying it *"was one black sheep, and the last of the first batch of ten. A leading engineer at Crewe told me when she was new that she was not quite 'square'. Anyway, she was always in trouble, and was banished to Shrewsbury in her early days to work trains between there and Hereford. Shrewsbury frequently had to help Crewe*

Webb LNWR "Renewed Precedent" Class 2-4-0 No. 1521 GLADSTONE at Shrewsbury shed, probably around 1920. This engine was built at Crewe Works in September 1889, and although allotted LMS number 5017 it probably never received it, as it was scrapped in March, 1926. These ' Jumbos' saw a variety of work between Shrewsbury and Crewe over the years. [LNWR Society]

Webb Class "A" 3 cylinder compound 0-8-0 No. 2528 stands in the shed yard at Shrewsbury alongside "Waterloo" (or "Whitworth") Class 2-4-0 No.404 ZOPHYRUS around 1920. The Webb 0-8-0s became synonymous with the operation of the "Jellicoe Special" coal trains that ran from South Wales to refuel the Grand Fleet at Scapa Flow. [LNWR Society]

Whale "George V" 4-4-0 LMS No.5344 BLOODHOUND stands in the centre road at Shrewsbury station, probably waiting to take forward a West to North express, in the company of a GWR Mogul. Built as LNWR No.1532 in May, 1911 it was withdrawn in January, 1937. [C.A.J. Nevett]

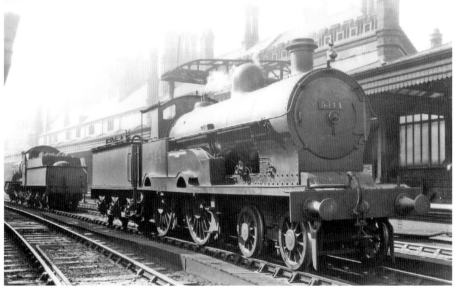

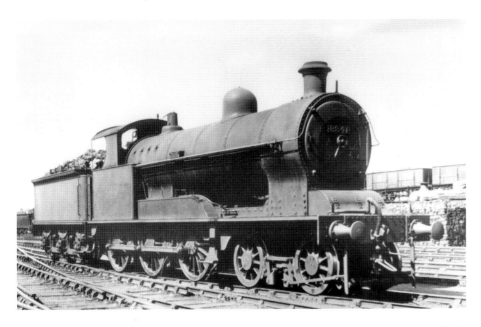

One of George Whale's '19inch' Goods' 4-6-0s, LMS No.8841 standing in Shrewsbury shed yard some time after 1933 when its Belpaire firebox had been removed. Despite their official class title, these were in fact excellent mixed traffic engines, capable of working heavy passenger trains to all but the most exacting timings. [W.S.Garlick]

Stanier's "Princess Royal" Pacifics were also frequent visitors to the line, as No.6212 DUCHESS OF KENT is seen here taking water before attaching to a return working to Crewe around 1935/6. The unusual perimeter 'dog catch' fixings to the smokebox door were possibly an attempt to cure a bad air leak, but did nothing for the aesthetics of the locomotive. [Lens of Sutton Association]

In its original form, Fowler "Royal Scot" Class 4-6-0 No.6126 ROYAL ARMY SERVICE CORPS awaits departure from Shrewsbury with a West to North express. Originally named SANSPAREIL the name shown here was added in 1935, and it was rebuilt with a taper boiler in 1945, dating this photograph to between those years. [Stephenson Locomotive Society]

Bowen-Cooke "Prince of Wales" 4-6-0 LMS No. 25674 SCOTT (originally LNWR No.1132) passes along the up relief road at the eastern side of Shrewsbury station with empty stock shortly before its withdrawal in February,1946. The bridge behind the locomotive's tender is over the sharply curved line into the Howard Street Goods Depot, alongside the prison, which can be seen above the engine. [Stephenson Locomotive Society]

out of compound difficulties by taking charge of 'lame ducks'. In their latter days Shrewsbury was simply bombarded with compounds, and became in effect a sort of 'marine stores' for them." Webb's continued work with compounds also resulted in the appearance of the "Jubilee" and "Alfred the Great" 4-4-0 classes for passenger work. But his largest influence was with the 17" 'Coal Engines' and 18" 'Cauliflowers' for goods work, particularly on the coal trains from South Wales. Local goods workings may well have seen the appearance of Webb's 'Coal Tank' 0-6-2Ts, but they were not especially suited to the through goods workings on the line. Tank engines generally were not suited to this line, and it is believed that Webb's 2-4-0T and 2-4-2T classes were similarly not likely to have appeared on anything like a regular basis. The same must be said for the Whale "Precursor Tank"4-4-2T, and the Bowen-Cooke "2665" or "Prince of Wales Tank" 4-6-2T. But without question the 0-8-0s designed by Whale, Bowen-Cooke and Beames in their various guises as four and three cylinder compounds and two cylinder simples were regular performers, especially on coal trains. The short lived 2-8-0 variants may well have made appearances.

LNWR passenger locomotives of Whale's 4-4-0 "Precursor" and 4-6-0 "Experiment" and "19" Goods" were frequently found on the line. Bowen-Cooke's introduction of superheating to the first two classes resulted in his 4-4-0 "King George V" and 4-6-0 "Prince of Wales" classes. Finally, his four cylinder 4-6-0 "Claughton" class also became regular performers, all of these principally on the "North & West Expresses". Shrewsbury had a small allocation of the Bowen-Cooke 0-8-2T and Beames 0-8-4T classes, although it is believed that they spent much of their time on the Central Wales line. After the Great War, the LNWR hired 150 of the Robinson GCR designed 2-8-0s that had been built for the Ministry of Munitions, and these too were used on the heavy coal trains from South Wales. However, they had all been returned by August 1921,

Webb "18" Goods" or 'Cauliflower' 0-6-0 LMS No. 28370 shunting empty stock at the north end of Shrewsbury station on 30 January 1948 having just passed into BR ownership. This venerable engine was completed at Crewe in August, 1895 and lasted until April, 1950. [P.Ward]

B.R. Western Region engines working to Crewe on through trains were a relatively rare occurrence, but those that did usually went to Crewe North shed for servicing. One such example is shown here, as having come off its train in the station, Collett "Hall" Class 4-6-0 No. 4986 ASTON HALL passes Crewe North shed (rear of which is in the background) on 19 July 1958. [B.Brooksbank]

although a further 30 were purchased, passing to the LMS and lasting until 1932. It is believed that they were not generally liked on this route, and their appearances are likely to have been few.

In to LMS days, there was naturally little change at first, and even the standard designs by Fowler, notably of his 4F 0-6-0 goods engines made little impression on the line, nor the vast number of the Johnson MR 3F 0-6-0 design found elsewhere throughout the LMS. Fowler's compound 4-4-0s are known to have been used on some passenger services, but not with any regularity. However, the Johnson 2P 4-4-0s were often used on the local and semifast services, and became the staple diet on the Tattenhall branch right up to the 1950s.

The Hughes mixed traffic 2-6-0s, popularly known as 'Crabs' performed on freight duties, express workings and excursion traffic from the 1920s up to the end of steam. The Stanier regime introduced a large number of classes : Class 5 2-6-0s, and 'Black Five' 4-6-0s for mixed traffic, 8F 2-8-0s for freight work; "Jubilee" 4-6-0s, "Princess Royal" and "Princess Coronation" 4-6-2s for express passenger work, along with Fowler's "Patriot" and "Royal Scot" 4-6-0s and their subsequent rebuilds by Stanier and Ivatt. The Fowler, Stanier and Fairburn 2-6-4Ts appeared on local passenger duties, but were more common (especially the Fowler version) on the Central Wales line from Shrewsbury. Photographic evidence suggests that the smaller 2-6-2Ts by both Fowler and Stanier do not seem to been used on the line.

The complexity of movements at the north end of Shrewsbury station are illustrated in this view from 14 September, 1959. On the left, Stanier Mogul no. 42980 is about to leave with the 7.30am Penzance to Manchester London road, whilst in the centre, 'Black Five' 4-6-0 no.44679 is moving forward on to the Chester line, presumably as a light engine. In the background, on the right a Gloucester RC & W DMU is waiting to leave with the 5.45pm all stations to Crewe. [M.H.C.Baker]

None of the Ivatt designs were in anything like regular use here, although some of his Class 2 2-6-0s were latterly used on the Cambrian branch, having been allocated to Oswestry shed. And so finally to the BR standard classes, of which perhaps only the Class 3 and Class 4 moguls and the Class 3 and Class 2 tank versions were not regular. The Standard Class 5 4-6-0s were popular with engine crews, and used on both passenger and freight work. Actually, the first ten of the Caprotti-fitted locos of this class, nos.73125 to 73134 were allocated to Shrewsbury shed when new, but the stay lasted only a few months as they were all transferred to Patricroft in September, 1958. The 2-10-0 version of the WD heavy freight locomotives are not known to have ever been used on the line.

Some of the last workings for the Stanier Pacifics were over this line during 1964, when they were rostered for the 6.25pm Swansea Victoria to York mail, from Shrewsbury to Crewe, returning with the 9.50pm working. BR "Britannia" Pacifics were still found on the line, notably on the 3.35pm Liverpool to Cardiff as far as Shrewsbury in March, 1964. In the final days of steam, Stanier and BR Standard 4-6-0s turned up on the odd passenger working. For example, the 7.50am

Manchester to Cardifff was noted on 29 May, 1965 running 39 minutes late, after 'Black Five' no. 45056 had deputised for a failed diesel at Crewe. A day earlier, no. 44685 and Standard no.73034 were noted on North to West expresses at Shrewsbury. 'Black Five' no. 44818 was used on an SLS Railtour of Shropshire that ran from Manchester Piccadilly to Shrewsbury and return on 11 September, 1965. These types were still appearing on freight duties in December of that year. But the 9F class 2-10-0s were regularly seen on the line, and are believed to have been the last steam types to have been seen on the line, in 1967, occasionally working freights from Crewe to the Coleham yard. That is, except for Gresley "A4" Pacific no. 60007 SIR NIGEL GRESLEY was outshopped from Crewe Works, where it had been since the preceding July, and was given a test run to Shrewsbury on 5 March, 1967.

In conclusion, it must have become obvious by now that virtually any class that was built or had overhauls at Crewe Works during LNWR, LMSR and BR ownership was likely to appear on the line, either by virtue of being 'run-in' after a works visit, or perhaps borrowed from Crewe North or South shed because of a motive power shortage.

Test Runs

Due to its proximity to Crewe, and the favourable nature of the line, it was inevitable that locomotives newly constructed or newly overhauled there would be tested on this line, which usually had a good deal of spare capacity. Consequently, any such tests could be carried out without disruption to other traffic.

It would appear that in the days of the LNWR, no special paths were provided for test runs, but under the LMSR such paths were incorporated into the Working Timetables and perpetuated by BR during its tenure. All such paths were designated as "Q" or "run as required". Locomotives under trial were coupled together, usually two, three or even four at a time. On arrival at Whitchurch, they would often be turned to even out the wear on new bearing surfaces.

The earliest times available are those from the 1929 Working Timetable, which gives two daily "Trial Run" paths, Monday to Friday. These ran from Crewe to Whitchurch, where after a pause for examination, the locomotives took the Tattenhall branch to Tattenhall Junction, and after reversal they continued along the Chester line back to Crewe. The first left Gresty Lane at 8.45am, arrived Whitchurch at 9.30am, departed at 11.10am and arrived at Tattenhall Junction at 11.55am. The second, which did not run on Mondays, left at 2.50pm, was at Whitchurch for one hour from 2.35pm and arrived at Tattenhall Junction at 5.20pm.

By 1936 there were five such working paths, but the locomotives did not proceed to Tattenhall Junction, instead returning

This Test Run is seen heading south of Wem on the embankment, and comprises "Jubilee" 4-6-0s Nos. 45648 WEMYSS and 45616 MALTA G.C., plus 'Black Five' No. 45313 in the mid 1950s. [J.Coltas]

Not a picture of the best quality, but this hastily taken photograph from a passing train portrays three engines at Hadnall, about to move into the up loop during a test run from Crewe in 1953. The nearest engine is "Princess Ropyal" 4-6-2 No.46203 PRINCESS MARGARET ROSE, now happily preserved, but the identities of the Stanier 2-6-4T and the "Jubilee" 4-6-0 are not known. [Kidderminster Railway Museum]

Most of the Test Runs latterly terminated at Whitchurch, where they used the turntable to even out the running-in. Here Aston shed's 'Black Five' No. 45094 plus another unidentified classmate sandwich a Stanier Class 4 2-6-4T No.42651 on 30 July 1956. [E.Hancock]

A further Test Run took place on 30 July 1956, and was recorded on camera with "Royal Scot" 4-6-0 No.46116 IRISH GUARDSMAN plus an unidentified Stanier Class 4 2-6-4T at Whitchurch. [J.A.Young / RCTS]

directly to Crewe. On their outward runs, the locomotives were scheduled to stop at Wrenbury for five minutes for "examination". All movements were from and to Crewe South Shed. In 1949 there were six trial runs, five of which left from Crewe North shed and one from Crewe station. Three returned to Crewe North shed, two returned to Crewe South, and oddly, there was no balancing return for the sixth. The 1961 Working Timetable gives four of the five runs starting from Crewe North and the fifth from Crewe South. Three returned to North shed and two to South shed. One of the outward runs continued from Whitchurch on to Hadnall, where it lay over from 11.45am until 1.20pm. For 1965/66 the situation was principally the same, but once again an unbalanced working appeared. Because the signal box was by then closed, the run to Hadnall was extended to Harlescott Sidings instead. In the final year of steam locomotive overhauls at Crewe, the timings for 1966/67 were very similar. Evidently, the new generation of diesel locomotives did not require 'trial runs' – although it could well be contended that they should have done, in the light of subsequent unreliability of certain classes.

Practices and Limitations

Contrary to the normal LNWR practice of mileages starting from zero at Euston and increasing in the down direction, the mileages on this line started from Crewe at zero, increasing in the up direction to Shrewsbury. However, the mileage posts were traditionally located on the down side.

In its earliest form, the line was fully equipped with telegraph, but train operation was by the "time interval" method, which

In August 1954, Hadnall was the destination for this Test Run which included Old Oak Common's 'Britannia' Pacific no. 70017 ARROW fresh from overhaul. This locomotive, and the two unidentified others are parked on the up goods relief line adjacent to the signalbox. [M.H.C. Baker]

was fraught with danger if trains had not cleared in the required time. Whilst this system worked acceptably (for the time), as traffic increased it became positively dangerous. It is unclear when this system was changed, but in June 1870 one incident occurred that suggests that "time interval" was still in operation then. The 11.33am passenger train from Shrewsbury failed to arrive in Whitchurch at its scheduled time of 12.13pm. It was eventually "found" between Shrewsbury and Wem, the locomotive having failed due to a leaking flue tube.

Eventually the "absolute block" system was adopted on both this line and the Tattenhall branch. Block posts were installed at Shrewsbury No.2 (Crewe Bank), Harlescott Crossing, Yorton, Wem , Prees, Whitchurch Cambrian Junction, Whitchurch Goods Yard, Whitchurch Chester Junction, Wrenbury, Nantwich Market Drayton Junction, Nantwich Station, Nantwich Newcastle Crossing, Willaston, Crewe Gresty Lane No.2, Crewe Gresty Lane No.1 and Crewe South Junction signalboxes.

For most of its life during LNWR, LMSR and BR days the line was subject to an overall speed limit of 75 mph, but this was increased to 90 mph in the mid 1970s.

A view inside Crewe Junction signal box at Shrewsbury on 19 August 1993. However, the interior had changed little during the past 100 years, apart from the signalman's comfy armchair and perhaps the slightly more modern cooking facilities. [K.Hughes / RCTS]

Shrewsbury Crewe Bank signal box was a WWII replacement for two smaller boxes, and was designed to withstand enemy air attacks. In this view from 1972 it was still in regular use, but with a decline in traffic for the Crewe Bank sidings was normally switched out for most of the time. The "32" milepost indicates the mileage from Crewe. [Shropshire Railway Society]

Harlescott Crossing signal box controlled the level crossing over the busy Harlescott Lane, but was extended around 1941 on the southern (left) side to accommodate additional levers for the expanded goods yards. The lack of windows for the operating room in the extension is apparent. This view was taken on 3 September 2012. [Author]

View inside Prees signal box in 1972, with the duty signalman about to operate the wheel to manoeuvre the crossing gates. Through the windows the plain corporate style station nameboard can be seen, and across the line, the goods shed is still extant at this time. [Shropshire Railway Society]

Following nationalisation on 1 January, 1948, the line from Crewe to Harlescott Crossing was placed in the BR's London Midland Region, Crewe District. From Harlescott Crossing into Shrewsbury the line was administered by the Western Region. A further reorganisation took place from 14 July, 1963 when the section from Crewe to Whitchurch was moved from the LMR Birmingham Division to the LMR Stoke Division, whilst the Chester to Shrewsbury section (via Tattenhall) was transferred to the LMR Chester Division.

The imposing Whitchurch Goods Yard signal box in 1978, which controlled movements to the north of the station, including both the up and down yards. The outside convenience for the duty signalmen would not encourage anyone to linger for longer than necessary, especially in Winter time. The building behind is part of W.H. Smith's iron foundry and engineering works. [Whitchurch Archaeological & Historical Group]

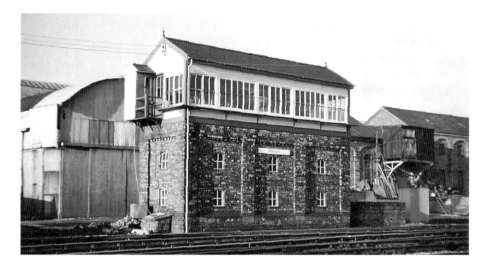

The original Nantwich Station signal box is seen here on 20 May 1951, prior to being replaced by the one from Aston Park (Wem) in 1967. This controlled the level crossing over the busy Wellington Road at the western end of the station, and was mechanically linked to the small Shewbridge Road level crossing further westwards. [Lens of Sutton Association / R.G.Nelson]

The original signal box at Willaston, dating from the opening of the line, was still in use when this view was taken on 28 September, 1952. It controlled not only the crossing over Wybunbury Road, but also the goods yard movements east of the station. The footbridge was mainly for the convenience of pedestrians when the crossing gates were shut against them, but also made an excellent vantage point for photographers - as several shots included in this volume will prove. [H. Townley / J.M. Bentley Collection]

Accidents, criminal acts and other malfeasances

The *"Shrewsbury Chronicle"* of 1 August 1860 carried an extensive report covering manslaughter charges being brought as a result of an accident at Whitchurch on 2 May previously. The circumstances were as follows, and it must be remembered that the line was still single, with a passing loop at Whitchurch, and that "time lapse" signalling was in operation:

The Crewe to Shrewsbury goods was due at Whitchurch at 6.50am, but did not arrive until 7.15am. This consisted of three engines and 75 wagons, and on arrival at Whitchurch the leading two engines were detached. At around 7.18am under the control of a pointsman, these two engines moved forward on to the single main line, then reversed off the running lines, probably to take water. The signal for a passenger train from Shrewsbury, due at that time, was then put to 'off'. However, the driver of the remaining goods engine began to move southwards, towards the single main line, in order to perform some shunting moves. The pointsman, being aware of the imminent arrival of the passenger train, waved his red flag at the driver to stop, but he did not. By then this was 7.21 or 7.22am, and so because of the movement of the goods engine, the approach signal for the passenger train was put to 'on'.

By then the passenger train was quite close, and seeing the signal at danger, the driver gave a continuous whistle. However, the goods engine had by this time run about 225 yards on to the single line. The passenger guard applied the brake in his van, but it had limited effect. At this time, locomotives only had a tender brake (effectively only a 'parking brake') so most braking effort was performed by the guard. Also, the brakes were not continuous, and so were pretty useless in emergencies. The passenger train collided with the goods engine at 7.29am, when it was estimated that the passenger train was travelling at around 15 mph. The passenger guard, John Jones of Whitchurch, was violently thrown about in his van, causing severe injuries to his liver and died as a result on 9 or 10 May. The jury found the goods driver, George Brown, not guilty of manslaughter and acquitted. But the passenger train driver, William Brindley, was found guilty by the petty jury, who nonetheless recommended leniency.

Another severe accident occurred in 1868, this time fortunately without loss of life, as reported in the *"Shrewsbury Chronicle"* of 10 July, 1868 :

WEM

"RAILWAY COLLISION. – About a quarter-past eight on Tuesday evening (7 July) a collision took place a short distance south of Wem station between a luggage train from Shrewsbury and a ballast train from Crewe. The luggage train was shunting and in the act of passing from the up to the down line, when the ballast train came up at the ordinary rate with the tender first, which caught the side of the luggage engine as it was passing over the cross points, from the up to the down line. The report of the collision was heard throughout the town; and for a short time the trains were enveloped in a cloud of dust and steam, and great anxiety was felt for the safety of the engine drivers and stokers. We are glad to say that those on the luggage engine received no injury, whilst those on the ballast train only received slight bruises with jumping or being thrown down the bank. John Galagan who had charge of the ballast break received a rather severe shock and a contusion at the back of the head, which, however, is not considered serious. Mr. S.B.Gwynne and Mr. Gill surgeons, were on the spot in a few minutes, and rendered their valuable assistance to the injured. The tender of the ballast train struck the goods engine obliquely, and was forced off the line down the bank, and lay with the wheels uppermost. The engine was thrown down the bank, and lay on its side. The luggage engine and tender left the rails, but sustained little damage. The rails on both the up and down lines for a few yards were considerably bent, and both lines were blocked. Mr Barratt, the station-master, sent telegrams immediately to both Shrewsbury and Crewe, when a staff of men from both places soon reached the spot, and worked with a will to clear the line and relay the rails. The down line was cleared by about one o'clock, and the goods traffic was worked on it between Wem and Yorton until five next morning when both lines were cleared. Mr. Barratt was exceedingly energetic in arranging for the convenience of passengers and the goods traffic."

The LNWR was advised in September, 1872 that in the vicinity of the Heath Lane Crossing, a horse had been killed on the main line. The Permanent Way Works & Estate Committee considered the claim by a George Batho for £50 compensation on the 17th of that month. The fencing along the line had been examined and found to be in good order. It was stated that 'considerable force would have been required to breach it'. The committee therefore denied the claim.

Whilst it is known that the LNWR was particularly parsimonious, it did try to maintain good relationships with landowners and local trades people. Nonetheless, there was a considerable feeling amongst many people that the railway companies in general were sitting on 'pots of gold'. Some people almost saw it as their duty to make spurious claims, so indicating that nothing really changes! For almost the same reason, railway stations have often been the target of thieves expecting a large amount of cash to be available. This incident, reported in the *"Whitchurch Herald"* on 12 October 1872 is a prime example :

"ROBBERY AT THE RAILWAY STATION. – Sometime during the night of Sunday last, some person or persons succeeded in obtaining an entrance into the Railway Station (at Whitchurch), and abstracting £3 16s. from the booking clerk's till. How an entrance was effected is not clearly known, unless it was through the ladies' waiting room window, which was found to be open on the Monday morning. None of the doors were open, neither were there any marks on them. On Monday a detective came over to enquire into the case."

Examination of subsequent newspapers did not reveal whether or not the miscreant was identified and apprehended.

Passengers at Shrewsbury in 1910 must have had a feeling of 'déjà vu' relating to the terrible accident of October, 1907 (see Chapter Three) when a minor incident occurred, as reported in the *"Shrewsbury Chronicle"* of 18 March that year :

"ALARMING ACCIDENT AT SHREWSBURY RAILWAY STATION
As the 7.22 p.m. passenger train for Crewe was leaving Shrewsbury Railway Station on Wednesday (16 March), the engine jumped the rails and caused considerable alarm. The matter, however, was soon put to right. Another engine was brought out, and the train got under way in about a quarter of an hour."

Although only a minor incident, considerable credit must go to the operating departments for minimising the delay to the passengers, and undoubtedly to other services at the station.

A serious accident occurred at Nantwich on 25 June 1964, when the 06.35 Plymouth to Manchester Piccadilly express comprising ten coaches and hauled by a BR Type 4 (later Class 47) diesel locomotive ran through the closed level crossing barrier at the station, having passed signals at danger. At the subsequent enquiry, the driver blamed drifting smoke from a passing steam locomotive hauling a freight towards Market Drayton Junction, for his inability to see the signals. The collision occurred at around 40 mph, hitting a Foden milk tanker, which was carried along the (fortunately deserted) platform and disgorging its load. Whilst four persons suffered injury, the only death was to a passenger in a Ford Zodiac car, stationary on the crossing at the time, and who succumbed to his injuries in hospital three days later.

The scene of the terrible derailment during the night of 15 October 1907 at Crewe Junction, Shrewsbury. The train engine, Whale "Experiment" Class 4-6-0 No.2052 STEPHENSON lies on its side amidst the wreckage of the wooden bodied carriages during the following morning. [Kidderminster Railway Museum]

Above Left: In the aftermath, Webb "Precedent" Class 2-4-0 No.381 PATTERDALE attempts to pull STEPHENSON from beneath the wreckage, using a wire hawser attached to the front buffer beam. [Kidderminster Railway Museum]

Above Right: The wreckage further down the train was equally appalling, and demonstrated the weakness of wooden bodied vehicles – although fortunately in this case there was no outbreak of fire, as often occurred in such mishaps. The early Travelling Post Office sorting vehicle was one of the casualties. [Kidderminster Railway Museum]

World War II

Shropshire would not be the most likely target for the Luftwaffe during this conflict, but it did receive attention, and the occurrences were mostly during 1940, remembered as "The Battle of Britain".

The "*Shropshire Chronicle*" of 11 August 1940 reported as follows:

"*A German plane dive bombed a working class district of a large market town in the West Midlands and did considerable damage to houses. The plane dropped two large high explosive bombs, both of which made huge craters. No one was killed, and the only casualty reported to the head warden of the district was a woman whose hand was slightly burnt.*"

Of course, reports such as this were heavily censored so that the enemy would not be aware of the success or otherwise

An unidentified "Patriot" passes beneath Rope Bridge with an up parcels train in August, 1944. The author has a sneaking suspicion that this train looks more like a pigeon special (hence the special reporting number), but lacks corroboration. [H. Townley / J.M. Bentley Collection]

Wartime photography was not only frowned upon, but it could easily be considered illegal. So the following small collection by Harry Townley, although not of great quality, are particularly valuable. In this view, we see a Riddles designed War Department 2-8-0 with Westinghouse air brake equipment approaching Rope Lane bridge, west of Crewe, in August 1944. Actually these locomotives were built to the order of the Ministry of Supply, who transferred them to the WD. [H. Townley / J.M. Bentley Collection]

of their actions, nor even where their bombs had fallen. That is why not even the town was mentioned, although it was Shrewsbury. The report went on to say that Mrs. Duckett, 67, had a collection of budgerigars and canaries, kept in her kitchen and in a hut, as an aviary, at the bottom of her garden. All were safe. This raid happened at about 7pm on the previous Wednesday, 9 October 1940.

The many airfields in Shropshire received attention, often when a group of enemy bombers were on their way, or returning from an attack on Liverpool. One such attack was concentrated on Shawbury airfield , where on 26 June 1940 five bombs were dropped.

Two months later, on 31 August, a bomb demolished a cottage at Ellesmere Road, Shrewsbury, killing a woman and two children. Her husband was extricated from the debris and was practically unhurt.

Three months later on 28 November 1940, four bombs were dropped in Cruckmoor Lane, Prees Lower Heath, damaging five houses. During the same attack, two parachute mines were dropped at Woodhouses, Whitchurch. Only one casualty was reported : one woman was slightly injured by flying glass, but many shop windows were smashed by the blast. It seems likely that the attack was aimed at Tilstock airfield, but these bombs had missed their target.

No reports of damage to the railway have been found, although as mentioned above, censorship at the time may have eliminated such reports from the newspapers, or details were so vague that it has not been possible to identify the locations.

A Bowen-Cooke 0-8-0 approaches Rope Bridge with a down freight in August, 1944 as the photographer's car lurks nearby to make a hasty getaway before officialdom spots his errant activities! [H. Townley / J.M. Bentley Collection]

Harry Townley managed to identify this streamlined Stanier Pacific as No.6228 DUCHESS OF RUTLAND. It is carrying the drab wartime livery, plus doubtless a good coating of grime, as it nears Rope Bridge with a down express on 19 August 1944. [H. Townley / J.M. Bentley Collection]

CHAPTER SIX

THE CAMBRIAN CONNECTION

The first connection to the Shrewsbury – Crewe line was the Cambrian Railways line from Oswestry, which has been described in R.W.Kidner's "The Cambrian Railways" (Oakwood Press, 1992). Therefore, once again, this chapter is simply a summary of the history and operation of this interesting connection as it pertains to our line.

Beginnings

The Oswestry, Ellesmere and Whitchurch Railway (OEWR) was locally promoted as an independent railway, although the intention was that it would link with the Oswestry and Newtown Railway (opened throughout in 1861) to provide the shortest route from Manchester and the North-West to that railway and others in Mid Wales planned or under construction at that time. It faced considerable opposition from the GWR, who had deposited plans of their own for various railways in the area, and were thus quite bitter about this rival upstart. However, having deposited its plans at Shrewsbury County Court on 30 November, 1860 the OEWR succeeded in obtaining its enabling Act of the same name on 1 August,1861 (Vict.24 & 25, chap.223). The LNWR were more amenable to the railway, and by 31 December,1860 had invested some £30,000 in the company, even though the LNWR Chairman Richard Moon described the line as passing through 'profitless country'. The Act denied running powers for the GWR over the OEWR, and the OEWR were not given running powers over the LNWR north of the junction to be made at Whitchurch, although local agreements enabled the movements of stock for the interchange of traffic. Whilst permitting immediate construction on the Ellesmere to Whitchurch section, Parliament included in this Act a specific suspension of work on the section between Ellesmere and Oswestry until 1 September 1862, in the hope that the GWR and OEWR would come to an agreement concerning their conflicting plans.

Construction

The line was engineered by the brothers Robert and Benjamin Piercy, with George Owen of Oswestry as Acting Engineer, and constructed by the contractor Thomas Savin for around £86,000. These latter three gentlemen, along with the local MP, one George Hammond Whalley, had been the original promoters of the OEWR.

The Shrewsbury turnpike road at Whitchurch required to be lowered by 3½ feet under the new single arch bridge, just before the connection with the LNWR. The formation of the line was built for the possibility of installing a double track railway, but only a single track was ever laid. It was noted that the rails were double sided and of 70 lbs per yard (quite substantial for the time) and in lengths of 24 feet. Considerable difficulty had been experienced in carrying the line over the Whixall Moss peat bog, for a distance of around three miles, but the traditional method of packing the bog proved successful.

Savin used one locomotive on the construction, which regularly appeared at Whitchurch, presumably to collect materials as the construction proceeded. This was a Manning Wardle "Old Class I" inside cylinder 0-6-0ST (works no.36) named "WHIXALL", despatched by the makers on 29 January 1862 to the contractor at Whitchurch. After a period of use on Savin's contract for the Carnarvonshire railway, this engine passed to the Brecon and Merthyr Railway, eventually becoming Cambrian Railways No.13 in 1867 by then named "GREEN DRAGON".

Captain Tyler inspected the line on behalf of the Board of Trade, and in his report to them dated 2 May, 1863 failed to confirm approval for the line to open to passenger traffic or not. However, in the Board of Trade Minute No.1103 dated 4 May, it was noted that his recommendation was "I think omitted by mistake" and so approval was given by the Lords of the Privy Committee on the following day. Captain Tyler's tacit approval must have been taken by the OEWR too, as services actually began on 4 May – the day before the Privy Committee had ratified the approval !

Captain Tyler's report mentioned that where the line crossed the bog, particular care should be taken to see if it required further packing, especially as it may settle after the passage of a number of trains. The report also contained other items of interest : "*LNWR are now altering Whitchurch station for the sake of obtaining extra accommodation there. They have not yet supplied an engine turntable, nor have they completed the Junction stage for the Ellesmere line….A patent locking frame for working the points and signals will be supplied within a fortnight, and the engine turntable should be supplied within 3 months. There is already an engine turntable at Ellesmere, and the Company will do well to work with extra caution as regards speed until that at Whitchurch has been completed. Train Staff will be adopted.*"

So it would appear that although the line was not really complete from an operational standpoint, the inspector had been assured that these measures would be put into place quite soon, and was happy to accept these assurances. All in all, quite a relaxed attitude.

Opening

Actually even before the inspection, on 20 April 1863, Captain Jebb and his Company of Rifles were transported over the line. As mentioned above, the line opened for all traffic between Ellesmere and Whitchurch on 4 May 1863, operated by the LNWR as the OEWR had no locomotives or stock. Local newspapers record that the initial trains in May, 1863 were hauled by a locomotive named "HERO" – this is almost certainly the Ramsbottom "DX" goods 0-6-0 no.192 completed at Crewe in August,1860 and lasting until June,1895. There were two other locomotives named "HERO" on the LNWR at the time, but these can be safely disregarded.

Having reached an impasse on the GWR plans for the area, construction eventually got under way for the remaining section, so that twelve months later the Ellesmere to Oswestry section was completed and traffic began on Wednesday, 27 July, 1864. However, just two days earlier a 'gaily dressed' commemorative train ran from Oswestry at 8.10am to Whitchurch, returning at 10.00am. On this same day, an Act was passed legalising the creation of the Cambrian Railways by amalgamation of the OEWR, the Llanidloes & Newtown Railway, the Oswestry & Newtown Railway and the Newtown & Machynlleth Railway. For the OEWR the authorisation was contained in the OEWR Act, 1864 (Vict.27 and 28, chapter 97) passed on 23 June, 1864. Coincidentally the last section of the line to Aberystwyth was also completed, and so through Cambrian Railways trains could run from there to Whitchurch. Once the somewhat chaotic situation regarding the ownership of locomotives had been sorted out, the Cambrian took over the running of trains into Whitchurch.

Operation

The single line from Oswestry divided into a double track just before joining the LNWR at Whitchurch, and this junction was controlled by a signal box, "Cambrian Junction", situated in the fork of the lines. However, bearing in mind the comments of Captain Tyler (above), it seems likely that the point and signal levers were not initially contained in a signal box, but remained in the open air, which was a common practice at the time. The signal box must nonetheless have been brought into operation fairly soon afterwards. The single line was controlled at first by train staff, but this was replaced by electric token apparatus, the exchange equipment being sited 11 yards south of the signal box. The original signal box was replaced in 1886 by a new one, sited on the down side of the main line, just north of the junction. Just to confuse matters, northbound trains on the Cambrian line were known as 'up', but from where they joined the LNWR, they became 'down'.

Whitchurch station was remodelled between 1862 and 1864, anticipating the arrival of this new line, with a new platform face added to the up platform, which thereafter became an island platform. This face was almost always used for departures southwards to the Cambrian line, whereas arrivals would either use this face, or the down main platform. A 42 foot turntable was installed, as promised by the LNWR at the time of the Board of Trade inspection, and was certainly used by LNWR locomotives that initially operated the line, and subsequently by Cambrian locomotives. The first shareholders' report of the Cambrian Railways, dated 23 July 1864, mentioned that 'sidings, turntable and station accommodation had been provided at Whitchurch'. The nearby single road shed, also erected by the LNWR in 1863 was used by the Cambrian for servicing and less frequently for stabling of locomotives.

The line received Royal patronage in 1911, following the Investiture of the Prince of Wales at Caernarvon and the laying of the foundation stone of the National Library of Wales at Aberystwyth by King George V, as detailed in this report from the *"Shrewsbury Chronicle"* of 21 July, 1911:

"The Royal Progress" Through Shropshire

Along the Cambrian Railways large numbers assembled at different stations, and flags and decorations were exhibited at many houses within sight of the railway. The Royal Welsh Warehouse at Newtown, which overlooks the railway station, was magnificently decorated for the occasion.

At Oswestry the public were excluded from the railway station, but many assembles at the Great Western Railway Station and at the Cambrian Railway (sic) cattle landings. A hearty cheer was raised as the train ran slowly through, and these salutations the Queen, who was plainly seen in one of the windows, graciously acknowledged.

Large numbers gathered round the Railway Station at Ellesmere to see the Royal Party pass through on the journey to Scotland. The school children, numbering four hundred, and their teachers, with flags, cheered heartily as the train passed through.

ENTHUSIASM AT WHITCHURCH

A large number of people assembled at the Whitchurch Railway Station on Monday last (17th July) to greet his Majesty King George V, on his passing through the station on his journey from Wales to Scotland ; and he was given a very loyal welcome. A stop had to be made at Whitchurch to change the Cambrian for a London and North- Western engine, and the company's latest engine "Coronation", together with the engine "King George V", were brought from Crewe for this purpose. The King was greeted before his arrival in the station by the school children of the town, who had been drawn up in a field below the railway, and on reaching the station he was given a right royal welcome by the crowds who had gathered there. His Majesty and the Queen stood at the entrance to the saloon as the royal train left the station, and the newly-invested Prince of Wales and Princess Mary were also seen by many before they left. The question of presenting an address had been discussed by the Urban District Council of Whitchurch, but owing to the shortness of the stay that was thought to be hardly feasible, so nothing was done officially in the matter, but great enthusiasm was evidenced and the loyalty of the inhabitants was shown by the heartiness of their reception."

The locomotives referred to in this report were both Bowen Cooke "King George V" Class 4-4-0s; the first member of the class, no. 2663 GEORGE THE FIFTH (built July 1910) and no.1800 CORONATION, the celebrated 5,000th engine to be built at Crewe Works, newly completed in June, 1911. Incidentally, such was the attention to detail that a 'trial run' of the Royal Train throughout its journey in North Wales and back to Crewe was undertaken two months earlier, on 16 May.

No accidents involving Cambrian or GWR trains in the vicinity of Whitchurch are known, but normal operating problems existed periodically, as this report from the *"Whitchurch Herald"* of 20 May, 1871 records :

"BREAKDOWN ON THE RAILWAY. – On the arrival, at Whitchurch, on Tuesday morning, about four o'clock, of the goods train from Oswestry, one of the steam pipes belonging to the engine burst, in consequence of which it was unable to return with the train it was supposed to take back. The guard and staff of the incoming train at once procured a conveyance and drove to Oswestry, and despatched another engine to fetch the outgoing train, to which was attached the disabled engine. The mishap caused considerable delay and inconvenience."

With Oswestry being just over half an hour away by rail, it must have taken a good hour to drive by horse and cart on the roads of the day – emphasising the problem of operating away from their home base and on 'foreign' metals.

The route from Oswestry was coded "yellow" by the GWR, which meant that locomotive classes of "uncoloured", "blue" and "yellow" were permitted, with the exception of the "28XX" and "ROD" 2-8-0 classes. In practice, the heaviest locomotives allowed were the "Dukedog" 4-4-0s, the "Manor" 4-6-0s, the "2251" 0-6-0s and the "43XX" Moguls. The BR Standard Class 4 engines of 4-6-0 and 2-6-0 configuration were permitted, along with their tank versions, and the corresponding classes of Class 3 and 2.

Passenger services

Weekday passenger services in October,1872 comprised five departures, with three trains from Whitchurch, at 9.30am, 1.52pm, and 6.10pm for Aberystwyth. Slow trains for Oswestry left at 7.40am and 8.08pm. There were five arrivals : at 12.43pm and 5.40pm from Aberystwyth, 7.03am and 8.03pm from Oswestry, and 8.50am from Newtown. There were no Sunday services.

The lack of running powers to Crewe obviously hampered the Cambrian's aspirations for through traffic, as any such through traffic inevitably involved attaching or detaching through carriages at Whitchurch. In fact, as early as 1865 the Cambrian had proposed a Bill in which it sought running powers to Crewe, but this was withdrawn in May, 1866 and any such hopes were thereafter stifled, although not altogether eliminated, as we shall see.

By 1888 the "Scotch Express" for Glasgow, Edinburgh and Aberdeen departed Euston at 10.00am, and included a through carriage for Aberystwyth which was detached at Crewe. This was then attached to the 1.30pm departure at Crewe for Shrewsbury. At Whitchurch this was again detached, and this time attached to the 2.10pm for Aberystwyth along with a buffet car. This working replaced the earlier 1.52pm departure. The balancing working was the 8.00am departure from Aberystwyth, which paused in Whitchurch from 12.20 to 12.27pm and arrived in Crewe at 12.50pm. The returning through carriage for Euston was attached at Crewe to the 12.00 noon from Liverpool Lime Street.

By 1904 the level had substantially increased, with departures totalling eight : for Aberystwyth at 2.25am, 10.07am, 12.17pm, 1.50pm (the through working from Crewe with a carriage from Euston), 5.20pm, to Oswestry at 8.20am,and 8.42pm, and Llanidloes at 6.40pm. Arrivals totalled nine : from Aberystwyth at 12.12pm, 12.55pm, 3.40pm, 6.10pm and 10.25pm, from Oswestry at 6.55am, 2.35pm, from Llanidloes at 9.25am and Welshpool at 5.10pm. The Oswestry services were local trains, calling at all stations, as did most of the services from Llanidloes and Welshpool. However, the Aberystwyth trains included three 'fast' services, which called at selected stations. The 12.17pm arrival and 3.40pm departure were designated as "The North Express", taking only 3 hours 20 minutes from end to end, against the normal express timings of 4 hours, and the slow trains of around 5 hours. This train conveyed through carriages to and from Manchester (London Road), being attached or detached at Whitchurch. There was now a single Sunday service, with the 'down' departure from Whitchurch at the unearthly hour of 2.25am and an 'up' arrival at Whitchurch at 10.25pm. The timing for this early train, and its weekday counterpart, was to facilitate the transport of mails, collected from the LNWR.

Four years later, in February, 1908 the Aberystwyth services had been cut by two each way, with dropping of the 12.55pm and 3.40pm arrivals and the 12.17pm and 5.20pm departures. One Oswestry train, the 11.27am arrival was also dropped. Two years later the service was very similar, with one further arrival from Aberystwyth (at 8.05pm), and the 6.55am arrival being replaced by the reinstated 11.37am arrival from Oswestry. Sundays continued with one train each way, as before. The through carriage from Euston attached to the Crewe – Aberystwyth service continued at least until 1914, and was resumed after the War.

After the disturbance caused by the Great War, other services returned to near normality, and in 1922 there were two

Former GWR 'Dean Goods' 0-6-0 No. 2409 prepares to leave Whitchurch in 1951 with a local train for Oswestry. The leading coach is an elliptical roofed design of uncertain origin and vintage. Unusually it is about to leave from the main up platform face. [Kidderminster Railway Museum]

Collett "2251" Class 0-6-0 No. 2204 stands at the island platform with a train for the Cambrian route on 2 July 1958. The first carriage is a Hawksworth brake second. In the far background, a Stanier Class 5 4-6-0 is arriving with an up stopping train. [Kidderminster Railway Museum]

WR "Manor" Class 4-6-0 No. 7823 HOOK NORTON MANOR slips away from the outer face of the island platform at Whitchurch with a stopping train for the Cambrian line on 27 August 1959, as an English Electric Type 4 (later Class 40) waits in the main up platform. [Kidderminster Railway Museum]

Hawksworth "Manor" Class 4-6-0 No. 7807 COMPTON MANOR strides out of Whitchurch for Crewe with the 3.50pm through service from Oswestry on 28 September, 1960. [Lens of Sutton Association – R.G. Nelson]

Collett "57XX" Class 0-6-0PT No.3770 provides ample power for this two coach stopping service for Oswestry, comprising only non-corridor stock, standing at Whitchurch's island platform on 12 July, 1962. [Lens of Sutton Association – R.G. Nelson]

Two miles north of Whitchurch, "Manor" Class 4-6-0 No. 7819 HINTON MANOR (now resident on the Severn Valley Railway) steams gracefully along with 12.45pm Aberystwyth – Crewe service, which has included a rake of milk tank wagons in its formation. The date is 30 August, 1962. [Lens of Sutton Association – R.G. Nelson]

departures to Aberystwyth, three to Oswestry (plus one SX), and two to Welshpool. Arrivals totalled four from Aberystwyth, one from Oswestry and two from Llanidloes. The timings were approximately those already mentioned, and the Sunday service continued.

However, Cambrian Railways had been formally amalgamated into the GWR as from 25 March, 1922 and the effect of this was eventually reflected in the 1924 timetable. This discloses six departures for Aberystwyth, two for Oswestry and one for Llanidloes. A further Saturdays only LMS Season Excursion is shown as running from Manchester between 13 July and 13 September (Whitchurch 2.50am, depart 3.07am after an engine change) and was to presage excursion traffic in the future. There were four arrivals from Aberystwyth, one from Oswestry and two from Llanidloes. The return of the LMS Season Excursion passed through Whitchurch between 2.00 and 2.10am on Fridays. The apparent curiosity shown in the timing of this excursion, is because it was not a 'day excursion', but was run for the benefit of holidaymakers, who would start their holidays on the Saturday and return on the Friday. The use of the term 'excursion' was to indicate that this was a cheap method of travel, and it did not involve changing trains en route between Manchester and Aberystwyth. Sundays continued as before.

By 1931, the pattern was still pretty much the same, but the numbers had changed again :
there were eight departures and eight arrivals, plus the LMS excursion, and still only one each way on Sundays. But by 1939, there were three LMS excursions, and these had moved to going outwards to Aberystwyth on Saturdays. They passed through Whitchurch at 2.50 to 3.02am, 9.41 to 9.46am, and 1.00 to 1.06pm. The return trips leaving Aberystwyth now on the Saturday morning at 11.05am, 1.00pm and 1.30pm, passing through Whitchurch at 2.37 to 2.42pm, 4.34 to 4.41pm and 4.34 to 4.59pm. However, the middle northward train terminated at Crewe. Thus holidaymakers now had the benefit of a good night's sleep at their resort before returning home. Also, the same engine could be used between Manchester and Whitchurch, even if two sets of coaches were still required. Otherwise, there were eight departures and arrivals, even if some of the destinations had move around between Oswestry, Llanidloes and Welshpool. Sundays continued as before.

As mentioned above, both directions of the through Crewe – Aberystwyth service resumed after the Great War and continued to carry the Euston carriage during the 1920s and 1930s, but this had ceased by 1939.

The Second World War obviously interrupted the normal services, so that in 1944 there were just four weekday departures from Whitchurch : 3.20am and 2.05pm for Aberystwyth, 8.17am for Oswestry and 6.50pm for Llanidloes. Arrivals were at 12.12pm, 4.41 / 4.47pm, and 10.17pm from Aberystwyth, 6.14pm from Oswestry and 9.11am from Llanidloes. The 4.41pm arrival was the continuation of the pre-war 1.00pm departure from Aberystwyth that worked through to Crewe in the Summer months, but now ran daily. Sunday services had been suspended.

Normal service had been resumed by 1949, with seven arrivals and departures. Of interest is that the Aberystwyth to Crewe service still operated, and during the Summer months the Manchester to Aberystwyth Saturdays only trains called at Whitchurch at 12.34pm southbound, and 3.06pm northbound. The engine and stock of the Aberystwyth through service is believed to have returned to Whitchurch as the 7.40pm departure from Crewe, then taken forward the following day on the 3.15am to Aberystwyth. The 6.55pm all stations from Oswestry, arriving at Whitchurch at 7.45pm and returning at 9.20pm was then operated as an auto-fitted push-pull unit, described as a "Motor Train". Sundays saw one departure for Oswestry (at 3.15pm) and one arrival (at 10.13pm) from Aberystwyth.

This pattern continued into 1951, but the "Motor Train" from Oswestry had been dropped. With slight timing variations, and the occasional change of destination, services remained at this level throughout the remainder of the 1950s. During the Summer months, a Saturday Manchester (11.57am departure) to Aberystwyth usually had a portion for Barmouth, normally detached at Dovey Junction; the return working was an 11.00am departure from Aberystwyth.

In almost the final period of service, the 1963 services still remained at this general level, a weekday summary at Whitchurch being :

For	Arrivals	Departures
Aberystwyth	4.29pm, 10.08pm	3.15am, 9.45am
Oswestry	2.25pm, 5.25pm SX, 6.12pm, 7.51pm SO	7.55am, 6.15pm SX, 9.15pm SO
Welshpool	12.12pm	1.30pm, 4.30pm
Llanidloes	8.58am	6.50pm

The 4.29pm arrival was the through train to Crewe, and Sunday services simply comprised the early morning 3.15am departure to Aberystwyth, and the 10.10pm arrival from there.

Many of the local passenger services in the early days ran as 'mixed trains' including goods wagons. This practice was not unusual on branch lines throughout Britain, and in some remote locations lasted until the 1960s. But the Cambrian chose to do things slightly differently, by marshalling the passenger carriages behind the goods wagons. This practice was usually only acceptable where trains travelled slowly, as the lack of proper braking of the passenger vehicle gave not only an uncomfortable ride, but also lacked adequate safety. The compulsory introduction of through automatic braking required in the 1889 Regulation of Railways Act, was eventually adopted by the Cambrian in 1894 on all of its trains. This meant

17 October, 1962 was a rather dull day, as "Manor" 4-6-0 No.7800 TORQUAY MANOR approaches Crewe with the 12.45pm from Aberystwyth, which on this day comprised only two coaches. [Lens of Sutton Association – R.G. Nelson]

B.R. Standard engines often provided the power for Cambrian line services in the latter days. Here we see Class 4 4-6-0 No. 75026 awaiting departure from Whitchurch in June, 1964. [J.Maden Collection]

Modern motive power for a Welshpool stopping train at Whitchurch on 30 October, 1964 with Ivatt Class 2 Mogul No. 46516 doing the honours. [Kidderminster Railway Museum]

Ivatt Class 2 Mogul No. 46512 (now preserved in running order) waits with the 9.45am departure for Aberystwyth at Whitchurch on 14 January, 1965 – just four days before withdrawal of passenger services. This stopping service took nearly 4 ½ hours to reach its destination – some 95 miles away. [Kidderminster Railway Museum]

that although the practice of mixed trains could continue the passenger vehicles had to be marshalled next to the engine, unless any intermediate goods wagons had through piping. So the local services between Oswestry and Whitchurch were changed in appearance.

Concerning the passenger stock, at the time of opening almost certainly the local services would have consisted of four-wheeled stock, but by 1882 most new coaches were six-wheelers. These would have found their way on to the line, particularly on the Aberystwyth trains. Oil gas lighting had been installed in most carriages by 1894, and because a number of vehicles were attached to LNWR trains at Whitchurch, it was important that some degree of compatibility was achieved. So in the following year, the first corridor coaches appeared, of the 'clerestory' design and mostly being composites of at least two classes, although some contained three classes. To facilitate their fairly long distance use, many incorporated a small luggage compartment. However, the GWR was keen on standardisation, and scrapped 80% of the Cambrian coaches before 1930, leaving only around 50 in use. Some of the Aberystwyth trains featured a buffet car during the 1930s, a feature that was not destined to last. But the standard GWR Collett and Hawksworth design of carriages soon became prevalent, with corridor stock on most trains, except for the local services to Oswestry.   Following nationalisation, the former GWR types continued to appear, but were supplemented by former LMSR corridor stock and eventually BR corridor and non-corridor types.

Mail services

Although mail was carried by the Cambrian from Whitchurch through to Aberystwyth from 1864, it was unsorted and carried in vans attached to the through express trains. However, from 1883 a sorting carriage was used (believed to have borrowed from the LNWR) and attached to the early morning departure from Whitchurch. By 1888 the Cambrian had their own carriage, which was worked through from Manchester, arriving in Whitchurch at 2.13am, where it was removed and attached to the 2.25am for Aberystwyth. This evidently required some swift station work! The return working arrived in Whitchurch at 10.15pm. By 1910 the sorting carriage was routed through from Crewe to Shrewsbury, and so a van carried the mails from Whitchurch to Aberystwyth, joining with the sorting carriage at Welshpool. It is not clear why this arrangement was made, although it is possible that it gave more time for sorting, especially for mail to be loaded / unloaded at Shrewsbury. However, sorting was suspended between 1917 and 1919, this believed to be caused by the shortage of men to do the work. When sorting was restored, the sorting carriage continued to run to Shrewsbury rather than via Whitchurch and Oswestry. However, the arrangement for a van of mail to be removed at Whitchurch for onward movement via the Cambrian continued, right through into BR days. By this time the southward train left Whitchurch at 3.15am including Sundays, with the return working arriving between 10.15 and 10.25pm.

Excursion Traffic and Through Workings

As early as 1867 the Cambrian began operating excursions to the resorts on its North Wales coast, such as Aberystwyth, Borth, Towyn, Aberdovey, Barmouth and Dolgelley. These were run in June 1867 in cooperation with the North Staffordshire Railway from starting points in Derby, Burton and Ashbourne to Crewe, where passengers changed to LNWR stock for a through train arriving in Aberystwyth at 6.40pm on Tuesdays. After either an overnight or seven day stay the excursionists returned at 8.00am on the Wednesday.

In subsequent years, through excursions from the North West were generally arranged by the LNWR, as mentioned in Chapter Three. However, in July 1886 through trains were introduced for the Summer timetable from Liverpool and Manchester to Aberystwyth that involved the use of Cambrian carriages and guards, but not, of course, locomotives.

This practice was to continue, with some changes reflecting the increased holiday entitlements of the general working population, until the outbreak of the Great War.

During the Great War, the railways were placed under the control of the government's Railway Executive Committee, so that some degree of common use of locomotives and rolling stock was introduced. During 1915 the Cambrian had arranged to work through goods trains to Crewe with their own engines, and the Traffic Manager hoped that it would set a useful precedent for the future, but whilst this arrangement continued during the War, it saw only limited application subsequently. This cooperation had become particularly necessary as the LNWR had sent a large proportion of its locomotives to France during the conflict, and so especially from 1917 onwards, was often desperately short of motive power. Cambrian engines also became regular visitors on passenger turns to Crewe at that time. In fact, the Cambrian loaned two of its passenger engines and one goods engine to the LNWR for the duration.

Into the 1920s the excursion traffic gradually built up once more, continuing along the same lines as before the War, and apart from the obvious suspension of day excursion traffic, continued until the early 1960s. The Summer weekend holiday traffic was a slightly different matter

Milk Trains

Milk was an important commodity on many rural lines, especially as it was obviously important to get it to the customer whilst fresh, particularly in the days before refrigeration was available. On many lines, the milk churns would be simply loaded into the luggage compartment of the last vehicle in a passenger train, or into a van attached at the rear. Latterly, special trains were run where the volume of milk required them, and where facilities allowed, glass lined tank wagons permitted the transport of milk in bulk from local dairies to city centre dairies or other food processing units. The area also produced much of the Cheshire cheese (even though it is in Shropshire), so this would also be transported. A major dairy, latterly owned by Dairy Crest, was opened in 1931 in Ellesmere on the wharf side of the Ellesmere Canal in the centre of the town. This replaced several smaller dairies nearby, and is believed to have been the major supplier of milk for the railway service.

On this part of the Cambrian system, milk was transported in daily trains from Ellesmere to Whitchurch, for onward movement to Crewe and dairies particularly in the Birmingham and Manchester areas. This pathing for this traffic was always listed in the succession of Working Timetables to be "as required". It would appear that the local dairy only supplied milk and related products to its contracted users when they had a requirement. Milk was considered as a priority for operating purposes, and so was included in the Passenger Working Timetables by the LMSR and BR.

A milk train from the Cambrian line enters Whitchurch behind Collett "2251" Class 0-6-0 No. 2233 on 5 October, 1960. [Lens of Sutton Association – R.G. Nelson]

There would not appear to have been any such specific traffic in the pre-grouping days, so any such milk traffic is presumed to have been carried in vans attached to passenger trains, as mentioned above. Consequently, the following details relate to the later period. In 1924, a daily milk train arrived in Whitchurch at 6.20pm (6.30pm Sundays) from Ellesmere, but there is no indication of its forward movement. However, there was a milk train from Whitchurch to Crewe at 9.30am but it seems unlikely that the traffic from Ellesmere would have been allowed to remain overnight there. The only premise is that this was attached to a suitable passenger or express goods, although there is no indication of such. The above working also appeared in 1931 and continued throughout the 1930s. In 1944 the timing had changed slightly, departing Ellesmere at 5.25pm (5.35pm Sundays) and arriving Whitchurch at 5.46pm (5.56pm). In 1949 and 1951 the timing was identical, and the corresponding light engine return to Oswestry was shown at 6.20pm (6.30pm). But by 1958 the arrival time in Whitchurch was 6.00pm, even though it still left Ellesmere at the same time. In the following year, a change was made, permitting a through working to Crewe from Ellesmere using a WR engine, although no corresponding return working or light engine movement is shown.

The milk train in 1962/63 from Ellesmere (Whitchurch at 6.10pm weekdays, 5.10pm Sundays) continued to run through to Crewe. A return working of empty milk was finally shown, leaving Gresty Lane at 7.56pm weekdays and 6.28pm on Sundays. It must be assumed that as no such working was shown in any of the earlier timetables, that the milk empties were returned in normal goods (or even passenger) trains.

Goods workings

The earliest available data for goods workings dates from the 1888 LNWR Working Timetable, which shows two southbound departures from Whitchurch on Monday, three on Tuesday, Thursday, Friday and Saturday, four on Wednesday, and two on Sunday. The additional Wednesday turn was for the weekly cattle market. These were balanced equally by arrivals, except that an additional one arrived on Monday, and none ran on Sunday.

In 1924 there was one more arrival and departure each day, except for Sunday which comprised just one each way. All ran between Whitchurch and Oswestry only, most calling at the intermediate stations. By 1929, the weekday services were similar at four on Monday and Wednesday, and three the remainder of week, in both directions. Interestingly, the 11.35pm from Oswestry (pausing at Whitchurch from 12.35am until 1.25am) ran through to Crewe, presumably requiring a change of engines at Whitchurch. There was one Sunday working southbound, but no return working.

By 1936 the services had shrunk, with just two southbound each weekday, except for three on Wednesday and Saturday.

The 'Dukedog' 4-4-0s were long associated with the Cambrian system, and in this delightful study is No. 9022 arriving at Whitchurch with a very short goods from the Oswestry direction, on 19 May, 1951. [E.R. Morten / J. Maden Collection]

Northbound, there was just one, with two on Monday and Wednesday. There were no scheduled services on Sunday.

After World War II, the 1946 timetable reveals three daily for Oswestry (at 6.40am MX, 12.30pm and 10.20pm, the last to "run as required"). The first northbound train was the 1.15am MX Oswestry to Crewe, booked at Whitchurch from 2.15am to 3.32am, and arriving at Gresty Lane at 4.06am. This was now a booked turn for a GWR locomotive, which returned as light engine at 5.00am, arriving in Whitchurch at 5.35am. The remaining northbound services consisted of arrivals from Oswestry at 4.30am MO, then at 11.37am, 7.10pm WO (cattle, return to Oswestry at 8.30pm as light engine), and from Ellesmere at 8.45pm. Sunday remained devoid of traffic.

After nationalisation, in 1949 there seems to have been a further reduction, with the elimination of the Oswestry to Crewe through goods, and the 4.30am MO arrival from Oswestry. The 12.30pm for Oswestry was cut back to Ellesmere, and the 10.20pm conditional departure for Oswestry was cancelled. It should be noted at this stage that a number of passenger and goods light engine and empty stock movements were necessary between Whitchurch and Oswestry, but not always included in the Working Timetables.

Much of the traffic involved coal, agricultural machinery, feedstuffs and fertilizer inwards, with agricultural products mostly outwards. The main changes for 1951 were that the early morning arrival from Oswestry was reintroduced, arriving at 2.15am MX and 4.48am MO. Also the 6.20pm WO livestock from Oswestry (Whitchurch pass at 7.10pm) now ran through to Crewe, with a WR engine throughout, it is understood. Sundays were not changed.

In the September 1958 to June 1959 Working Timetable, the 2.15am MX arrival from Oswestry was now shown as going forward at 2.58am for Crewe Gresty Lane (arrival 3.37am). The only other addition was a 7.45pm WSX empties from Oswestry (Whitchurch arrive 8.46pm), which in the Summer 1959 timetable carried on to Crewe. So it would appear that by this date, that there was a continuation of some cooperation between BR regions to introduce the economies of through running.

This pattern for normal goods continued into the final years of the Cambrian line from Oswestry, with the 1961 timetable giving two weekday workings, except for three on Wednesday, one on Saturday and none on Sunday. Southbound the frequency was two daily, with one on Wednesday and Saturday and none on Sunday.

Overall, the line produced very little in the way of goods traffic, which can be said of most rural lines, and because it never formed part of a major route, there was even less through goods traffic.

Locomotives

The Cambrian Railways locomotives were initially extremely varied, resulting from the three small companies that contributed to its stock on formation. For example in 1868 the stock comprised one 0-4-0, six 0-4-2, sixteen 2-4-0, fifteen 0-6-0, one 0-6-0T, eight 0-6-0ST, six 0-4-0ST, one 0-4-2ST and three 2-4-0T. Whilst adequate for the time, some of these were obviously pure shunting types, whilst it is clear that the 2-4-0s would have been used on passenger work, and the 0-6-0 were the standard goods types. However, replacements were obtained for some of the elderly types, notably seven 0-6-0, one 0-6-0T and two 4-4-0s in the 1872-6 period. The latter types were intended for the fast and longer distance passenger work. Furthermore, with the acquisition of the Mid Wales Railway in April 1888 a further five 0-4-2 and six 0-6-0

The history of the 'Dukedogs' is convoluted, and in this shot from early 1946 we see No.3209 EARL OF RADNOR reversing to the shed at Whitchurch for servicing, while its train stands in the platform to the left. This engine was built in 1937 using "Bulldog" class frames and a "Duke" boiler. It was renumbered in July of the same year as the photo, to No. 9009 and lost its name. [P. Ward]

locos were added. Almost all of the tender types could have been seen along the line to Whitchurch, and probably a number of the tank engines on local goods or passenger work. However, as the Cambrian developed its own locomotive works at Oswestry, and eventually began construction there, some semblance of standardisation began to emerge. Nonetheless, the company still relied heavily on outside manufacturers, notably Beyer Peacock and Sharp Stewart, who had also developed their own standard types specifically for goods or passenger work. These were well proven designs, supplied to railways all over the world, and certainly appropriate to the Cambrian. By 1908, the fleet comprised 78 locomotives of eight different wheel arrangements, including two built at Oswestry.

It is not at all surprising after inclusion into the GWR in 1922, that the latter company would attempt to standardise the locomotives. Obviously, the older and weaker engines were the first to go, but the last Cambrian engine actually survived into BR days, when 0-6-0 no.855 was withdrawn in October, 1954. Actually, one of its predecessors, no.844 survived even longer as a stationery boiler at Oswestry Works. For passenger work, the GWR " Barnum", "Stella" and "3232" class 2-4-0s firstly held sway, supplemented by the "Duke" 4-4-0s. The main goods types were the Dean "2301" class 0-6-0s, and these survived in good numbers into BR days. Many of the Churchward and Collett designed 0-6-0PTs appeared on both local and passenger duties, but as freight duties were not really arduous, it is not believed that the larger GWR types would have been required on this line. In any case, the route was designated as 'yellow' by the GWR, indicating that a maximum axle weight of only 16 tons was permitted, although this was later raised in BR days, in 1960, to 18 tons.

Eventually the "Dean Goods" 0-6-0s were supplanted by the Collett "2251" class 0-6-0s which proved their worth on both passenger and goods duties. It should be noted that many of the turns to Whitchurch may have involved passenger in one direction and goods in another, and so the 'mixed traffic' type of engine was most appropriate here. One of the most popular types to become familiar was the Collett rebuild of Dean 4-4-0s that became known as "Dukedogs", from the two classes that supposedly donated parts : the "Dukes" and the "Bulldogs". These survived into BR days, when replaced by the more modern "Manor" 4-6-0s, and subsequently by the BR standard 4-6-0s, 2-6-0s, 2-6-2Ts and 2-6-4Ts as they became available.

As the Cambrian, and the GWR as its successor, did not have running powers between Whitchurch and Crewe their locomotives were normally changed at Whitchurch for the few through workings that did take place. However, on occasions these 'interlopers' did work through as far north as Crewe, where they were serviced at Crewe North shed. One such possible through working was on the Crewe – Aberystwyth service, which ran from the 1880s to the 1930s, but the balancing working for the 'foreign' engine is not at all clear. In BR days such through workings became more commonplace, as would be expected of a unified system. However, they were mostly limited to workings that terminated at Crewe, except for special workings such as excursions and troop trains - but even so, the engines would nonetheless always be changed at Crewe.

No diesel locomotives are known to have run over this line, nor any diesel multiple units, although it is possible that excursions or special trips formed of the latter may have appeared before closure.

Finale

The line became part of the Shrewsbury District of the Western Region of BR on 1st January, 1948, but was moved into the London Midland Region from 1963. Goods facilities at intermediate stations except Ellesmere were withdrawn from Wednesday, 4th March 1964. It was originally scheduled to close the line to passenger traffic in November,1964 but this closure was delayed because adequate alternative bus services could not be arranged in time. All passenger services were eventually withdrawn with effect from Monday, 18th January 1965. Goods traffic between Whitchurch and Ellesmere survived until Saturday, 27th March 1965. All track had been removed by 1966,including the junction at Whitchurch, although the under and over bridges remained in place for many years.

CHAPTER SEVEN

THE MARKET DRAYTON LINE

The detailed history of this line may be found in my book "By Great Western to Crewe" (Oakwood Press, 2005). Therefore, this chapter gives a summary of the development and operation of this line, so far as it is relevant to the Shrewsbury to Crewe railway.

Origins and Construction

The Nantwich and Market Drayton Railway Company (NMDR) was formed in 1860 to build a line of 10 miles 6 furlongs 2½ chains (10¾ miles) from Market Drayton to join the Shrewsbury to Crewe line just west of Nantwich. The line was built by Thomas Brassey in partnership with William Field, and opened as a single track line on 19 October 1863. It was originally proposed that the line would be worked by the LNWR, however no agreement on terms could be reached, and so the GWR was approached. The GWR was already interested in the area, having backed the formation of the Wellington and Drayton Railway (WDR) in 1862, for a line from Wellington to Market Drayton that would join by an end on junction to the NMDR. So the GWR operated the services of the NMDR from the outset, even though in 1863 this was a remote outpost of its system.

In 1864 Brassey and Field began construction of the double track WDR, and a year later the directors of both the NMDR and the WDR agreed to operate under one Board. In 1866 it was agreed to double the NMDR track, and work began in March of that year, again using Brassey and Field. This was completed in July 1867 and the complete line from Wellington to Nantwich opened on 16 October that year with double track throughout. The GWR had earlier obtained running powers over the LNWR from Nantwich as far as Manchester, as part of its GWR and West Midland Railway Amalgamation Act, 1863 (Section 2, Article 5). So it was then in a position to commence northbound services from Wellington (and further afield). However, the GWR never operated north of Crewe; all such through services required a change of engines at Crewe. Whilst the GWR did manage to create through services to Manchester in an entirely different direction, using running powers from Chester into Manchester Exchange, it never achieved a major status in that city. Its passenger services over the WDR and NMDR into Crewe thus remained mostly a purely local service, although some services originated as far south as Worcester and some through carriages from even further south were conveyed to Crewe from further afield, as we shall see.

Passenger traffic

At the opening of the NMDR there were four weekday trains in each direction, terminating in Nantwich and none ran on Sundays. These arrived in Nantwich at 9.5am, 12.30pm, 3.20pm and 8.20pm, returning at 9.30am, 1.00pm, 4.00pm and 9.05pm. All trains conveyed 1st and 3rd class passengers and were mixed, so no individual goods trains operated. The locomotive and stock were stabled at Market Drayton. By 1865 one additional service operated, on Wednesdays only, leaving Market Drayton at 10.30am and returning from Nantwich at 11.00am.

With the opening of the line from Wellington in October 1867, the four weekday trains were no longer mixed and continued into Crewe, with approximately the same times, except for the last train, which ran two hours earlier. A Sunday service was implemented, departing from Crewe at 7.10am and 6.10pm, with returning services arriving at 10.20am and 9.15pm. Thus the operation of services was moved to Crewe, where arrangements for the stabling of locomotives and stock had been made. Northbound trains were able to set down passengers at Nantwich, but not pick up; correspondingly, southbound trains calling there could not set down passengers, but could collect them for the onward journey into GWR territory. No trains called at Willaston en route to or from Crewe, and these limitations (with two exceptions that we shall see later) continued after nationalisation, and until closure of the line. However, just one month later in November 1867 the services improved dramatically to six each way on weekdays. The two additional trains were expresses that did not even stop at Nantwich and were timetabled as through services from Wolverhampton to Manchester, although they must have changed engines in Crewe.

This level of service continued through 1872, and 1883, but by 1888 the Sunday service was reduced to one train, departing Crewe at 7.20am and returning at 9.00pm.

Moving on to 1898, there had been substantial changes. There were now 8 down (northbound), but these included one through train from Worcester, and two of the other services included coaches slipped from Paddington trains at Wellington, being worked through to Manchester. The 7 up (southbound) services included through coaches from two Manchester services, to be attached to southbound trains at Wellington. The Sunday services remained at one each way.

This basic pattern continued until the Great War, although the down trains now balanced the up trains at 7 each way on weekdays. After the War, the service was slightly reduced, with one of the hitherto daily trains running on Saturdays only. However, by the Summer of 1922 there was an indication that the through services were becoming more important, as 3 of the 6 down trains were through : one from Worcester to Crewe, one to Manchester, and one comprising four carriages to Manchester detached from a Bournemouth – Birkenhead train at Wellington. In the up direction, there were 5 trains including the return working of those through services just described. In 1931 the service had increased back to 7 weekday each way. A further empty stock working was made from Crewe at 10.50am (MX) to Worcester.

On Sundays an additional train ran, arriving in Crewe at 10.21am and returning at 11.00am to give two each way. In 1939 the overall number remained the same on weekdays, but yet another Sunday service was added, the up train departing from Crewe at 8.05pm, and the down train arriving there at 11.08pm.

Wartime conditions obviously affected services, even if this line did serve a number of RAF and Army installations. In 1942 there were 4 up weekdays plus one Wednesdays only, 4 down and two each way on Sundays. In 1944 there were additional trains arriving in Crewe at 12.26am on Mondays only (MO) and at 11.21am on Wednesdays only (WO).

In 1947 and just prior to nationalisation services had not returned to normal and were at almost the lowest level of frequency since opening, with just 3 each way on weekdays and 2 on Sundays. But by 1949 matters had improved somewhat and had reached 6 up plus one MWSO, 5 down plus one WO, and 2 up and one down on Sundays. The route was then attracting long distance parcels traffic, with one each way on weekdays between either Portsmouth or Southampton and Crewe. In 1953, the 5.10pm from Crewe was the only WR train that was scheduled to call at Willaston and was to remain so, as Willaston closed to passengers from 6 December 1954. By this time, passengers at Nantwich could finally take advantage of the WR trains to Crewe in each direction : the restriction imposed by the LNWR (and later, the LMSR) on GWR trains calling had been removed, as the competition element no longer applied to the nationalised service.

Again, the service pattern was to remain unchanged, this time until 1957, when the Sunday service was stabilised at 2 each way. In 1958 services were fragmented so that up weekdays saw 5 plus one WO and 1 MO (which ran through to Donnington, for the benefit of workers at the Ordnance Depot), and down were 4 plus 1 SO. Sundays were unchanged, but one of the parcels trains now began from Bristol. For the final three years of passenger operation up to withdrawal on 9 September 1963, the number of services remained unchanged but for one additional down service. The weekday parcels traffic comprised one SX up to Bristol, and one down from Evesham. Other parcels services from the south were being

Dean double-framed "3201" or 'Stella' Class 2-4-0 No. 3201, built in 1884, standing in the bay platform at Crewe with a Wellington train. The date is probably sometime in the late 1920s. The carriage set has been labelled on the end as "Wellington and Crewe No.2" indicating its dedicated usage. [A.V.W.Mace / Milepost 92 ½]

A stopping train from Wellington enters Crewe, probably in the late 1920s, with Dean "3206" or 'Barnum' Class 2-4-0 No. 3223 at its head. The first carriage is a comparatively modern Collett non-corridor brake third, whilst the second is a Churchward clerestory corridor composite and probably downgraded from main line service. The magnificent LNWR gantry in the background completes the picture. [A.V.W.Mace / Milepost 92 ½]

Collett "5101" Class Prairie Tank No.4154 runs through the mist into Willaston station with a stopping service from Wellington on 25 September, 1952. Despite nationalisation, this train will pass through the station without stopping, as part of the original working agreement with the G.W.R. [H. Townley / J.M. Bentley Collection]

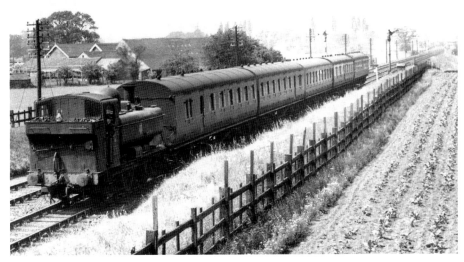

A strengthened Wellington train of five coaches (three non-corridor and two corridor) bustles along west of Willaston on 23 June, 1956 behind Collett "57XX" Class 0-6-0PT No.9630. [H. Townley / J.M. Bentley Collection]

concentrated at Market Drayton, to avoid congestion at Crewe. This required a light engine from Crewe North (usually a Pacific turn) to Market Drayton, from where empty parcels vans, sometimes numbering as many as 20 bogie vehicles, would be taken to Willesden.

The line was regularly used by excursion traffic during the 1950s, mostly from Manchester and Liverpool to Birmingham, but also in the opposite directtion from the West Midlands to such destinations as Blackpool and the Lake District. Football specials also frequented this route in both directions. The line received its highest accolade from 10 September 1962 when a titled train was scheduled to run. This was "The Pines Express", whose original route had been from Manchester (London Road) via Crewe, Stafford, Walsall (engine change), Camp Hill line at Birmingham, Bristol, Bath and Bournemouth. However, because of electrification work south of Crewe, it was routed over this line to Wellington, Birmingham (Snow Hill), Banbury, Oxford, Reading, and Basingstoke to Bournemouth. The southbound "Pines" passed through Nantwich at 10.57am, and the northbound at 4.07pm. This was scheduled for haulage by a Type 4 diesel locomotive (usually an English Electric Class 40) but during this period steam occasionally deputised. "Royal Scot" 4-6-0s were noted, as were LMS 'Black Fives' and BR Standard 4-6-0s. However, following the withdrawal of passenger services between Wellington and Nantwich, and the consequent downgrading of the line to 'goods only' status from 9 September 1963, "The Pines" was routed to carry straight on at Nantwich to Shrewsbury, then take the Wellington route from there southwards. The timings remained pretty much the same, passing Nantwich at 11.02am southbound (10.58am Saturdays) and 4.05pm (4.10pm Saturdays) northbound. Intriguingly, the Monday to Friday service (both directions) was scheduled to call at Shrewsbury, whilst the Saturday service passed through non-stop. Motive power between Oxford and Crewe was scheduled for a "Warship" diesel-hydraulic, but steam still deputised on a few occasions, notably "Castle" Class 4-6-0s. With the completion of the electrification works, from 1967 the route was once more revised southwards from Manchester to run via Macclesfield, Stoke, Wolverhampton (High Level), Coventry and Leamington to join the WR route onwards.

In summary, the number of passenger services varied from a minimum of three daily weekday trains each way, to a maximum of seven, with an average of around five, with between one and three on Sundays. Considering the changes to the individual timings of these mostly local services, these mostly only varied by a few minutes. So the reader has been spared the tedious detail of such changes!

Ivatt Class 2 2-6-2T No. 41232 stands in bay platform No.3B at Crewe with the 5.20pm for Wellington on 19 April, 1962. Meanwhile, the DMU on the right is forming the 5.10pm departure for Shrewsbury in platform 4B. [B. Brooksbank]

Goods workings

As we have seen the transport of passengers was never of major importance, particularly as the route passed mainly through agricultural land, and served no large towns. It was the importance of this line for goods traffic that was evident from the moment that it became a through route connecting to the GWR system. The January to June 1870 Working Timetable gives 7 up and 8 down goods workings on weekdays, of which one up and two down were local goods workings. On Sundays there was but a single up through working. However, the frequency soon increased, and the following tables will give some idea :

UP GOODS WORKINGS

	Mon	Tues	Wed	Thurs	Fr	Sat	Sun
June 1872	7	10	10	10	10	10	4
June 1888	7	11	11	11	11	11	5
September 1929	13	13	14	13	12	14	5
September 1936	8	11	11	11	11	12	2
May – October 1946	7	8	8	8	8	8	3
Sept 1958 – June 1959	14	18	18	18	18	18	4
June – Sept 1961	14	12	12	12	12	7	5
June 1965	13	18	18	18	17	16	0
Oct 1966 – Mar 1967	14	19	18	19	18	16	0

DOWN GOODS WORKINGS

	Mon	Tues	Wed	Thurs	Fri	Sat	Sun
June 1872	4	8	8	8	8	8	4
June 1888	8	13	13	13	13	13	5
September 1929	10	15	15	15	15	16	6
September 1936	10	18	18	18	18	14	6
May – October 1946	7	10	10	10	10	10	5
Sept 1958 – June 1959	10	15	15	15	15	16	7
June – Sept 1961	10	14	14	14	14	10	5
June 1965	17	18	19	18	19	18	0
Oct 1966 – Mar 1967	17	19	19	19	19	18	0

The number of local or pick-up goods workings varied, but was usually two or three each way on weekdays. With the withdrawal of passenger workings in September 1963, and the consequent desire to reduce operating costs, signal boxes

One of Churchward's original "28XX" Class 2-8-0s, No.2819, comes to a halt at the Willaston down distant signal, which protected the level crossing, with a lengthy down goods working on 4 July, 1953. Meanwhile, hay making continues in the field in the foreground. [H. Townley / J.M. Bentley Collection]

were usually unmanned on Sundays and so no goods workings were scheduled. However, the line still functioned as a useful diversionary route, especially at weekends, and so goods workings could be seen even after completion of the electrification in 1965, but these obviously did not appear in the Working Timetables.

It can be seen that goods workings were generally three times as many as the passenger workings. Furthermore, the

An up Class "F" express goods for the Wellington line passes through Willaston station on 28 September, 1952 behind Collett "Hall" Class 4-6-0 No. 5988 BOSTOCK HALL. [H. Townley / J.M. Bentley Collection]

On the same day as the preceding photo, Banbury shed's Collett "43XX" Class Mogul No. 6334 takes a Class "H" goods southwards through Willaston station, bound for the Wellington line. [H. Townley / J.M. Bentley Collection]

On the outskirts of Crewe, Collett "57XX" Class 0-6-0PT No. 3770 fusses along with a short freight from the Wellington line on 17 October 1962. [Lens of Sutton Association – R.G. Nelson]

through workings were of considerable length. The destinations and points of origin were considerable, although the most frequent were those remarshalled at Oxley yard in Wolverhampton, and at Crewe, Basford Hall and later Gresty Lane yards.

Some ran as through (often fitted) freights to or from such northern locations as Leeds, Liverpool, Manchester, Carlisle, Heysham, Tees Yard, Haverton Hill (Middlesbrough) and southern locations served included Birmingham, Worcester, Cradley Heath, Paddington, Reading, Basingstoke, Southampton, Bristol, Avonmouth, Tavistock Junction, and Marazion (Penzance). Whenever through freights reached Crewe, there was of course, the inevitable engine change. There was a notable frequency in the Summer and Autumn of fresh agricultural produce from the South and South West to the North West, particularly fruit, broccoli and other vegetables. One commodity that did not seem to be regularly transported was coal, except when included in local goods workings to the intermediate towns and villages along the line. An interesting working was the British Leyland car carrying service which in 1963 ran from Morris Cowley to Bathgate (near Edinburgh) thrice weekly with an unbalanced twice weekly return. This was initially the duty of a BR Standard Class 9F 2-10-0, but as there was a substantial stud of "Britannia" Pacifics at Crewe North at this time, they were often used, However, by 1964 the ubiquitous Brush Type 4 diesels (later Class 47) had replaced steam on this duty. By 1965 this working was elevated to three northbound workings (Monday, Wednesday and Friday) and three southbound (Tuesday, Thursday and Saturday). The following year the destination was changed to Johnstone High (near Paisley) and the unbalanced working of 1963 was reinstated.

Goods traffic finally came to an end as from 8th May 1967 when the line was closed completely. The final rites were carried out during the following months with the removal, firstly of any vehicles in sidings, then useful lineside equipment and finally the track. Although the track was not removed immediately, the clearance had been completed by 1970.

Locomotives and rolling stock

At the opening of the line in October,1863 the GWR had an number of small locomotives inherited from its nearby constituents. It seems fairly reasonable that one or more of these various 0-4-0 tank locomotives would have been pressed into service on the undemanding duties for the 10½ miles from Market Drayton to Nantwich. Also, the West Midland Railway had been absorbed into the GWR in August of that year, and they had a sizeable stock of tank engines of the 0-4-2, 2-2-2, 2-4-0 and 0-6-0 wheel arrangements that would also have suited. The first passenger trains consisted of four wheeled stock, and this would have continued in use for some years after the line from Wellington was opened. Certainly by the late 1880s six wheeled coaches were in use on the local services, but it would be into the early 20th century before bogie vehicles were used. In common with many other secondary routes, main line stock was cascaded down into use here, to end their days in revenue earning service. The early Dean clerestory carriages were still in use in the 1930s, but eventually more modern GWR stock was introduced. After the Second World War some Churchward and Collett stock

Wellington shed's B.R. Standard Class 3 2-6-2Ts made frequent appearances on the stopping trains to Crewe in the 1950/60s, and here we see No. 82009, in lined green livery, backing down to its return train after running round in Crewe station. In the background Stanier 'Black Five' No. 45394 prepares to depart with a southbound main line train. The date is 19 June, 1957. [B.Brooksbank]

appeared, and eventually in the 1950s some new Hawksworth carriages made their debut. In BR days the local services were almost entirely comprised of non-corridor stock, normally in two or three coach formations. Diesel multiple units were never used on the local services.

Returning to the locomotives in use, in 1868 Wellington locomotive shed was opened, whose allocation included some of the Wolverhampton built Joseph Armstrong 2-4-0Ts and 0-6-0STs. These would have been equally happy on the local goods, as well as local passenger turns. Wellington shed became quite synonymous with aging types working out their lives on less demanding turns. Three of the "481" class 2-4-0 tender engines built in 1869 were allocated there before being withdrawn between 1899 and 1906. Several of the double framed "149" class were also working the line at the start of the 20th century until withdrawn between 1916 and 1920. One of the Dean single framed "3226" class, no. 3231 worked the line just after the First World War, and the last Armstrong double framed "806" class no. 810 was shedded at Wellington until withdrawn in 1926. The "Stella" or "3201" class of small wheeled double framed 2-4-0s, nos. 3204 and 3507 worked the line between 1922 and 1925, and other members of this class continued the tradition until 1933. The last class of 2-4-0 to be seen on the line were the Dean "Barnum" or "3206" class, some of which were still active here until 1937. However, from the 1920s onwards many of the passenger turns were being taken over by larger 4-4-0 types that had similarly been cascaded down from main line duties. The GWR shed at Gresty Lane included members of the Dean "3252" ("Duke") and "3300" ("Bulldog") classes in 1921, and some lasted until the outbreak of World War II. However, by this time, Collett "5101" class 2-6-2Ts had been allocated to Wellington, primarily for local passenger duties, but equally at home on goods duties. Similarly, whilst several members of Dean's 0-6-0PT classes had been handling goods work, they were gradually being replaced by Collett's "57XX" class, which when vacuum fitted were equally happy on local passenger turns. Both of these types were periodically allocated to Gresty Lane shed, which in GWR days was treated as a sub-shed of Wellington. The Dean "2600" or "Aberdare" 2-6-0s were frequent visitors to Crewe on goods turns, but the long lasting "2301" or "Dean Goods" had become well established. The Churchward "43XX" 2-6-0s were a mixed traffic type that most often appeared on the through goods work, and the occasional passenger turn. However, most of the local passenger duties were still rostered for tank locomotives, as they did not require turning at Crewe, which was obviously an otherwise time consuming task at that very busy station. As the volume, and weight of the goods traffic mounted, so the engines involved became larger, and so any of the GWR 4-6-0s (except for the "Kings") could be seen. Admittedly, the use of "Castles" was not commonplace, but at the very end of steam use, they did make appearances on freight duties. Possibly the last appearance of one of this class, was on 11 December, 1963 when no.7012 BARRY CASTLE worked the 12.30pm Wellington to Crewe parcels. The GWR Churchward "28XX" and Collett variants of the "2875" class were also stalwarts for goods work, as indeed were the GWR "ROD" 2-8-0s of which a few were allocated to Oxley shed. During the Second World War, the Riddles "Austerity" 2-8-0s were noted, as well as the LMSR Stanier 8Fs built for the War Department.

With the changes in BR regional boundaries in 1950, the LMR took over control of the line to Wellington from Nantwich as far as Crudgington, although for administration purposes only. However, from 19 April 1953 the former GWR shed at Gresty Lane became a part of the Crewe Motive Power District. It was not long before an allocation was made here of Ivatt Class 2 2-6-2Ts for the local passenger duties, and they continued in this role until the withdrawal of passenger services ten years later. However, these were shared with Wellington shed who also obtained some new locomotives in the form the BR Class 3 2-6-2T of the 82XXX series for their branch services, which inevitably resulted in their appearance on Crewe stopping trains.

In the final years of goods only working, the GWR types still predominated, but former LMS "Black Fives", 8F 2-8-0s, Ivatt Class 4 Moguls and BR Moguls also made appearances. Although the line was not officially authorised for passenger use, a number of specials, excursions, diversions still occurred. Also one or two enthusiasts' railtours made visits, perhaps the most exotic being "Merchant Navy" Pacific no. 35022 HOLLAND-AMERIKA LINE which visited enroute from Waterloo to Crewe and return to Paddington on 27 November, 1965. Possibly the last, was when sister engine no. 35026 LAMPORT & HOLT LINE passed through at the head of the Warwickshire Railway Society's three-day "Aberdonian" railtour, on the first leg of its journey from Waterloo to Scotland, via Crewe on 24 June 1966.

During the few years that diesel locomotives did operate here, many of the main line classes available at the time put in appearances. Those not already mentioned also include the BR Type 2 (Classes 24 and 25), and English Electric Type 2 (Class 20) and Type 3 (Class 37). The Crewe built "Westerns" were tested over the line prior to acceptance by the Western Region and sent to Swindon. Even the humble "08" diesel shunters ventured on to the line for track removal duties, along with the Sulzer "24" and "25"s.

CHAPTER EIGHT

THE TATTENHALL BRANCH

This line, running from Chester Junction, Whitchurch to join the Crewe – Chester line at Tattenhall Junction has been the subject of several articles in the railway press, and in local history papers. However, it has not been totally researched before, and as it forms an important connecting line to the Shrewsbury to Crewe line, this chapter is devoted to a detailed study of the history and operation of the line.

Beginnings

The LNWR decided that this line would be a vital link in its network, to connect its traffic from South Wales to the Merseyside docks and to the Holyhead route for Ireland, avoiding the congestion that had built up around Crewe. Indeed, C.P. Neele in his book "Railway Reminiscences" (originally published in 1904) described the line on 2 October, 1872 as "creating a direct line of our own from Ireland to Hereford and South Wales, and a competing route between Shrewsbury and Chester, unsatisfactory, probably, to the Great Western Company, who had hitherto possessed a monopoly of traffic." The LNWR were at pains to emphasise that it was not meant as a competitor to the GWR route from Shrewsbury to Chester, as it desired to keep on good terms with the GWR. Nonetheless this new route would be some 3¾ miles shorter than the GWR route, and did not include gradients as steep as Gresford Bank, which was nearly four miles at 1 in 82½, and thus made for heavy going for southbound freights.

Plans for the route were deposited at Shrewsbury County Court on 30 November,1865. Details of the construction powers were included in section 4 of the London and North Western Railway (New Lines) Act, 1866 (Vict.29 and 30, chapter 168) which received Royal Assent on 16 July, 1866. The line was to be 14 miles 3 furlongs and 8 chains, "from a junction at Whitchurch, Salop with Shrewsbury and Crewe branch of Company to junction at Hatton with Chester and Crewe Branch of Company". The railway was to be double track throughout. Section 17 required completion of the railway within five years.

Like most new railways, some changes were made to the route, and so on 15 July, 1867 further powers were granted in section 4 of the London and North Western Railway (New Lines) Act (Vict.30 and 31, chapter 113), to permit two deviations. These were minor changes around Malpas. The Act also extended the time for completion by one year. However, it would appear that there was some delay in the acquisition of land, and so the Company applied for a further extension of time in their London and North Western Railway (New Works and Additional Powers) Act, 1869 (Vict.32 and 33, chapter 115). This was passed on 12 July, 1869 and permitted a further three years from that date for completion.

Negotiations for land continued, with some difficulty being experienced in gaining rights from the freeholders to cross the Bradley and Edge commons. Other major landowners in the area to be traversed included Sir Philip Grey-Egerton (Lord of the Manor of Broxton), John Hurleston Lache (Carden Hall), Robert Barbour (Bolesworth Castle) and Thomas Tyrwhitt Drake (Lord of the Manor of Malpas).

Construction

Even so, it was not until February, 1870 that the following notice was published, inviting tenders for the construction:

THE WHITCHURCH AND TATTENHALL RAILWAY
London and North Western Builders
To Contractors and Builders

The Directors are desirous of receiving Tenders for the construction of the Whitchurch and Tattenhall Railway in the County of Cheshire, a length of 14 ¾ miles

Parties desirous of Tendering may see the drawings Specifications and Quantities, or may obtain copies of the same, on payment of Six Guineas, upon application to Mr. William Clarke, 38 Parliament Square, Westminster, S.W. on and after Tuesday 1 March between the hours of Ten and Four o'clock

Tenders addressed to the Secretary at Euston Station, and marked outside, 'Tender for Whitchurch and Tattenhall Railway' to be sent in or before Four o'clock
Wednesday 18 March 1870.

The Directors do not bind themselves to accept the lowest or any Tender.

S.Reay, Secretary Euston Station, February, 1870.

The following tenders were received :

Scott & Edwards, Wigan	£79,398
Eckersley & Baylis, Westminster	£79,800
E. Knight, Manchester	£82,494-16-6d
J.& J. Jackson, Kent	£85,022
J. & C. Ridley, Carnarvon	£85,243
A. Pilling	£85,658
Engineer's Estimate	£88,500

plus 15 other tenders, the highest being £154,688.

The contract was awarded by the LNWR Permanent Way Works & Estate Committee (PWWEC) to Scott & Edwards, along with free railway travel passes to be issued to one member of the firm and one foreman from Wigan. The *"Whitchurch Herald"* of 2 April, 1870 confirmed that the contract had been let, so this must have occurred just a few days earlier. It also mentioned that the appointed Principal Engineer was William Clarke, of 38 Parliament Street, Westminster.

With these formalities over, attention turned to the site, and the usual ceremony of "Cutting the Sod". However, this was not to be a lavish occasion, as had hitherto been normal. The *"Whitchurch Herald"* of 23 April, 1870 reported the event as follows :

> "CUTTING THE FIRST SOD OF THE NEW RAILWAY – *An event that may prove of vast importance to present and future generations, occurred on Tuesday last (18 April) . The first sod of the new line of railway between Whitchurch and Chester, near to the Whitchurch Station, was turned up, with little ceremony, without the ringing of bells, or amidst the cheers of a large assembly. There were simply there Mr. Clarke (the engineer for the line), Messrs. Scott and Edwards (the contractors), and a few others connected or interested with the proceedings; and so quiet was the whole affair , that it was quite accidental that we witnessed the beginning of a work that will bring us nearer to friends at Malpas, Broxton, and other places between here and Chester, and give them the benefit and accommodation which a railway always affords to a district. The ceremony being concluded, a few bottles of wine appeared to be enjoyed, under a brilliant sun, by those employed in the work and by the visitors present, who drank success to the line, and wished the contractors a profitable return for the work in hand."*

By 27 July, 1870 works were already in operation, and on this date a locomotive to assist with the construction was despatched by the makers. This was CHESHIRE, an 0-6-0ST with 13" x 18" inside cylinders, and 3' 6" wheels built by Manning Wardle & Co. Ltd. of Leeds . It was works number 291 of 1870, and was one of their Class "M" locomotives, a type popular with railway contractors. It is not clear exactly where the locomotive was sent to, but from later events, it was obviously in use on an isolated section of the railway under construction.

By 22 August, 1870 the PWWEC were informed that two bridges had been built and works were progressing satisfactorily. A month later, five bridges had been completed, and a further one was ready to receive its girders. New lines had been laid at the Tattenhall end of the line, and the contractor's engine was working there. A further month later, it was reported on 29 October, 1870 that the contractors had driven through the heaviest cuttings at the Whitchurch end of the line, and that "an engine is now working thereon". This could suggest that another locomotive was in use, but there is no evidence that Scott & Edwards had a second locomotive at this contract. Bearing in mind subsequent events, it is in fact more likely that this refers to an excavating engine. There was also a brick making steam engine located at Mr. Snow's farm at Tushingham (mid way between Whitchurch and Malpas), which reputedly could produce 16,000 bricks per day. It was, of course, standard practice for contractors to use the raw materials (in this case, clay) available in the immediate area. The report goes on to say that an engine was at work in the Broxton area, near to where the line formation was already complete. This would be the Mannning Wardle "CHESHIRE". Girders for most of the bridges had been delivered, but about five miles of the middle portion of the line had not yet been started.

Work seems to have slowed considerably, and perhaps not unexpectedly during the Winter months, and on 16 March, 1871 the PWWEC were informed that works had stopped because the frosts had recommenced, making excavation extremely difficult. However, the central section was then reported to have commenced, and the junction at Tattenhall was being made.

A report in the "Whitchurch Herald" of 29 April, 1871 gives some more detail on the progress of works, and are interesting as it relates to the methods adopted to cross the canal at Grindley Brook:

> "WHITCHURCH AND CHESTER RAILWAY. – *The works on this line have not of late shown the advance on the rate of construction which appeared to the eye before Christmas, though since the stoppage by the long frost the navvies and bricklayers have been steady at their labours. The heaviest piece of work of the whole length has just been completed, viz, the bridge at Grindley Brook, above which the line and its high embankment passes over. It is several months since the canal was diverted out of its course, and since the bricklayers and others have been*

busy – first of all laying many thousands of bricks in concrete to form the bottom or bed of the waterway : this and the foundations were the principal difficulties, an engine having to be kept in use for running out the water for a considerable time. The bridge is built upon the principle of a large culvert. The arch and approaches are now complete. The canal has again been turned into its proper course, and by this time the two high embankments have been made to meet, thus forming a continuous and ready way for the rails. Near Whitchurch, commencement has been made in laying down the permanent rails. At the Tattenhall end, the difficulties being less, a greater distance has been cut."

Work continued apace, but in May 1871 the locomotive "CHESHIRE" broke down. As it was a vital piece of equipment, immediate repair was essential, and so it was sent by road to Whitchurch for remedial work. According to the *"Whitchurch Herald"*, this caused ' a great deal of curiosity' in Broxton, as it was pulled by 22 carthorses. To overcome the loss of the locomotive, the LNWR provided a temporary replacement locomotive, at a charge of 3 guineas per day, so as to ensure that the works were not delayed. Meanwhile, there were so many navvies in the neighbourhood that the Egerton Arms at Broxton was forced to convert their hayloft into lodgings.

Difficulty in obtaining men was reported on 15 June, 1871, although most of the heavy embankments and approach roads had been completed, and all bridges well advanced. Five miles of the permanent way had been laid, albeit only as a single track at that time.

Recruitment of men was still a problem by September, due to them preferring harvest work at that time. However, the single line had advanced to 10 miles. Surprisingly, work progressed well in the following two months, with 21 miles of single track having been laid. The station buildings at Hampton Heath (Malpas), Broxton and Tattenhall had been started, but once again frost interrupted progress. The PWWEC was informed that the line could be ready in April, 1872 if sufficient men could be obtained, but the engineer was confident that it would be finished by 1 June. Through January and February 1872, progress was reported as slow, with incessant rains causing problems. Alterations at Whitchurch and Tattenhall for the new alignment had been approved by the Chairman of the PWWEC. These included the installation of the bay platform at Whitchurch station for the branch trains. This was achieved by removing that part of the main down platform next to the large brick wall that had been installed to prevent the ingress of coal dust from the goods yard. Thus the width of this platform was effectively halved, and a single track laid in. As there was no room for a run round loop, this presented an operational problem that was never satisfactorily solved : incoming trains would have to reverse out into the down goods yard to permit an engine release. Alternatively, and more commonly, incoming Chester trains would use the up island platform, then after the engine had run round, the stock would be moved into the down goods loop, from where it would be reversed into the bay platform ready for its next departure. The entire platform area was covered by an overall roof supported by the large brick wall on one side, and by cast iron pillars on the platform. This overall roof was of wood and glass construction with detailed featherboard edgings, but only extended from just in front of the footbridge to less than half way along the bay platform.

On 14 March, 1872 it was reported that the roofs were on the station buildings at Broxton and Tattenhall, and the station buildings and goods shed at Malpas were up to plinth level. Good weather had permitted favourable progress.

The LNWR submitted its 1st Notice of Intention to open the line to the Board of Trade on 10 May, 1872 – but this seems to have been somewhat premature, as in his final report to the PWWEC, on 19 August, 1872 the engineer stated that it would not be possible to get the line ready for inspection for at least another two to three weeks. Continued wet weather had caused numerous slips of embankments and cuttings.

Nevertheless, the LNWR Company Secretary, Stephen Reay, sent a 2nd Notice of Intention on 4 September, and Colonel Rich made his inspection on 21 September. His report, dated the next day, mentioned that the line was laid with steel rail of 84 lbs per yard, which was the highest grade of rail available at the time. Raised cabins had been provided at each of the stations to house the levers operating the points and signals, which were interlocked. However, at Whitchurch there was no such provision, although it was noted that the LNWR intended to erect such a cabin to centralise the operation of the points, which were at that time scattered about the yards. Although generally favourable his report did highlight some minor matters for rectification :

"The following points are required on the New Line.

The permanent way from about the 4th to the 8th mile post requires lifting and regulating.

The view of the Station South Distant Signal at Malpas and Tattenhall, as they are approached from the South, and that of both Station signals at Broxton require to be cleared from overlapping trees.

Boarded foot ways between the platforms required at all the stations.

Padlocks are required for all the Accommodation Gates.

The Engineer (Mr. Clarke) has promised that these small works shall be completed at once, before any passengers are carried on the line.

I submit that the Board of Trade may sanction the opening of the Whitchurch and Tattenhall Railway."

Opening

Despite wishing to remain on good terms with the GWR, the LNWR lost no time in advertising the benefits of their new line, as this advertisement from the "Whitchurch Herald" of 28 September, 1872 reveals :

Railway Notices

LONDON AND NORTH - WESTERN RAILWAY

On and after OCTOBER 1ST, the NEW LINE between TATTENHALL and WHITCHURCH will be opened for Passenger Traffic , affording the SHORTEST ROUTE between Chester, North Wales, Birkenhead, Shrewsbury, and South Wales.

For full particulars see Bills W. CAULKWELL, General Manager Euston Station, September, 1872.

The "*Whitchurch Herald*" of Saturday , 5 October 1872 included the following report, and the "Shrewsbury Chronicle" of the same date, ran an absolutely identical report. Evidently, syndication of news reports is not a modern day phenomenon.

"OPENING OF THE WHITCHURCH AND TATTENHALL RAILWAY

This line of railway was opened for general traffic on Tuesday last, (2nd October,1872) the first train leaving Whitchurch at 7.25 a.m. The number of passengers who went by this train was not great, certainly not more than a score. It was accompanied by Mr. Wood, of Shrewsbury, Mr. John Weston, Mr. Hewitt, Mr. Edwards (of the firm of Scott and Edwards, contractors) and others. There were a good few Whitchurch persons on the ground to witness the departure of the first train. As it proceeded out of the station a number of fog signals were fired. The traffic on the line during the day was very fair, and we noticed in our town not a few strangers, but where they hailed from is not in our power to tell.

The opening of the new line was celebrated at Tattenhall, but the proceedings were anything but of a lively nature, and hardly worth the journey which we took from Whitchurch. All the stir – what was – was at the Aldersey Arms. Here a tent was erected close to the house, where, at one o'clock over 200 of the navvies and others sat down to a most excellent dinner, provided by Mr. And Mrs. Jones, the worthy host and hostess of the Aldersey Arms. The dinner was presided over by Mr. Edwards; Mr. Smith, engineer, being in the vice-chair. Among those present, and whom we noticed on the ground during the afternoon were Mr. John Weston, Mr. West, of Shrewsbury, Mr. Dewitt, Messrs. Scott and Edwards, the contractors, Mr. D. Hamilton, engineer, Mr. Totnes, Mr. Fray, Mr. Barnes, and Mr. Beckett, of Manchester, contractors, Mr. Veitch, civil engineer, Inspector Lowe, of Salop, Mr. Job Thompson, inspector of railways, Mr. Johnson, inspector of Crewe yard, Mr. F. Arthen, &c., &c. There was no after dinner speeches, but the workmen gave many hearty cheers for their kind and hospitable entertainers (Messrs. Scott and Edwards). In the yard adjoining the Inn Mr. Webster, of Chester, photo'd a large number the navvies, their employers and others connected with the line. Taking everything into consideration, Mr. Webster succeeded in obtaining a pretty good picture.

Soon after three o'clock the advertised sports began, in the presence of some 500 or 600 spectators.

(There then followed a lengthy list of the various races, and the resultant first three places in each event.)

The sports over, the majority of those present wended their way homewards. Adjoining the field of sport were a number of gingerbread, nut, and other stalls, but from what we saw the owners of them did anything but a "roaring trade".

Following the completion of the line, an auction was advertised in the "*Whitchurch Herald*" of 12 October, 1872 of the contractors' surplus materials and equipment, as was normal at the conclusion of a contract. Interestingly, the advertisement only specifies one locomotive, confirming the belief that they did only employ one here. The details confirm the identity of CHESHIRE.

Advertisement :

MESSRS. CHURTON, ELPHICK AND CO.

BEG to announce that they have been favoured with instructions from Messrs. Scott and Edward to SELL BY AUCTION, (in consequence of the completion of the Whitchurch and Tattenhall Railway,) on TUESDAY, the 15th day of October, 1872, and following day if necessary (and not on Tuesday, the 8th, as previously advertised), at the Depots at Whitchurch, and Hampton Heath, the undermentioned valuable PLANT, MACHINERY, and EFFECTS, including about 200 tons of contractors' rails, from 48 to 56lb. per yard, which have only been used about 12 months; quantity of fish plates and bolts, cast iron and steel crossings, a first-class LOCOMOTIVE TANK ENGINE, 6 wheels coupled, 3ft. 6in. diam. 13 in. cylinder, by Manning Wardle & Co., of Leeds, built in 1870; one sett cast girders, for a 10ft. cattle creep; smith's tools, quarry tools, wrought and cast scrap iron, earth wagons with wrought wheels, barrows, planks, huts, stables, sheds, boarding, sleepers, balk timber, battens, scaffold poles, culvert and bridge centering, 18 one-horse carts, two four-wheel timber carriages, one excellent mortar mill, a new and first class drum with break, suitable for a sharp incline; together with seven very valuable young WAGON HORSES, harness mare, and a large quantity of excellent gears and harnesses, the greater part of which was made new for these works.

Full particulars, with catalogues, will shortly be published.

Unfortunately, this newspaper did not give full details of the proceeds of the sale, as witness this report one week later:

"SALE OF RAILWAY CONTRACTOR'S PLANT, HORSES, &c. – On Tuesday and Wednesday last, Messrs Churton Elphick and Co., held a sale at the Malpas and Whitchurch stations, of the materials used in the construction of the Whitchurch and Tattenhall Railway, now completed, also the horses, gear, &c. Tuesday being a beautiful day, there was an enormous company, and the numerous lots realized good prices. Eight Cart Horses sold for £509 5s., or an average of £63 13s., each."

However, whilst it is known that the locomotive CHESHIRE was acquired by the firm of Falkner & Tancred in 1872, who renamed it as "MARY", its subsequent history is unknown.

Passenger services

The initial services in 1872 comprised seven 'down' departures from Whitchurch at 7.25am, 9.05am, 10.42am, 1.05pm, 3.40pm, 6.35pm and 8.50pm. The seven 'up' trains left Chester at 8.05am, 8.55am, 12.10pm, 1.10pm, 3.05pm, 5.15pm and 8.20pm. The second 'down' ran from Hereford and ran non stop between Whitchurch and Chester, taking 38 minutes. The second and fourth 'up' ran non stop from Chester, with the second continuing through to Hereford. Oddly, the prepenultimate departure from Whitchurch did not stop at Tattenhall, otherwise all other trains stopped at all stations, and took between 43 and 50 minutes for the journey. There were no Sunday services.

Shortly after the line opened, it was the scene of a tragic and fatal accident, as reported in the *"Whitchurch Herald"* of 19 October, 1872 :

"FRIGHTFUL RAILWAY ACCIDENT. – Yesterday, (Friday) afternoon (18 October, 1872) a frightful accident occurred at Grindley Brook, crossing on the Whitchurch and Chester Railway. Mrs. Matthews, a widow, 70 years of age, who resides at Grindley Brook, was proceeding to Mr. Robert's farmer for some supping. As she was crossing the line the passenger train due at Whitchurch at a quarter to two o'clock came up, and dashed the poor woman to pieces, legs, head, intestines, &c., being strewn about the line. When we saw the engine – on its arrival at Whitchurch – two of the wheels were smeared with blood. It is conjectured that the woman did not see the train as it came up. About 40 yards from the crossing the line curves, so it is not astonishing the train came on the deceased unawares. The engine driver blew his whistle, but the woman – who is said to be somewhat deaf – either did not hear or could not get away in time. The guard put on his break when he saw the danger deceased was in, but was not able to pull up in time to save her life. An inquest will, of course, be held. The sad affair has cast a gloom over the neighbourhood."

Obviously, this poor woman was just not used to there being trains running on the line and the one she met was the 'express' from Chester. Given her disability, this adds to the tragedy.

The same issue also recorded a distinguished visitor to the line, who had travelled at little earlier on the same day, as follows :

"DEPARTURE OF W.E.GLADSTONE, ESQ. – Yesterday (18 October, 1872) the right honourable gentleman, accompanied by his brother left Cloverley Hall, and proceeded to Chester by the train which leaves Whitchurch at one o'clock. There was no demonstration beyond the firing of a few fog signals."

William Gladstone was at that time, two-thirds the way through his first period (1868-1874) as Prime Minister, and had a further three terms later. He had been visiting John Pemberton Heywood, who was the principal partner in his family's Liverpool bank, which was subsequently sold to the Bank of Liverpool, which itself was acquired by Martin's Bank, now part of Barclays Bank.

By 1888 the services had been increased to seven departures from Whitchurch at 7.48am, 10.31am, 12.00noon, 3.07pm,

Webb "Renewed or Improved Precedent" 2-4-0 LMS No. 5036 NOVELTY (built in 1892 as LNWR No. 1682) leaving Whitchurch for Chester during the late 1920s. A horse box has been marshalled next to the engine. The various Webb 2-4-0 classes were difficult to differentiate at a glance, and so were collectively referred to as 'Jumbos'. [G. Coltas Collection]

Standing in the Whitchurch bay platform, a very smartly turned out Webb "Renewed Precedent" 2-4-0 LMS No. 5029 SPEKE awaiting departure to Chester in 1929. This engine was completed at Crewe in June 1891 as LNWR No. 1684, and was finally scrapped in 1931. [J.M. Bentley Collection]

Webb "Renewed Precedent" 2-4-0 LMS No. 5020 DELHI runs forward 'wrong line' from the up main line platform at Whitchurch with the set of carriages for a Chester service. It will pause behind the photographer, then reverse into the bay platform to the right of the down platform occupied by a Whale 4-4-0 or 4-6-0 waiting with a Crewe train. The scene is likely to be in the late 1920s. [Kidderminster Railway Museum]

5.18pm, 6.20pm, and 8.30pm. The second service was a through train from Shrewsbury. All other services gave an 'across the platform' connection from Shrewsbury to Crewe stopping trains at Whitchurch. Chester departures were at 8.55am, 11.05am, 12.45pm, 3.20pm, 4.25pm, 5.35pm and 8.45pm. The first and third departures from Chester ran through to Shrewsbury, and once again there were good connections at Whitchurch, although it is possible that the fifth train in each direction conveyed through carriages.

The times had varied by 1908, but there were still seven trains in each direction, of which one ran through to / from Shrewsbury. Two years later, the services were identical, but for the 4.25pm from Whitchurch, which was revised to run on Saturdays only. The Working Timetable for October 1914 showed no great change, as the effects of the Great War were yet to be felt. In fact, there had been a slight increase in the number of services to seven each way on weekdays, plus one Saturdays only. Only the 10.00am departure from Chester ran through to Shrewsbury, and there was no corresponding down working.

After the Great War, the services returned to normal, and in 1921 the number was identical to 1908, apart from some small timing changes. However, in the following year (1922), one train was introduced to start from Malpas at 7.55am to Chester, and the 5.25pm from Whitchurch was dropped. This Malpas service involved the running of a light engine from Whitchurch at 7.10am, although there is no mention of where the passenger stock had been held. It was presumably worked in to Malpas on the previous evening.

Coal shortages arising from the General Strike prompted the LMS to issue a temporary timetable as from 31 May, 1926. This limited the services to just four in each direction, with one down train being the 8.05am (retimed 10 minutes later) starting from Malpas.

Moving forward to 1931, there were six 'up' services and one SO. In the 'down' direction, there were seven plus one SO, and the morning Malpas to Chester train. The light engine to serve this train was then shown alternatively as a local freight "to run as required", hopefully making better use of the resources.

By the Summer 1939 Working Timetable, there were had been a number of changes. There were then eight 'up' weekday services, plus two more on Saturdays. The first train (8.45am from Chester) ran through to Shrewsbury, and the 8.02pm ran through to Wem. The 2.30pm departure from Chester was a through service from Llandudno. 'Down' weekday services totalled seven, plus one SO and the Malpas to Chester morning train. The 8.53pm departure ran through to Birkenhead (Woodside) and the 5.26pm SO ran through to Llandudno. Sunday services had been introduced, with four each way, all starting or terminating at Shrewsbury. One in each direction ran through to / from Bangor. These services were shown as "Season Excursions", so evidently not to be run during the Winter months.

With the outbreak of War, an Emergency Timetable was introduced in September, 1939. This provided for a basic service of five trains each way, with none on Sundays. However, by the Summer of 1944, there were six 'up' weekday trains with one less on Saturdays. The 'down' trains totalled the same, but the 9.48am from Whitchurch ran through to Rhyl.

With the War over, and nationalisation having occurred a year earlier, the 1949 timetable showed little variation, with precisely the same number total number of services, although some timing changes had been made. Sunday services had not been restored. Three years later, the Summer timetable for 1952 showed one train less in each direction, but the 1.10pm (WO) from Chester then ran through to Shrewsbury. During 1956/57 nothing more had changed, the timings being also unchanged. Although there were a number of trains running only on specific days, the overall effect worked out at

Unusually this Chester train is seen leaving from the main down platform at Whitchurch, and so may be one of the through workings from Shrewsbury. It is headed by Fowler 2P 4-4-0 No.40529, one of the 1913 batch of rebuilt Johnson engines. [Whitchurch Archaeological & Historical Group]

five trains each way, in the final year of service. It seemed that BR had given up on this line, but in all likelihood, it was the passengers that had given up, making the service uneconomic.

The last train ran from Chester General on Saturday, 14 September 1957, hauled by Ivatt Class 2 2-6-2T no.41266 at 11.10pm for Whitchurch. An interesting, if somewhat overly romanticised account of its departure appeared in the *"Chester Chronicle"* on the following Saturday :

LAST OF THEIR LINE

Class 2 Passenger engine No.41266, with a number of carriages behind, stood in the Bay on No.7 Platform at Chester General Station on Saturday night ready for the journey which would mark the closing to passenger traffic of the Chester – Whitchurch line.

On the platform stood a tall man in a white mackintosh, with a god-like forelock framing his forehead, as of another world, but, in fact, direct from Liverpool's last train.

He spoke : "I am Ralph Jackson. And I attend them all." This transport "undertaker" thought it "perfectly natural" never to miss the last train, tram or bus.

But why ?

"One doesn't question these things", said he, clutching tighter his mysterious brief-case, "One simply obeys." He added humanly, "Send a paper. It'll help." Meanwhile three men chatted on the footplate. "It would've been good", grieved Fred Evans, the guard (who retires in six months) "to've ended the 37 years on the ol' line." His Whitchurch neighbours, driver Jimmy Major Picton and fireman Peter Heatley, nodded. Then they nodded to the steam gauge. It was nearly time.

The top-hatted stationmaster, Mr.E.I.Thompson whispered "Forty-five."

I stiffened. "Forty-five?" I said.

"Forty-five" he repeated. "I know. I've counted them."

"Aha!" I'd caught on. "Forty-five general mourners eh : Well we'll have a word with them."

Meanwhile the clock fingers were at 11-3. And snug in the misty-windowed compartments, two misty-eyed lolling lovers unclinched, blushed and said the buses wouldn't be so useful. A worried mother predicted her small daughter's travel sickness would restart on Monday, and a youth in a tattered "mack" complained that Malpas by bus was two pence dearer.

Not welcoming the end of a thirty year's habit were Mr. And Mrs. Sydney Penk, Higher Wyche, Malpas. Very disgruntled about the whole thing was Mrs. Alice Allman, Well-lane, Malpas.

And very sorry the line was closing was Miss M.L. Seddons, Old Hall-street, also Malpas. Then : No. 41266 whistled thrice, then moved from the dank, black station. Fog signals which had been placed on the line detonated. The last passenger train was on its way. And the clock fingers showed 11-10….."

The "Chester Courant" had earlier recorded this event on Wednesday, 18 September. Their report included many interviews with passengers, which are not relevant, but the following abstracts add a little flavour :

THE LAST TRAIN TO WHITCHURCH

Exploding Detonators Provide Railwaymen's Farewell

> …"To the accompaniment of a shrill blast from the engine whistle, and exploding detonators which had been placed on the line to speed her on her way, the train – the last passenger train to run along a stretch of line which has been operated since 1870 (sic) – drew out of the station almost unobtrusively.

> …It was sad to realise that the steam leviathan which had for almost 90 years chugged its way along the rural route from Whitchurch to Chester, has now been replaced by a fleet of 'buses operated by Crossville Motor Services.

> …Mrs. Alice Almond, who was accompanied by her 11-year old daughter, Deirdre, was even more forthright in her condemnation of the decision to withdraw the service. "Those of us who live in Malpas may now as well be dead," she commented. "It will be very difficult for us to travel to Chester."

Alice Almond's reaction seems a little excessive, but she evidently felt very strongly.

Passenger traffic was officially withdrawn as from Monday, 16 September 1957, but the Saturday departure was the last service, as there were no Sunday trains. A small matter of conjecture remains, concerning the pathing of diversions and excursions from 1957 until 1963. In the Summer months there were huge numbers of day excursions taking people from the East and West Midlands to the North Wales coast, and possibly from other locations. The use of this route to avoid Crewe seems obvious, and indeed the LMR Sectional Appendix for October 1960 states that although "no passenger trains are booked over this line, passenger trains may use it with no special permission".

Goods Workings

In the 1870s and for many years afterwards, British merchant and naval ships were coal-fired. Also much of the coal was sent abroad, even as close as Ireland, so there was a ready market at the ports, not only for bunkering, but for exports too. It is this traffic that the line was primarily built to serve.

The earliest traceable goods workings are for June 1888, summarised as follows:

	Mon	Tues	Wed	Thurs	Fri	Sat	Sun
UP	11	9	9	9	9	9	1
DOWN	8	10	10	10	10	10	2

All down daily workings, except one, were Abergavenny to Birkenhead coal trains. The exception was the 10.10am Shrewsbury to Chester local goods. In the up direction, all workings were the returning coal empties from Birkenhead, except for the returning daily local goods (3.25pm ex- Chester) and the 12.45am MX Chester to Whitchurch (arrive 1.55am) non stop goods. Thus, the primary purpose for the line had evidently been achieved, by successfully routing this coal traffic away from Crewe.

During the Great War, it British Naval Fleet was largely relocated from its southern bases (Portsmouth, Plymouth, etc.) to Scapa Flow in order to have effective control of the North Sea. The Admiralty required steam coal from the Aberdare and Rhondda pits in South Wales for its Fleet, so this had to be sent about as far as it is possible to go northwards. In practice, this meant to Grangemouth, on the Firth of Forth, where it was transhipped into colliers, which would then load directly into the warships at Scapa Flow. Some other destinations for this traffic included Glasgow, Newcastle and Immingham – but these were to a much smaller extent. This vital coal traffic became known as "The Jellicoe Specials", which by 1918 totalled 15 trains per day. Much of this traffic was handled by the GWR northwards to Chester, where it was handed over to the LNWR, or at Warrington. It has been thought that some of this traffic used the Tattenhall route, but this has been disproved. Probably what gave rise to the assumption in the first place was the Admiralty coal traffic passing over this line to Birkenhead and Holyhead, where some of the requirements still needed to be met. During this time, about 15 trains per week of this Admiralty traffic used the Tattenhall branch to Birkenhead, and about a further 60 wagons were sent weekly to the Admiralty base at Holyhead. However, by the end of the Great War the advantages of oil fired ships became apparent, and the Navy began building or rebuilding its fleet accordingly. Similarly, but rather more slowly, the merchant ships were converted.

The Working Timetable for September 1929 shows a consequent and dramatic decline in goods traffic with just two workings each way on most days. The 'down' workings comprised one daily local goods, calling at all stations, and one MSX Abergavenny Junction to Mold Junction coal train. In the 'up' direction, the return coal empties from Mold Junction to Abergavenny ran on Mondays only. Other southbound workings were a non stop freight from Chester to Whitchurch (MX), a local goods (SX) and a SO Broxton to Whitchurch local goods. There was no traffic on Sundays – so the line could be closed completely for that day.

By 1931 the Abergavenny – Mold workings had been suspended, leaving just one local goods each way, plus a MX Chester

A hive of activity as the Cheese Train of 1907, sponsored by the Yorkshire chain of grocers by the name of Driver, being loaded at Broxton and headed by a Webb "Cauliflower" 0-6-0. The bowler hatted gentleman in the foreground is William Bamber, whose father started the local Cheshire cheese wholesaling business and owned the warehouse is seen in foreground. The large half timbered building in the background is the Egerton Arms Hotel, once used for accommodation by the navvies constructing the line. [Whitchurch Historical & Archaeological Group]

Stanier 8F 2-8-0 No. 48630 approaching Broxton station on 16 July, 1965 whilst engaged on track removal duties. These were taking place further west, as the removal had commenced from the Chester end of the line. [D.P.Rowland]

to Coleham (Shrewsbury) through freight. There was also a SO Broxton to Whitchurch, and a Whitchurch to Malpas local goods. The line was beginning to look like the typically bucolic British country branch line.

Undoubtedly, the war years of 1939 to 1945 would have seen the line being pressed into further use, but no details are available. So we must look next to 1946 when there were two daily local goods each way, one of which ran between Whitchurch and Malpas only, the other reaching Chester. There was one through goods in each direction : 2.55pm daily Harlescott Sidings to Birkenhead, and 3.48am MX Chester to Coleham.

With the cessation of passenger services in September 1957 the locomotive shed at Whitchurch had also closed for normal operations, so there was no motive power available from Whitchurch for local goods. The only local goods working was a through daily working between Crewe Gresty Lane and Broxton, also calling at Malpas. It was diagrammed to leave Crewe at 6.35am, arrive Whitchurch at 8.38am and depart at 9.08am, arriving in Broxton at 10.10am. It returned at 11.00am from Broxton to Whitchurch, where it laid over from 11.20am until 1.30pm until continuing its journey to Crewe Gresty Lane. As if to compensate, a small amount of through traffic had been introduced in the September 1958 to June 1959 Working Timetable. In the 'down' direction, a Bordesley Junction (Birmingham) to Birkenhead ran MX. In the 'up' direction, a through Chester to Coleham ran MX, and a Birkenhead to Cardiff ran SX. By 1961 however, the line had become the preferred option for oil tank workings from Ellesmere Port, Hooton and Stanlow, destined mainly for the Midlands. There were four such workings on most days, with the MX Chester – Coleham and the Broxton – Crewe workings continuing. Northbound, the empty tanks were returned in five workings. The apparent unbalanced nature of these workings is due to some taking the GWR route at Shrewsbury to Chester.

Around this time, with the electrification works being carried on near to Crewe, it is almost certain that the line saw a number of diverted freight, and even passenger workings. But such diversions were not timetabled, and local recollections of any such workings do not seem to have been recorded.

However, even this significant amount of traffic was insufficient to save the line, and it was officially closed completely, as from Monday, 4 November 1963 including all remaining goods facilities. In fact, an earlier proposal had been made, in June 1959, for the line to be completely closed, but nothing more came of that. It is believed that the last revenue earning working passed over the line in January, 1963 with Stanier 8F 2-8-0 no.48165 at the head of a Stanlow to Rowley Regis oil train. The track was taken up during 1965, except at the Whitchurch end, from the junction with the main line for about 200 yards (passing beneath the Black Park Road bridge). This was used as a shunting neck for the down side goods yard, but was eventually removed during the rationalisation of the track layout in the late 1970s.

Locomotives

There is no record of locomotives used on the Tattenhall line at the time of its opening. But very soon afterwards, the passenger services became well known for the use of the Ramsbottom and Webb 'Jumbos'. There were many classes of these excellent 2-4-0s that initially thrived on main line work, but could also be found on secondary work, such as this route. The first to appear was Ramsbottom's "Samson" class in 1863, to be followed by his "Newtons". Webb continued with developments, such as the "Precursor", "Precedent", "Improved Precedent", and "Waterloo" (or "Whitworth"). The last one of the final class was built in 1896, but members of this generic class could be found on these workings well into the 1920s. In 1917, the Whitchurch shed allocation comprised five engines, all of which were 'Jumbos' : No.604 NARCISSUS, No.609 EARL OF CHESTER, No.737 ROBERTS, No.763 VIOLET and No.901 HERO. Others later based here included No.628 TARTARUS, No.737 HECLA, No.793 MARTIN, No.1132 NORTH WESTERN and No.2157 UNICORN. Despite the apparent stronghold that this class had on the passenger services up to the 1920s, other types would almost certainly have put in appearances, particularly on the through workings to/ from Shrewsbury or to North Wales destinations. Indeed, Ahrons commented that in 1877 the much rebuilt Ramsbottom 2-2-2 CORNWALL with its 8' 6" driving wheels "*was doing duty between Chester and Shrewsbury via Whitchurch. I fancy the engine must have been stabled at Crewe, at all events she was there in 1880*". This locomotive, dating originally from 1846, is now in the care of the National Railway Museum. Types more appropriate would be the LNWR "Precursor" and "George the Fifth" 4-4-0s, or even Webb's 2-4-2Ts on local services. But by the early 1930s, it would seem that the Johnson, and later Fowler Class 2 4-4-0s of Midland Railway and LMS origin had become the staple diet for passenger services, with several allocated to Whitchurch, as a subshed of Crewe North. This major shed had several of these engines, primarily for use as 'pilot engines' on heavy West Coast main line trains. Eventually, under BR, the passenger services in the 1950s were handled by Stanier and Fairburn Class 4 2-6-4T, and Ivatt Class 2 2-6-2T locos.

Around 1960/61 the line was used on occasions for the training of drivers on the new diesel locomotives then being introduced in some numbers. Also at this time, the experimental gas turbine 4-6-0 locomotive GT3 was garaged at the closed shed at Whitchurch. This promising 2,700 hp locomotive, was built speculatively by English Electric using a 4-6-0 rolling chassis and supplied with power from a static bed gas turbine. It was tested along the branch and on to the North Wales Coast route, subsequently at Rugby Locomotive Testing Station, on the West Coast main line over Shap, and on the former GCR between London and Leicester. However, it failed to impress the BR board, and was returned to English Electric at the Vulcan Foundry works at Newton-le-Willows in 1962. It was later sent to Crewe Works, where certain items were removed, and finally sent for scrap to T.W.Ward in February,1966.

For goods traffic, Ramsbottom's famous "DX" goods would have been used from the outset, this class having been introduced in 1858 and eventually numbering some 943 members. Trevithick's earlier Goods 2-4-0s of three variations, were quite long lived, so may well also have appeared. The introduction of Webb's 0-6-0 'Coal Engines' and "Cauliflowers" would prove a long lasting presence on the line for a wide variety of goods workings. Eventually, the heavier coal trains needed the use of the many variants of 0-8-0 (some rebuilt as 2-8-0) introduced and / or subsequently rebuilt by Webb, Whale, Bowen-Cooke and Beames. These mostly excellent machines did exactly what was required of them on these duties and acquired an enviable reputation for their slogging sure-footed power. Otherwise local goods workings were often hauled by Fowler 4F 0-6-0s, which had become the standard LMS goods design on the 1920s. Before the Second World War, some vestige of modernity would have shown itself in the appearance of Stanier 8F 2-8-0s on through workings. After nationalisation, and with little local goods traffic, these designs continued in use, although there is some evidence that the mixed traffic Stanier Class 4 2-6-4Ts were also used on this traffic. Stanier 2-6-0s and 'Black Five' 4-6-0s often worked the Bordesley to Birkenhead freights. With the introduction of the heavy oil trains, this work was almost entirely entrusted to Stanier 8Fs and BR Standard 9Fs.

A final note on working is that breakdown arrangements in 1960 were given by the LMR that the WR No.11 crane (30 tons) at Shrewsbury would be available for any eventuality on this line.

Typical motive power for the Tattenhall branch from the 1930s until closure were the Fowler 2P Class 4-4-0s, which were rebuilds of Johnson engines of Midland Railway ancestry. Here No. 40413 poses outside Whitchurch shed in 1953. [Kidderminster Railway Museum]

Description of the route

As already intimated, Chester trains usually starting or terminating their journeys at Whitchurch, did so from the bay platform adjacent to the down main line platform. Using an independent down running line, they threaded their way past Whitchurch Goods Yard signal box to reach the Tattenhall branch, just over a ¼ mile distant. Here the line swung away on a 12 chains radius curve in a westnorthwest direction from the Crewe line in the area of Yockings Gate. "Whitchurch Chester Junction" signal box was sited in the fork of this junction to control all movements on and off the Tattenhall line, and some nearby sidings that led from the branch. This was the start of the line, double tracked from the outset, and worked on the absolute block system, with each of the ensuing signal boxes acting as block posts. The line climbed away on varying gradients between 1 in 176 and 1 in 331, before crossing Alport Road. It had originally appeared that it would be necessary to have two underbridges here : one also for Wirswall Road. However, approval was given for the diversion of Wirswall Road into Alport Road, so that only one bridge was required. The line then continued directly at 1 in 170 up to the district of Hinton, where it passed beneath the Tarporley Road (originally A49, now B5476). This had required the raising of this road by some 25 feet to enable the railway to pass under. Following, the line descended at 1 in 140 to **Grindley Brook**, where it turned into more northwesterly direction. At this point, with the line crossing into Cheshire and running on a substantial embankment, it passed over the Llangollen Canal, just where the canal is descending in a series of seven locks. As mentioned above, the work required to divert the canal during construction of the railway was particularly tricky. Slightly to the north of this crossing point an unstaffed halt, **Grindley Brook Halt** (2½ miles) was opened on 4 July, 1938, with simple pedestrian pathways being linked to a nearby lane at the western end. No photographs are known to exist of this structure, but it is believed to have consisted of a basic wooden construction, possibly redundant sleepers, and if any shelters were provided, they would also have been simple wooden affairs. The halt continued in use to the end of passenger services. The immediate area here today is very busy during the Summer months with much canal traffic, which has become very well developed.

Continuing in the northwesterly direction, the line once again climbed, firstly at 1 in 239 then at 1 in 140 to cross beneath the Chester Road (A41) carried on a red brick skew bridge. The original road here had to be raised by five feet for this construction. The countryside now opens up into pleasant agricultural land, with fine views in most directions as it switchbacked from ascent to descent, crested near to the hamlet of Bradley Green, then once again began a descent into a small but wide valley. The profile changed yet again, as it climbed at 1 in 122 for nearly a mile to an overbridge carrying the road from No Man's Heath (on the right) to Malpas (on the left). But we have to travel nearly another mile, now descending at 1 in 383 mile before reaching the station for **Malpas** (6½ miles). This was located just on the north side the overbridge carrying the road from Hampton Heath to Malpas, and is in fact, on the very edge of the village of Hampton Heath. So much so, that the local populace almost always referred to the station as "Hampton". The LNWR were much criticised for the siting of this station so far away from the village – but, in mitigation to move the line further westwards and nearer to the village would have entailed considerable earthworks on the southern approaches to the village. As the line was not expected to glean much from its wayside traffic, one can sympathise with the LNWR for adopting the course duly chosen.

Malpas was a sizeable village which grew to a population of 1,628 by 2001, and the name of the village comes from the French for "poor or bad passage", possibly deriving from its position on an old Roman road, from Bovium (Tilson) to Mediolanum (Whitchurch).

Whitchurch station in the 1950s with Stanier Class 4 2-6-4T No. 42677 waiting to remove the stock of an arrival from Chester to the down line, from where it will reverse it into the bay platform on the right, ready for its next trip along the Tattenhall branch. Meanwhile 'Black Five' 4-6-0 no. 45109 passes through the down platform with a northbound express. The famous station running-in board, dating from LNWR days is portrayed on the left. [A.W.V. Mace / R.S. Carpenter]

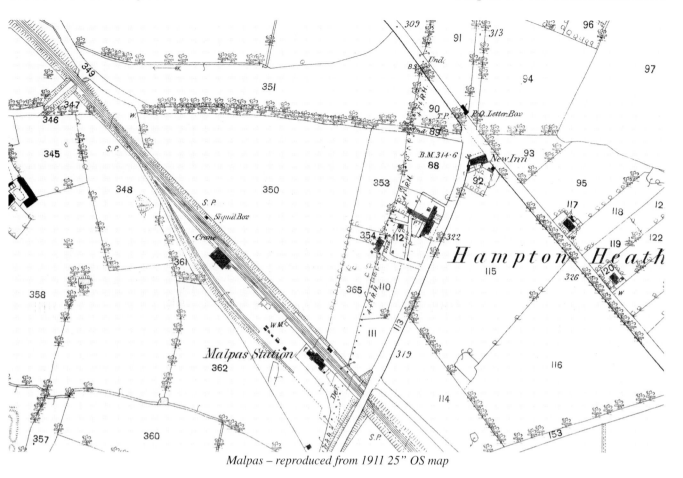

Malpas – reproduced from 1911 25" OS map

The signal box at Malpas, seen on 16 July 1965 after closure of the line, but prior to removal of the track. This was a standard small LNWR design of signal box. [D.P.Rowland]

The station buildings comprised a substantial two storey stationmaster's house, plus booking hall, waiting rooms, staff offices and toilets, all executed in local red sandstone, and on the down platform. The gable ends of the stationmaster's house were positioned side on to the railway, whilst the roofline of the remainder of the buildings paralleled the track. Two pleasing bay windows faced out on to the platform. An attractive wooden canopy over a portion of the platform in front of the booking office and waiting rooms was provided, enhanced by ornate cast iron supports and feathered and pierced canopy edges. By contrast, the up platform featured only a relatively small timber waiting shelter with a canopy cantilevered out from the roof line. Steps down from the road overbridge were provided for passengers wishing to reach the up platform, but access between the two platforms was by way of a boarded crossing, there being no footbridge ever provided. To the north of the station lay the goods yard, being furnished with a substantial goods shed (actually the only one on the line) of red brick, a cattle dock and a substantial 10 ton crane. There was a trailing crossover between the running lines to give access to the down goods loop and to the goods yard, just beyond the northern end of the station platform. At the northern end of the goods yard, a facing crossover gave access to the goods yard throat and to the other end of the down goods loop. From the goods yard throat, one siding ran parallel with the up goods loop, and through the single road goods shed to the cattle dock and end loading platform. Two further sidings ran from the throat around the western side of the goods yard, leaving a large open area in the centre. This was mainly used for coal, which was of necessity kept some distance

The divergence of the Tattenhall branch from the Crewe line and the associated WhitchurchChester Junction signal box, as seen from a passing train in the late 1950s. The sharpness of the curve to the left is apparent, hence the 15 mph speed restriction. [Mr. Brough / RCTS]

The station buildings at Malpas on 16 July 1965, before the track had been removed. The pleasing sandstone construction is seen to good effect. [D.P.Rowland]

Malpas was provided with a substantial brick built goods shed, with one road passing through. This view, taken on 16 July 1965, is looking south-west towards Whitchurch. [D.P.Rowland]

Broxton station looking northwest towards Chester on 19 April, 1962 shortly before closure. The privately owned cheese warehouse can be seen to the left alongside the mileage siding. [B. Brooksbank]

Tattenhall station on the last day of passenger services, 14 September 1957. This station was not provided with a goods yard, and so there was no pointwork, and consequently the signal box was a very small wooden building at the far end of the station buildings. It was taken out of use during the Second World War, and the signals thereafter controlled from a small frame housed in plain brick building seen in the centre of the picture. [C.Gammell / H. Davies Collection]

Tattenhall station looking west on 16 July 1965, after the track had been removed. Despite looking rather neglected, the station buildings were still in sound condition. [D.P.Rowland]

from other traffic because of the dust nuisance. The westernmost line was extended between 1877 and 1898. A weighbridge and office were sited at the road entrance to the goods yard, and a yard crane was positioned at the north end of the yard. Total sidings capacity was given as 32 wagons. The station and yard was controlled by a small standard wooden LNWR signal box mounted on a brick base, with about 20 levers, sited on the up side near to the northern crossover.

Malpas achieved an honour, when in May 1917 the Royal Train carrying King George V and Queen Mary was stabled for the night at Malpas station. The Royal Train was guarded by troops from the Household Division during this stay, and the next day their majesties carried to an official visit to Chester. The royal couple travelled over the line again three years later on their Royal Tour of 16 and 17 July, 1920 but in the opposite direction. Their tour had started from Holyhead via Denbigh, Rhyl, Mold, Chester, Whitchurch, and Craven Arms to Swansea.

A further visit occurred on 1 November, 1955 when the Royal Train conveying the Queen and Prince Philip again stayed overnight at Tattenhall Junction. The train had left Euston at 10.00pm behind Stanier Pacific no.46250 CITY OF LICHFIELD, which ran through to Tattenhall Junction. On the following morning, a pair of 'Black Fives', nos. 44865 (Holyhead Junction) and 45043 (Mold Junction) took the train to Whitchurch, where the Pacific took over for the short run to Nantwich. Here the royal couple disembarked for a trip to Wedgwood Hall. Meanwhile, no.46250 continued on to near Wedgwood Hall, where the couple rejoined the train after their visit and returned to London.

Northwards the line continued a gradual descent, firstly at 1 in 383, then 151, 119, 115 and 112 for the 3½ miles to Broxton. On the way, the line crossed Edge Common, and an interesting lane called "Brassey's Contract Road" that runs from the Chester Road to Edge Hall. This name possibly derives from when Thomas Brassey was engaged in construction of part

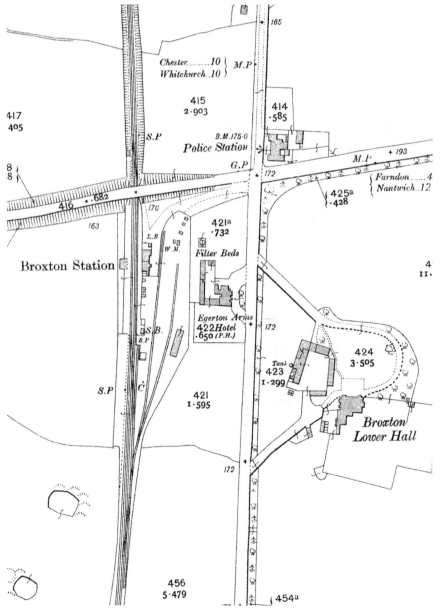

of the Crewe and Chester Railway in 1837, and may have quarried sandstone at Edge for use on that project. Approaching Broxton, to the right stand the Peckforton Hills with the noble Peckforton Castle, and the Rawhead sandstone escarpment, whilst to the left are excellent views of the Welsh mountains, weather permitting. Half a mile after passing through a lengthy cutting, the line reached **Broxton** (10 miles) where the station was situated at the foot of Bickerton Hill, and on the southern side of the Wrexham to Nantwich road (now A534). Broxton was a rather small community, but the choice of the site for the station was determined by the road mentioned, which nearby crossed the Whitchurch to Chester road, giving access for passengers and goods from the neighbouring communities. Notable were the twin villages of Farndon and Holt, situated four miles to the west, on either side of the meandering River Dee. The main station buildings were identical to Malpas, except that no canopy was provided, but were located on the opposite, up side. Again, a small waiting shelter was provided on the down side, with access between platforms being by a boarded crossing. Additionally, steps led down from the road bridge to the up platform only. A small Saxby and Farmer signal box was situated on the southern end of the up platform. This controlled a trailing crossover that gave access

Broxton – reproduced from 1911 25" OS map

from both lines to a long headshunt running south, from which access into the goods yard was achieved after reversal. The yard comprised firstly, a short siding to the cattle dock and end loading platform sited at the southern end of the up platform. Nearby a concrete feed store mounted on raised concrete beams, was erected around the 1930s, of the familiar type adopted by BOCM for such products at country locations. Secondly, one siding ran into the centre of the yard where coal stages were provided. A 5 ton crane was situated in the yard. The third siding reached the eastern perimeter of the yard, and was flanked on its outward side by a sizeable warehouse, the property of Messrs. Bamber & Son. Its function was primarily the storage of cheese, for which the area was particularly well known, and this became the railhead for the congregation of products from several dairies for onward distribution. Special trains often became necessary for the transport of the large quantities of cheese produced, and bearing in mind the product, these would be rated as 'express freight'. One such special occurred in 1907 when a grocer by the name of Edward Driver, with a chain of stores in West Yorkshire, purchased 50 tons of the local cheese and hired a special train for its conveyance. This train was highly decorated so as to gain the most possible publicity, bearing the title "Driver's Christmas Cheese Train", utilising around 20 ventilated fruit vans for the purpose. The exercise was repeated in the following year, but does not seem to have been perpetuated thereafter.

In Summer, Broxton also became a focal point for fruit and vegetable distribution to other parts of the UK. Many local farmers brought their produce here, particularly strawberries from the areas around Farndon and Holt, which were to the west, on the banks of the River Dee. Dissatisfaction grew amongst local growers in the later years of the 19th century, concerning the amount of transhipment required for their produce. One local grower, a Mr. Edwin Bellis protested in February, 1895 to the Welsh Land Commission (in London) "that as all produce had to travel five or six miles by road, to be loaded into a train causing loss and damage to soft fruit, plus extra time and cost in transit, that serious consideration should be given to providing Holt with its own railway connection..." It seems unlikely that any serious consideration was given to this request, or to that of a roadside tramway, which was also discussed, as the amount of purely seasonal traffic would simply not have been sufficient to justify the outlay. During the Spring, cabbages from these area would be transported here, to be packed into nets and loaded into cattle wagons that had been specially washed out. These wagons would then be attached to the next available working to Whitchurch, and so eventually reach their intended market, possibly the Manchester Smithfield. A further market was tapped in the 1930s when the Forbes Brothers of Clutton would send a consignment of day old chicks, mostly ducklings, from their farm to Essex where they would be fattened for the London market. Such consignments were considerable, often requiring two 50 foot full brakes twice a week during Spring and Summer. Rated as 'express freight', these would be attached to local passenger workings.

Beyond the goods yard to the east, lay the substantial premises of the Egerton Arms Hotel, built in 1896, actually at the junction of the Chester and Wrexham roads.

Continuing our journey, the line had

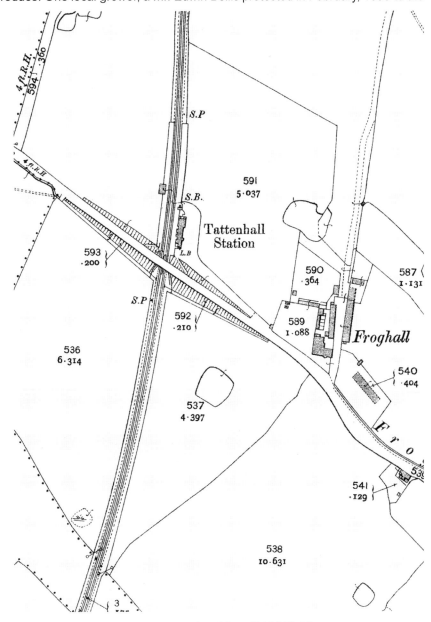

Tattenhall – reproduced from 1911 25" OS map

then reached a fairly flat portion of land involving only a slight undulation, and now travelling almost due north it crossed the Chester Road once again and reached **Tattenhall** (12¾ miles). This community is very old, and is mentioned in the Domesday Book (1086) as "Tatenale", meaning " a meadow". The name went through very many spellings over the long years, such as "Tatenhala" (1280), "Tattenhall" (1289), "Tatnall" (1473), "Tottenhall" (1553) and "Tettenhall" (1649). Notable in the village are a group of houses designed by Sir Clough Williams-Ellis, and St. Alban's Church with its 15th century tower.

The station was actually sited on a level section at the foot of the steepest gradient of the line, falling at 1 in 114 towards Chester, this unfavourable location being mentioned in report of the Board of Trade Inspector, Colonel Rich, and described as being "an afterthought". Whilst this certainly may have not made life easy for southbound trains starting away from here, it was by no means insurmountable, even for 1872. Furthermore, the location was very convenient to the village – which is more than can be said for the other two stations.

The range of station buildings here were identical to Broxton, and were situated on the on the up or southbound side. This station was more conveniently located to the nearby village, but was never furnished with any goods facilities, other than for milk and parcels traffic to be dealt with by passenger trains. Local milk was sent here in churns from Cooke's Creamery just down the lane. Steps were provided from the Station Road overbridge (now Frog Lane) down to each of the platforms for the benefit of pedestrian passengers, and for crossing from one platform to another, although it is suspected that most people used the boarded crossing at the south end of the platforms. Alongside these steps was a ramp on the up side for milk churns to be loaded down to reach the platform directly from Station Road. The down platform was provided with the usual small wooden waiting shelter of the same style as at Malpas and Broxton. As there were no sidings provided here, a very small signal cabin was situated on the up platform to control the few signals, and a trailing crossover sited in the centre of the platform lengths. This rather square box was of a curious but pleasing design, being of mainly wooden construction mounted on a dwarf brick plinth, with a large brick chimney at the rear, and sited just to the north of the range of station buildings. This signal box went out of use with the closure to passengers and was shortly after removed entirely, thereafter eliminating this block post.

As the line continued northwards for its last 2¼ miles, the countryside was rather flat, but still managed to produce a further undulation, albeit of modest gradients, which required a low embankment and later a low cutting. Upon reaching **Tattenhall**

Today Tattenhall station is a private residence, and almost all of the original construction has been saved and restored sympathetically. This view was taken on 9 July 2012. [Author]

This subsequent view of the Chester Junction at Whitchurch was taken in 1972, when although a stub of the branch remained, the signal box had been completely removed. [Shropshire Railway Society]

The roadside view of the station at Malpas, as seen since having been purchased by the firm of Miles Macadam in 1985 and sympathetically renovated for use as offices. [Author]

Junction (15 miles), a single relief siding was available on the down side, protected by catch points. It is not clear if this was provided at the outset, but if not, it was certainly installed by 1877, when at that time it would have been used to ease congestion on the Chester line which had no other relief loops westwards until Chester. In fact this spur remained in place long after the branch tracks had been removed. As the branch joined the Chester line, so it turned on a 40 chain curve to the left towards the north west. The junction was controlled by Tattenhall Junction signal box, which was an LNWR 30 lever frame box of 12½ feet by 12 feet and sited on the down side of the main line, just west of the junction.

The switchback nature of the line did not unduly affect the lightly laden passenger trains, as most of the gradients were not severe, nor were they particularly taxing from any of the station stops. However, it was not the same story for freight workings, as the switchbacks meant that extreme care had to be taken in maintaining taught connections on the largely loose coupled trains worked here. It required a special degree of cooperation between the footplate crew and the guard operating the brake at the rear of the train to ensure that no 'snatching' of couplings occurred, with the possible result of breakages and train separation. For these reasons, this route was never particularly popular with train crews, who would often prefer the harder grade of the lengthy Gresford bank between Chester and Shrewsbury, as it was a constant factor that could be addressed much more easily.

Remains

Most of the route is easily traceable, as the earthworks (except at the northern end) are still extant, as are the numerous over and under bridges. Malpas station and goods yard was taken over by Miles Macadam in 1985 and have been developed sympathetically since. The original station buildings were used as offices for many years and have been well cared for. However, during 2011 a new office block in a rather tasteful style that suggests a signal box has been erected in what was the station courtyard. The original station buildings have been retained and are to be further restored. The remainder of the goods yard has disappeared beneath this firm's factory development. At Broxton, the entire station and goods yard have been demolished and converted into a picnic area. However, the stationmaster's house at Tattenhall has been tastefully converted into a private residence, although the waiting rooms and other ancillary buildings were demolished in 2005.

A trackside view on 9 July, 2012 of the renovated Malpas station. Even the cast iron supports for long gone canopy have been retained.
[Author]

CHAPTER NINE

DESCRIPTION OF THE LINE

In this chapter, a description will be given of the line and its many features, capturing those that existed during the extent of its working life. Many of the buildings and other lineside equipment have disappeared today, but the memory of these features and the contribution that they made to the operational interest of the line are worthy of comment. The original signal boxes and ground frames dating from the opening of the line were all replaced by the LNWR in the 1870-90 period, except for the one at Willaston, which lasted until 1958. There were many level crossings on the line, and these are mentioned below. These were all initially gated crossings, but around 1967 a programme of modernisation started that meant while the major ones were converted to automatic lifting barrier operation, others were downgraded to user operation, some to footpath crossings and some closed completely. To avoid repetition, these conversions to lifting barriers are not hereafter mentioned individually. Similarly, a description of the 'second class stations' built at Hadnall, Yorton, Prees, Wrenbury and Willaston is only given for Hadnall, although this is referenced at the other locations. Although the mileage posts (sited on the down side) start from the junction at Crewe, this narrative begins at the southern end of the line, Shrewsbury.

As mentioned in Chapter One, the station in Shrewsbury opened on 1 June 1849 with the completion of the joint line from Wellington, Stafford and (eventually) Wolverhampton. The Shrewsbury and Chester Junction Railway had already opened their line into Shrewsbury in 1848, but used a temporary station near to Coton Hill, about ½ mile north of the new station. This new station was named "Shrewsbury General", not really to distinguish it from any other stations in the town, because there were no others at that time. This was quite simply to convey to travellers the importance of the station and the three companies then using it. It was not until 6 December 1853 that passengers were able to use the station for services on the Shrewsbury and Hereford Railway.

The southern approaches to Shrewsbury in 1875. The original bridge over the River Severn contained only three running lines, and the platforms did not extend on to the bridge. Two small signal boxes are evident, and the 'Abbey curve' opened in 1867 completed the triangle of lines. Numerous four wheeled vehicles, and the slotted signal posts complete this period scene.

[Shropshire Records & Research]

Viewed from almost the same vantage point in Shrewsbury Castle, but some 132 years later, as "Princess Royal" Pacific No. 6201 PRINCESS ELIZABETH enters the station with the "Welsh Marches Express" that it has worked from Newport on 13 October 2007. The increased width of the bridge and the lengthening of the platforms are apparent when compared to the 1875 illustration, even though the running lines and platforms had been much reduced in recent times. The magnificent signal box and the Abbey survey the scene. [Author]

The station façade was, and is, impressive by any standards. It was designed by Thomas K. Penson of Oswestry, and intended to complement that of the nearby 16th and 17th century Shrewsbury School (now the public library). It was constructed by Thomas Brassey, who won the contract with his tender of £30,963-11s-2d, although after taking into account the land costs and other extras, the final costs came out in the region of £100,000. The façade was finished in Grinshill stone, quarried just six miles north of the town and the rather pleasing style has attracted several attempts at classification, namely – Tudor Gothic, Tudor Revival and Neo Jacobean. The tower in the centre of the façade was furnished in 1850 with an eight day clock using a 12 foot pendulum by the notable makers, J.B.Joyce of Whitchurch, who we shall meet again later in this chapter. To the southern end of the station, the bridge over the River Severn was designed by William Baker, who was the engineer for the joint SUR / SBR line. Originally it carried three tracks only, and consisted of seven elliptical arches each of 45 feet span, that were 18 feet above the springings and the rails were 36 feet above the mean water level. The station was originally constructed with two main platforms, each 16 feet wide. In the fashion of the day, there was a departure platform of 650 feet on the western side adjacent to the main station buildings, and an arrivals platform of 450 feet to the east. A 70 feet overall roof span was supported on pillars at each side. The track layout, and the early signalling were designed by Henry Robinson and Robert Stephenson. At the north end of the station, there was a four track bridge over Castle Foregate consisting of a 64 feet wrought iron span by Brymbo Ironworks. For the installation of the approach lines of the Crewe line in 1858 a further girder was required to be placed alongside so as to carry these lines over Cross Street, which formed a junction with two other streets at this point.

Between 1861 and 1863 a new platform face was added to the Howard Street side of the arrivals platform, thus making this an island platform. A separate new platform was also added slightly further to its east, giving one through face and one south facing terminal face. Connection to all of the platforms was from a public footbridge that also ran from the Castle to Howard Street directly opposite the entrance to the prison, and named "The Dana". The two main platforms were both extended by 400 feet for which the existing roof was extended by some 250 feet, and a separate awning provided for the new platforms.

However, by the 1880s the station had become a notorious rail traffic bottleneck. The Joint Committee decided on a major remodelling that was carried out between 1899 and 1902. Firstly, new girder bridges were built on either side of the existing ones at the north end of the station, to carry additional tracks across the road junction formed by Cross Street and Castle Foregate. Major work was required on the main station buildings, with the most notable addition being the addition of an extra floor. This was not done by building upwards, but by digging out the whole of the station forecourt, and then constructing this additional floor 12 feet <u>underneath</u> the existing structure, utilising in part the cellar area. So well done was this, that even now it is only by very close examination that it becomes apparent. The effect was that it was then possible

Work underway to add a third floor to the office and passenger accommodation at Shrewsbury station around 1900. The left hand wing was also extended at this time. The rather unique process of building directly underneath the existing building required the removal of the station forecourt down to the new level, so that passenger access to the platforms would henceforth be by subway. [Shropshire Records & Research]

A view of Shrewsbury General station shortly after work had been completed on the extension and three storey conversion. Shrewsbury Castle dominates the scene from the background. Apart from the horse drawn cabs awaiting custom, the scene remains pretty well unchanged today. [Real Photos]

The crew of Webb 'Coal Engine' 0-6-0 LMS No.8153 relax as they survey the scene northwards at Shrewsbury station, during a spell as station pilot in 1946. This engine did not last much longer, being withdrawn in February, 1948 after 70 years service during which it was on loan to the Railway Operating Department of the Army from 1917 to 1919. Left of centre in the background can be seen the 1848 locomotive shed of the Shrewsbury & Chester Railway, which survives today in commercial use. [Stephenson Locomotive Society]

A view looking north inside Shrewsbury General station around 1952. By this time the overall roof made the platforms rather gloomy, but remained in place for another 10 years. The curious 'dog-leg' of the main down platform is clearly visible, and was another feature to disappear in the 1960-63 remodelling. The two bay platforms (right of centre) were primary used by trains for Wellington and Stafford, although some Hereford local services also participated. A North to West express appears to be occupying the main up platform on the far right. [R. Mulford]

Unnamed "Patriot" Class 4-6-0 No. 45517 draws two coaches into the south end of Shrewsbury station in 1952, probably to add to an incoming West to North express. The south end footbridge frames the picture, but was rarely used, being in the wrong position for most passengers. It was removed entirely around 1962. [R.Mulford]

The divergence of the Chester and Crewe lines at Shrewsbury was unsurprisingly called Crewe Junction. The building on the left is the warehouse of the former G.W.R. Castle Foregate goods yard, which was situated at a lower level. Stanier "Jubilee" 4-6-0 No. 45657 TYRWHITT is running in on the right with a North to West express around 1960. [A.V.W.Mace / R. Carpenter]

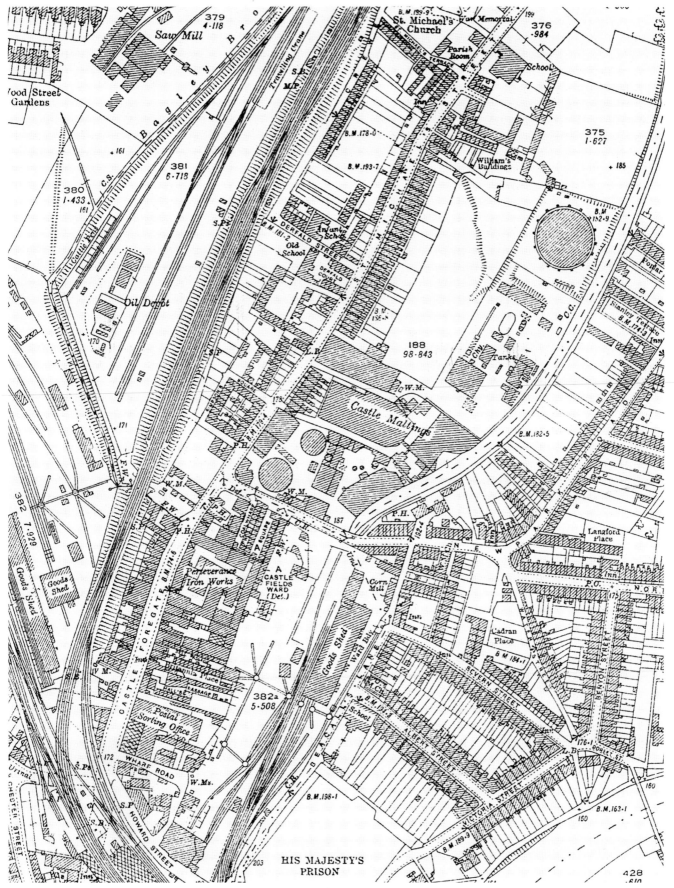

Reproduced from 1926 25 OS map, the line from Shrewsbury General (bottom left) runs upwards to Crewe Bank. Howards Street Goods Depot is centre, lower.

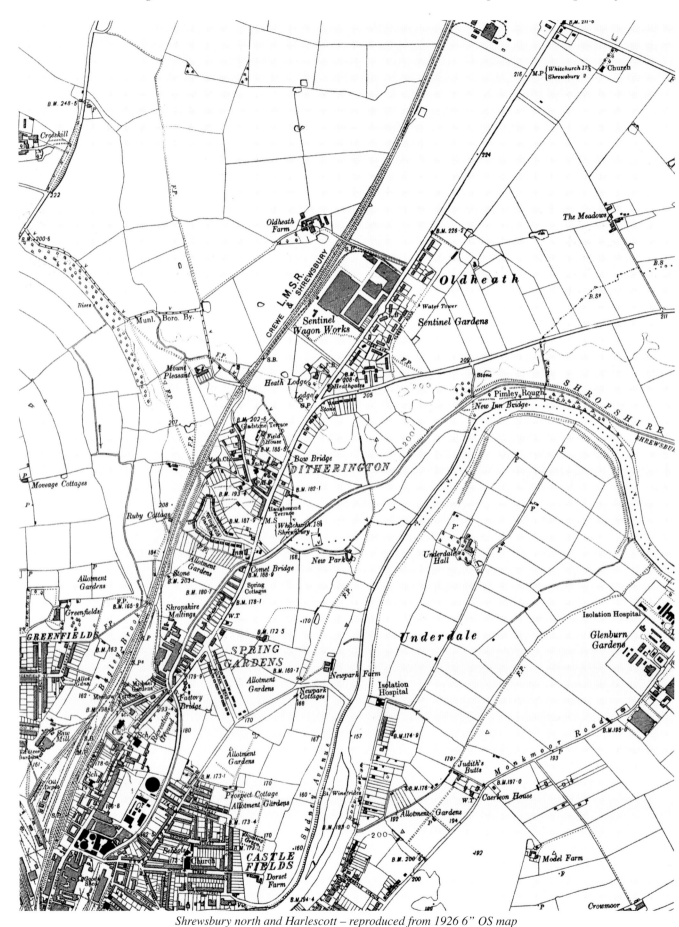

Shrewsbury north and Harlescott – reproduced from 1926 6" OS map

An unidentified Class 08 0-6-0 diesel shunter ambles along the up relief road at the eastern side of Shrewsbury station with some parcels vans around 1971, as a Swindon 3-car 'Cross Country' set (Class 120) stands at the up platform having arrived on the former G.W.R. line from Chester. Shrewsbury prison can be seen towering in the right background, with the Dana footbridge linking to it, crossing the picture. In the centre, some vans can be seen stabled on the severely curved line to Howard Street goods yard that passed beneath the plate bridge. [Shropshire Railway Society]

to make a subway connection to the various platforms directly from a new entrance hall, as well as to provide badly needed extra space for the operating departments. The station buildings were further enlarged on the northern side by an additional matching section, noticeable only when comparing illustrations of the building in its earlier and later condition.

Two further bridges over the River Severn were constructed, one each side of the existing original bridge. Thus the platforms could now be extended actually over the river. The original departures platform next to the main station building was lengthened to 1,000 feet and reached across the river. In order to utilise the length of this platform for two trains at once (i.e. one behind the other) a curious 'dog-leg' was introduced, so that a train at the rear could depart before any train in front of it. This seemingly useful feature eventually caused more problems than it was designed to solve, especially with the increased lengths of trains as time went by. At its southern end, on the western side, a new double sided bay platform of 350 feet was added. The other existing platforms were mostly replaced by one large new island platform, which also extended across the river, and also incorporated a new double sided bay at its southern end. These two sets of bays were generally used by trains terminating from the Hereford, Central Wales, Welshpool and Severn Valley lines (on the down side) and from Wolverhampton, Wellington and Stafford (on the new island platform), but either could be used in emergencies. A new wood and glass footbridge was constructed at the south end of the platforms, and "The Dana" was closed to rail passengers, from which time it has become a pedestrian right of way. The existing overall roof was retained, but for the benefit of passengers a vast new roof was added, extending southwards over the new platforms. This was of an entirely different construction, being steel frames supporting a ridge and furrow design situated at right angles to the running lines. This roof was clad with glass, but even so soon became a rather gloomy area once soot from passing trains had blackened it. The easternmost platform was removed, so that the area between the island platform and Howard Street was given over to two goods relief lines. These therefore bypassed the station platforms in the up direction, and also gave access to the Howard Street goods yard.

By 1924 the old overall roof at the north end of the station was in need of replacement, and so was dismantled. The new roof over this area consisted of individual platform canopies, giving a much brighter appearance on the platform, even if weather protection was compromised.

After nationalisation, there were many improvements to made across the network, so it was not until 1961 that BR's Western Region got around to looking for improvements here – not only to replace time expired structures, but to reflect its new image and the impact of diesel services on its timetables. The 'dog-leg' was removed, enabling a third through line to run the almost the entire distance through the station, even if did mean that one of the southern bays was seriously reduced in width. The wooden footbridge at the southern end of the platforms was removed, as it was rarely used, being too far from the subway to be convenient for passengers. This work continued until 1963, in which year the overall roof was removed, to be replaced by individual platform canopies on the main platforms. Passengers using the bay platforms did not receive any weather protection. Eventually, in 1974 the exterior stonework was cleaned which certainly helped to enliven the station frontage. There was a further rationalisation of trackwork in the station area during 1980, and during the 1990s the two westernmost bays were taken out of use, and that on the island platform other was reduced to one line.

The Howard Street Goods Depot was opened in 1858 (as described in Chapter One) and was more convenient to the town centre than the original SUR depot at Abbey Foregate. In that same year, the LNWR acquired the adjacent Butter Market, which had been built in 1835 to serve the canal wharf, and converted it into a grain store. Although the shunting neck from behind the station's up platforms into this new depot was rather sharply curved, it did fan out into an array of sidings that served the three road goods shed, lines to the canal wharf, and via a headshunt to the Butter Market. With the reorganisation of the lines in the 1899 – 1902 period, the up goods loop more usefully served this depot. However, also in 1902 the LNWR built a new larger goods depot at Coleford, which despite being more modern was still some distance from the town centre. Howard Street Goods Depot closed officially as from 5 April 1971, but still stands, now in commercial use and the former goods yard is a public car park. The former Butter Market also still stands, as does the prison, although this closed in April, 2013. Current speculation is that the prison may be converted into a hotel !

As we move out of Shrewsbury station and take the right hand curve at Crewe Junction, we pass the signal box of that name, situated on the down (west) side opposite the junction of the Chester and Crewe lines. This was one of the larger LNW type of signal boxes with a brick base and wood and glass cabin, and having 120 levers. It was constructed by the Joint LNWR / GWR committee in 1903, following the major track reorganisation. The line is level at this point, and features both up and down relief lines mainly for the benefit of goods trains. It was here that the terrible accident of 1907 (see Chapter 3) occurred. Working regulations required that upon leaving Shrewsbury station, drivers should exercise caution, even though the signals may be 'off', and be prepared to stop short of any train that may be in front. The GWR Castle Foregate Goods Depot (now in commercial use) is on the left at a lower level, and as the line straightens we reach the site of a 'ticket platform' that existed from 1862 to around 1910. As many principal stations were operated as 'open' stations to avoid queues, the checking of passengers' tickets took place at the station immediately preceding the principal station. Shrewsbury was one example where this was not practical, so the LNWR erected wooden ticket platforms on each of the main lines leading to the station, as an alternative to checking at the preceding station. However, it became clear that in some circumstances the holding of trains at these locations seriously disrupted services by occupying track space on congested lines.

Nearby, at Crewe Bank, a further signal box was installed, when the lines into the LNW Castle Foregate Goods Yard were connected before 1880. The original signal box was known as "Crewe Junction No.2", but was replaced during World War II by a brick faced concrete "ARP-style" box containing 45 levers and named "Shrewsbury Crewe Bank", but by 2007 had been switched out. The yard lay on the down side of the line and featured four terminal sidings, to which a further two were added between 1902 and 1927. A further private siding led from the throat of this yard into the saw mill of William Jones & Sons after crossing Bagley Brook. The keys for unlocking the points to this siding were kept in the No.2 cabin.

At some point this yard became known as New Yard presumably to distinguish it from the nearby GWR Castle Foregate Goods Yard. The LNW goods depot itself was not large, but did contain a sizeable overhead gantry crane, although an equal purpose of the site was for coal distribution, which by the 1920s had been partially converted to handle fuel oil. Two sidings were later used by the Engineering Department to store rails. But the yard continued to handle coal and oil, right up until 1974 when it was rearranged as a Coal Concentration Depot. This had the capacity to handle 60,000 tons of coal per year, delivered by rail in 25 ton hopper wagons. It was closed around 2000 and only part has been converted to commercial use. The line leading into this yard remains, but heavily overgrown and somewhat truncated.

The line now begins a slight descent at 1 in 209, into a cutting and passing beneath "Bulls Bridge" before reaching another level section and passing, on the right, the impressive Ditherington Mills building. Designed by Charles Bage, this was originally built in 1796/7 as a flax mill, and is the oldest iron framed building in the world. Because of its unique construction, it is considered as the 'grandfather of skyscrapers', predating the use of this method of construction for large buildings by over a hundred years. In 1886 it was converted into the Shropshire Maltings, but finally closed in 1987. After a period of total disuse, its architectural heritage was finally recognised when a major project was launched in 2005 to restore the building, which is still continuing. This mill had been sited adjacent to the Shrewsbury Canal, but with coming of the railway, was given a lengthy private siding, running from the up main line. The key for the operation of the points accessing this siding was kept in the "Crewe Junction No.2" signal box.

Shortly after, the line passed into what was originally open countryside, but housing and commercial development

The view northwards at Harlescott as an unidentified English Electric Class 37 passes the former down side yards, by this time (c1972) reduced to a couple of loops. The signal box protecting the level crossing over Harlescott Lane is visible in the background. [Shropshire Railway Society]

A specially posed photograph at the rail entrance to the Sentinel Company's works in Shrewsbury, recording the shipment of an order of "Super Sentinel" road vehicles to Czechoslovakia The date is unknown, but the locomotive, one of C.J. Bowen-Cooke's "1185" Class 0-8-2T No. 2294 was built in 1917 and did not receive its LMS number (7896) until June, 1927. As it is in plain LNWR livery, this puts the date somewhere between the two, but almost certainly not immediately after the Great War. The company's single connection to the LNWR line, seen here, faced southwards. [LNWR Society]

increasingly spread alongside the railway. After passing beneath Mount Pleasant Road, the next feature was the works of the Sentinel Waggon Works Ltd. on the up side. This company was famous for its production of road and railway vertical boilered steam locomotives. The business was started by Stephen Alley and John Alexander MacLellan operating from the Sentinel Engineering Works in Polmadie, Glasgow in 1876. In 1880 they moved to new nearby premises, where they specialised in the manufacture of compressors, lighting plant, marine and stationery engines, ships' machinery and prefabricated ships, of which latter they built nearly 500. In 1903 they acquired the business of Simpson & Bibby, of Horsehay (now part of Telford), who made steam road vehicles. They transferred this manufacture to their Polmadie works, and in 1905 produced the first Sentinel steam waggon. Production continued there for ten years until being moved to this new works on a 16 acre site at Shrewsbury in 1915 where they had also built a large housing estate, "Sentinel Gardens" (on the eastern side of the works) for their workers, which included the unheard of luxury of hot water in each home. But in 1917, the company was taken over by large Scottish engineering group William Beardmore & Co. Ltd. who shortly afterwards experienced financial problems, and so the Shrewsbury business was reorganised as Sentinel Waggon Works (1920) Ltd. Production of railway locomotives and railcars began in 1923, using their own technology which had developed high pressure, water tube boilers and was very successful. In 1947 the company became Sentinel (Shrewsbury) Ltd., and was taken over by Rolls Royce in 1956, in which year production of road vehicles ceased. The production of railway steam locomotives totalled over 850 built up until 1959, of which many were exported all round the world. Their railcars were supplied to both the LMSR and LNER, with the coach bodies being supplied by Metro-Cammell. Rather surprisingly, railcars and locomotives were also sold in some numbers to the Delta Railway in Egypt. One of the three-car railcars has been repatriated and is under long term restoration at the Quainton Railway Centre in Buckinghamshire. Gradually production of steam locomotives was switched to diesel locomotives, which began in 1959 and lasted until 1971 totalling some 200 locomotives. After that time, the factory continued to make diesel engines, but was sold to Perkins Engines Ltd. of Peterborough in 1985, who in turn were taken over by the American firm of Caterpillar Inc in 1998. Perkins switched the manufacture of engines to their nearby works at Harlescott. Consequently, the factory site was unwanted, and a Morrison's supermarket was firstly developed on part of the site. The company was served by a single siding from the up main line, that branched into double track running parallel with the main line until reaching the northern extremity of the works. At this point it reverted to a single line, and turned through 90 degrees terminating near to Whitchurch Road (now A5112). The company never used a particular locomotive for its internal works shunting, relying instead on any that were to hand from the production run.

The line is now climbing at 1 in 124, then levels out as we pass the single up loop and two (originally three) down reception loops as we approach Harlescott level crossing and its associated signal box. A single siding had led from a trailing connection on the up loop to a World War II Ministry of Defence Depot, later designated as a Mechanical Transport Repair Depot, but this was removed in the 1960s. The down loops were originally arranged in the 1920s by the LMS as sorting sidings, but were gradually enlarged to become a major marshalling yard with around 10 north facing and two south facing terminal roads. This yard was removed in the 1960s and rearranged partly for a single loop, and partly redeveloped as a small industrial estate. Both up and down loops were finally removed in the 1990s. "Harlescott Crossing" was a standard LNW box dating from 1881, comprising a brick base containing the mechanism room with a wood and glass cabin above, and housed 38 levers on an LNW tappet frame. Just beyond the crossing, a single siding led from a trailing crossover and connection to the up line, into a Ministry of Food "Buffer Depot" which was another World War II construction, this time to house emergency food supplies. Shunting into this siding unfortunately involved occupying the level crossing, so that

As the line leaves Shrewsbury it passes into the rural countryside at Battlefield, where we see Bulleid "Battle of Britain" 4-6-2 No.34067 TANGMERE making a rather smoky departure with "The Great Britain II" railtour on 8 April, 2009 that it worked from Bristol to Preston. The county town can be seen in the distance, and beyond the Shropshire Hills. [Author]

inevitable and unpopular delays occurred. To cater for the extra sidings put in here in 1941, "Harlescott Crossing" signal box was itself extended to accommodate the extra levers, and the additional brickwork (on the south end of the building) can be seen. A little further on, now on the down side was a single trailing connection into the works of the Hall Engineering Co. Ltd. This factory was built in 1928 by the Chatwood Safe Company for the manufacture of bank safes. This was an old established company, originating in Bolton in 1854, with a later factory in Speke, Liverpool before opening this additional location. This company was acquired by Hall Industries Ltd. in November 1955, and merged with the Chubb Safe & Lock Co. Ltd. in 1970. However, the factory here is believed to have closed during the early 1970s. In the meantime, the rail access had been shunted by the company's own locomotive, which was a product of the nearby Sentinel Works, being a four-wheeled vertical boiler type, works number 8098 supplied new in 1930. This engine never carried a running number or name, and was scrapped on site by George Phillips & Son of Shrewsbury in September 1965. It is believed that the rail connection was taken out around this time, and the site has since been redeveloped for commercial purposes.

Now the line starts a climb for nearly two miles at 1 in 127, crossing a lengthy embankment as it approaches Battlefield. The name of this place commemorates the Battle of Shrewsbury that took place here on Sunday, 21 July 1403, between the Lancastrian King Henry IV and the Percy family from Northumbria. The Percy family had helped Henry to claim the throne in 1399, but felt that their support had not been adequately rewarded. The battle began after lengthy negotiations had broken down and was over in a few hours, with the field, previously used for growing peas, not visible beneath the piles of thousands of bodies. The battle finished when Sir Henry Percy (also Earl of Northumberland, and popularly known as "Harry Hotspur") was killed and the King was victorious. Initially, Sir Henry Percy was buried at Whitchurch, but there were rumours that he was still alive, so his body was disinterred, salted and impaled on a spear in Shrewsbury market place for public display. Later it was quartered, and the four pieces sent to Chester, London, Bristol and Newcastle-upon-Tyne, whilst his head was displayed on the North Gate in York. His followers faced similar gruesome endings after being found guilty of treason. The King built a chapel on the site of a mass grave of the battle dead, replaced by a church, St. Mary Magdalen, which was renovated in 1862.

The line now reaches a summit, and begins a descent at 1 in 155, winding slightly as it approaches **Hadnall** (4½ miles). The village is more correctly known as Hadnall Ease, and although quite pleasant has little other history, being mostly located on the Shrewsbury to Whitchurch trunk road, now A49. The station was a short walk from the village, and was sited alongside

Stanier "Jubilee" 4-6-0 No.45644 HOWE runs into Hadnall station with a down stopping train in the mid 1950s. The station staff are waiting to load a crate on a platform trolley into the arriving train. The waiting rooms on the line's platforms opposite the main buildings varied considerably in style, and here the structure was a simple wooden affair. In the right background, a row of passenger carriages and parcels vans are stabled in the mileage siding. [Ivy – Hadnall Local History Society]

A postcard view of Hadnall station around 1910, showing the standard style of construction for the line's secondary stations. The children on the up platform are evidently enthralled by the activities of the photographer – a sight probably more unusual than the trains at this time. [Kidderminster Railway Museum]

An unidentified Stanier Class 5 4-6-0 runs into Hadnall station on a sunny day in the 1950s, with a down West and North express. The station staff were evidently very keen to maintain the station platforms in a pleasant and welcoming manner. [M.H.C. Baker]

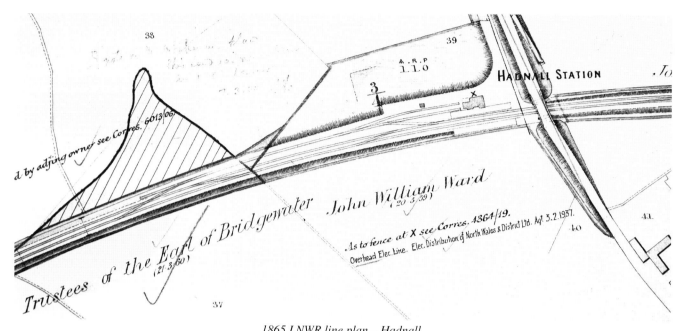

1865 LNWR line plan – Hadnall

what became logically enough Station Road. This crossed the line at the southern end of the station on a bridge made of the local Grinshill stone, and from which steps led to the down platform. The main station buildings were positioned on the up side, constructed in red brick, and were of a standard design for all of the secondary stations along the line. The gabled roof of the main building incorporating the stationmaster's house lay parallel to the running line and incorporated some staff offices on the ground floor. Three elegant tall chimneys protruded through the tiled roof. Abutting this building was a single storey extension towards the platform that contained the entrance from the station forecourt, booking hall, waiting rooms and toilets. This was fully glazed on the platform side and a small canopy forming an extension of the flat roof was cantilevered outwards for the protection of passengers. A further two rather shorter chimneys led from this extension. The brickwork for the

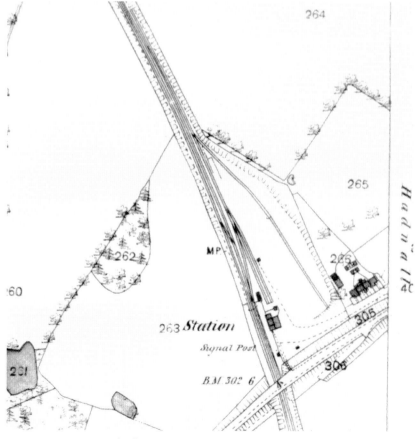

Hadnall – reproduced from 1883 25" OS map

entire station ensemble was relieved by pale stone quoins around the edges of the building, beneath the gable ends, around the doors and windows, and on the chimney surrounds. This enlivened what would otherwise have been a very plain red brick construction. A similar style, which we have seen was built by Daniel Climie, was also used by this contractor for stations on the Coalport branch built immediately afterwards. Originally, a wooden store shed was positioned at the north end of the up platform, but this replaced by a larger unit at the south end of the platform at some point in time. The down platform contained only a rather rudimentary wooden waiting shelter, which was fully enclosed, and glazed on the platform side. It was finished with a tiled, gable ended roof, through which a stovepipe chimney gave evidence of some form of heating for the passengers in Winter. Passenger transfer from one platform to the other was by means of a boarded crossing at the southern end. The platforms were actually rather short, so that lengthy stopping trains had to pull forward sometimes in order for passengers to alight. The road bridge

North of Hadnall, Stanier 'Black Five' 4-6-0 no. 45426 approaches Haston bridge with a Plymouth to Liverpool express containing a variety of coaching stock and liveries, on 5 September 1958. [M.H.C. Baker]

and the rail entrance to the goods yard precluded any extension on the up side. The last stationmaster here was a Mr. Hollingsworth, who was reputed to have been rather authoritarian.

The goods yard was sited on the up side, being accessed from the lengthy up goods loop with a capacity for 58 wagons, that ran from north of the yard and continued to a headshunt running north. This loop could be accessed from the down line by a trailing crossover at its northern end, and a further trailing crossover from the down line was positioned at the northern end of the platforms. The yard contained two groups of sidings. Two were sited just behind the main station building, that terminated in a side and end loading platform with a cattle pen. A separate mileage siding was situated on the eastern side of the yard, a typical feature that will be found at other goods yards along the line. Mileage sidings were provided mostly for bulk traffic such as coal, iron ore, stone, manure and other fertilizers, whose carriage was paid for on the basis of mileage travelled. Other commodities were usually paid for on the basis of their weight. Because such 'mileage' goods were often bulky, and frequently messy when being loaded or unloaded, the sidings for these were kept separate from those for other 'cleaner' goods. In this case, these would have been incoming coal and probably fertilizers, and possibly outgoing stone from local quarries. Also a good deal of freight was handled here during the construction of the RAF airfield at Shawbury, and for the construction firm of Balfour Beatty, who also had a depot at Shawbury. This mileage siding was supplemented by a further two some time after 1902. Unusually, no goods shed was provided. Further inward traffic also consisted of livestock, agricultural machinery, and outward traffic was mostly seasonal agricultural produce including milk by passenger train for Liverpool and Manchester, sugar beet in open wagons, and potatoes. One apocryphal story is that an entire wagon load of potatoes was stolen over a weekend during 1943. Because the station was only two miles from Shawbury, it gave rise to a considerable number of RAF personnel using it over the years.

The LNWR standard wood and brick signal box was sited in the fork of the goods yard lines just beyond the station

Immaculate Stanier "Princess Coronation" Class 4-6-2 no. 46224 PRINCESS ALEXANDRA from Glasgow's Polmadie shed was evidently on a running-in turn after overhaul at Crewe Works in this undated view, as it enters Hadnall with a stopping train from Crewe. [M.H.C. Baker]

The main station building and waiting room on the up side at Yorton in the late 1950s, still displaying an LMSR nameboard amidst a fullsome rose bush. Looking south, the signal box is visible in the distance, as is the tall home starter signal, repeated for the benefit of enginemen's sighting. [A.Harden Collection]

The waiting room on the down platform was (and still is) a sizeable and handsome structure in red brick, presumably for the benefit of visitors, including royalty, to nearby Sansaw Hall. A DMU is disappearing into the distance, having collected any passengers here. [A.Harden Collection]

Yorton's signal box was removed to the Severn Valley Railway, and now operates at Arley. However, on 23 October, 1969 it was still in operation, even though the connection to the former small goods yard had been removed. In the foreground is the only means of passenger connection from one platform to the other, except for a lengthy walk down a lane and up a rather steep set of steps alongside a field, which eventually terminated by the lamp post on the right. [D.P.Rowland]

platforms, with a loading gauge alongside. The up goods loop and crossovers were used for "Trial Runs" of locomotives from Crewe Works as described in Chapter 5. Around 1964 BR Standard Class 5 4-6-0 no.73026 on an up freight came to grief in the catch points at the southern end of the loop, finally coming to rest on its left hand side, and requiring the assistance of the Shrewsbury travelling crane. The station here was the third, and last on the route to have closed, this being with effect from 2 May 1960. Goods facilities were withdrawn as from 2 November, 1964 and the signal box was closed on 9 November 1965. The platforms were completely removed, along with all other railway structures other than the station building. Since that date the goods yard area has been developed for commercial purposes, and the station house renovated and used as offices. At the time of writing, the whole property consisting of some sizeable modern buildings as well as the station house, has been vacated and is for sale.

Northwards the line completes another gentle reverse curve, then starts a short climb and descent through two cuttings, the latter being on the western edge of Sansaw Park. Further to the east rises the hill at Grinshill, source of much local stone, notably for the main station building at Shrewsbury, as described earlier in this chapter. Finally, after a further short cutting, we arrive at **Yorton** (7 miles) situated on a ¾ mile ascent at 1 in 167. The station served the nearby very small community of Yorton, as well as another hamlet, Alderton, to the west, but mostly it served the large village of Clive, a mile to the east. Although geographically correct to name the station as Yorton, it would surely have been more appropriate for it to be named Clive.

The main station buildings are once more located on the up side, with road access up a short steep drive from a lane that, joined by another passes beneath the line at the northern end of the station. Immediately on the other side of this road underbridge, a steep set of steps leads to the centre of the down platform, and is the only access to that platform. Originally, the steps continued on to a pathway behind the down platform, to give access at the south end of this platform, where was a boarded crossing provided a route to the up platform and station facilities. However, this pathway and the boarded crossing have now been removed.

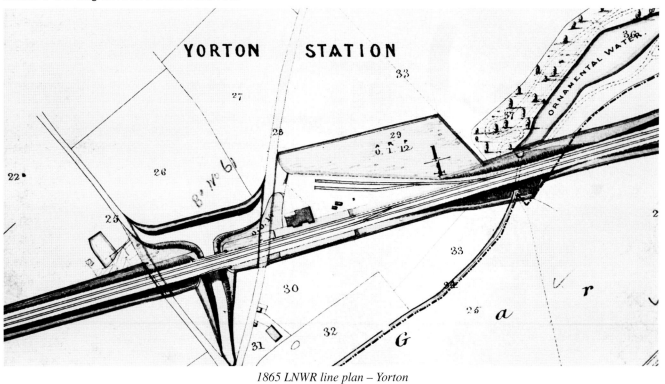

1865 LNWR line plan – Yorton
Interestingly, the plan shows how the two original roads were combined, so that only one bridge was necessary.

The station building is identical to Hadnall, and remains open, although the stationmaster's house and adjoining waiting rooms and booking office are now a private residence. It was reduced to unstaffed status from 15 August, 1966. A small steel and glass 'bus shelter' has been erected for the benefit of passengers on the up platform. However, passengers on the down platform, no doubt exhausted by their climb from the roadway below, have the benefit of a most attractive brick built waiting shelter, maintained in superb condition. However, although the level of the up platform was raised to conform with the later design of carriages, that on the down side has not. Consequently, a set of wooden steps is provided for those wishing to alight here. The station today is, of course, unstaffed and most services require prior notice to be given to the guard if wishing to leave a train at this station. Passengers joining here must make an appropriate signal to stopping trains as they slowly approach.

The reason for the lavish waiting shelter on the down platform lies with the nearby Sansaw Hall built in 1773, once the home of John Bibby (1775 – 1840) the founder of the Bibby shipping line and later, a major cattle feed business. James Bibby (1813 – 1897) expanded the shipping business and retired to this Hall in 1873. Many of the Bibby Line ships were pressed into naval use during both World Wars and the Falklands War. Queen Mary is said to have often visited her brother, whilst he was staying at Sansaw Hall, and for that reason the waiting shelter was provided in such comparative luxury. Almost certainly, it therefore replaced an earlier structure of more modest means.

The goods yard was situated south of the station on the up side, accessed by a trailing connection from the up line. This was controlled from Yorton signal box, positioned at the south end of the down platform, opposite the connection. There was no direct connection from the goods yard to the down running line, but a crossover was positioned about halfway along the platform faces. The goods yard comprised just two sidings, fanning out eastwards and terminating near to the station entrance. No goods shed was built here, but a small lock-up was situated in the yard close to the station, and perhaps rather surprisingly, a 5 ton yard crane was listed in the Railway Clearing House Handbook of Stations for 1904. However, these modest goods facilities were withdrawn as from 6 April, 1964 and the sidings removed shortly afterwards. However, the signal box remained in situ as it provided a useful block post, especially after Hadnall signal box closed. It was felt at that time, that otherwise this would have created an excessively large block section between Harlescott and Wem of some 8¼ miles. However, a change in policy resulted in its closure as from 15 April 1973. It was subsequently purchased by the Severn Valley Railway, where it now enjoys a new life at Arley station. The signal box was a standard small LNW type built entirely of wood, with 18 levers in the fully glazed cabin. As the size of the goods yard did not attract much traffic, the box was not continually manned, being operated on two shifts only during BR days, and switched out at night.

Now the line continues its northwards direction, making a slight turn to the right as it descends, mostly at 1 in 208, beneath Holbrook Bridge carrying the Shrewsbury to Wem road (now B5476). The road here was altered to a 'dog-leg' so that the bridge could make a right angled crossing of the railway, and is another structure made from the nearby Grinshill stone. All other bridges on the line were made of Staffordshire blue brick. Shortly after, the line runs on to an embankment then over a user operated crossing at Shooter's Hill (now known as Lyons Hill Farm Crossing) which is still extant with the vehicular gate controlled by telephone communication to Wem signal box. Pedestrians are required to use stiles at each side of the rarely used lane. This was originally an occupation crossing without a resident keeper. About a mile to the west is Sleap (pronounced "Slape") airfield. Opened in April 1943 as No.81 Operational Training Unit (part of Bomber Command), initially using Whitley bombers for training. Two of these aircraft were involved in separate incidents during 1943 when they hit the control tower, killing aircrew and ground personnel. But from 1 January 1944, the emphasis switched to training pilots to use the Horsa heavy gliders that were used during the D-Day landings, and in November 1944 Wellingtons were drafted in. On one occasion during this conflict a whole squadron of USAF B-52 "Flying Fortresses" landed here when due to adverse weather conditions they were unable to land at their home base. The airfield closed on 28 Decembner, 1945 and was put on a Care and Maintenance Basis until 1956, when it reopened as a satellite to RAF Shawbury (about 3 miles to the east). Although this use terminated in 1964, the site is still used by trainee helicopter pilots as a landing and hovering site, although the Shropshire Aero Club are the primary users of facilities here.

Continuing through a further cutting, the line curves to the northeast as we approach the site of **Tilley Crossing** (9 miles) where a level crossing was provided for the road from the Shrewsbury – Wem road into the village of Tilley. The gates here were originally controlled by a resident crossing keeper, for whom an adjacent cottage was provided, sited just north of the crossing on the up side. On 7 May, 1860 the LNWR Permanent Way Estates and Works Committee fixed the rental

Wem station looking south around 1960, with the platform gardens in full bloom. The appearance of the footbridge is commented upon elsewhere in this work, and is only partially visible here. However, the location of the public footbridge in the distance can be appreciated in this view, near to the rail entrance to the goods yard, just beyond the down side station buildings. [R.S.Carpenter]

Many people are not aware that the Stanier Pacifics were used so regularly on this line, but some of the North and West expresses were heavily loaded, especially in Summer. Here, No.46235 CITY OF BIRMINGHAM passes beneath the unusual footbridge at Wem with a rather shorter, six coach southbound express around 1964. [P.Ward]

for this cottage at 1s 3d per week. A small wooden signalbox was sited south of the crossing on the down side, with a 12 lever LNWR tumbler frame for operation of signals only. This was closed sometime between 1933 and 1937, and replaced by a ground frame, which in turn was removed along with the signals on 17 January 1971. The gates were altered to swing away from the line, instead of across it, as previously. Subsequently, the road was terminated either side of the crossing, which was then altered to give a pedestrian only gate at each side and a boarded crossing. No restriction or telephone communication is provided. By the 1980s the crossing keeper's cottage had been demolished entirely.

The line then makes a further slight movement to the east, crosses the Shrewsbury – Wem road again, and runs on to an embankment as the precursor to crossing the River Roden on the three arched brick built bridge that collapsed when first constructed. The arches of this bridge are constructed of Grinshill stone, with the bed and parapet in red brick. A tall chimney on the left marks the site of Wem Corn Mill once an important employer in the town. It was built in 1834, closed in 1980 and has now been tastefully converted into residential apartments. A handsome lengthy pedestrian suspension bridge spanned the line at the south end of the goods yard, but was replaced in the 1990s by a modern footbridge constructed of steel panels, and sited about 100 yards further north, so as to line up with housing developments under way. We then reach **Wem** station (10 ½ miles), which is sited conveniently close to the town centre. The town gets its name from the Saxon "Wamm" meaning a marsh, but the area was settled by the Cornovii, who were an Iron Age people. Later, the Domesday Book (1086) records the town as having four Manors, and in 1202 it became a Market Town. During the Civil War the town supported the Parliamentarians, and 40 of the townsmen along with the town's women, fought off an attack by Lord Capel. Later, in 1677 many of the buildings in the town centre were destroyed by a catastrophic fire. The town's other claim to fame at around this time was the ennoblement of Baron Jeffrys of Wem, who may be better known as "The Hanging Judge", which soubriquet was applied because of his ruthless sentencing of the supporters of the Duke of Monmouth who attempted to overthrow the Catholic King James II.

A more modern tribute for the town is that Henry Eckford developed the Sweet Pea plant into its modern form here. It is also the birthplace of actors and comedians Peter Jones, Peter Vaughan and Greg Davies.

To the south of the station, the line first passes the goods yard, situated on the down side. Rail access was from a facing point, adjacent to a trailing crossover which permitted movements from the up line. This led to the down loop, with a capacity for 53 wagons, that joined the down running line just before the station, and to two groups of two terminal sidings each, and a south facing headshunt. Access to these sidings was controlled from a ground frame, unlocked from the signalbox. Moving from the running line, the first siding was positioned alongside a large brick built goods shed, and the second ran through it. These two sidings were connected by wagon turntables at their extremities. A 5 ton crane was situated in the yard. The next two sidings ran to the far end of the goods yard, and first passed beneath a large gantry of Messrs. Isherwoods, a large timber merchant, whose yard was sited at the western boundary of the goods yard. This concern was notable in the 1920s for its production of butchers' blocks. A further trailing crossover was located adjacent to where the loop rejoined the main line, at the south end of the station. Also at the end of the loop, a short siding led to a side and end loading dock and cattle pens which saw much use during the Wem cattle market days.

The main station buildings were sited on the down platform, and were of a standard design in blue brick for principal stations of the line, being replicated at Whitchurch and Nantwich. A single storey booking office and waiting room with a pitched roof running parallel to the platform was flanked at each end by two two-storey gabled ended structures at right angles to the platform. These contained accommodation for the stationmaster, and on the ground floor additional offices for staff, handling of parcels and toilets. An enclosed footbridge was installed between 1918 and 1926, of plate steel construction with wood and glass panels and a pitched roof, connecting the two platforms from at the north end of the station building. The central portion of the footbridge had no roof, at least from 1950 onwards, giving the whole structure a somewhat comical appearance, as will be seen in the accompanying photographs. It has not been possible to determine whether this structure was originally completed in this manner, or whether the central section was removed at a later date. But as each end of the truncated roof section was finished with decorative edging, this suggests that if the central part was removed, some consideration was given to a tidy finish. A sizeable wooden waiting shelter, mounted on a dwarf brick base, provided protection for passengers on the up platform. Chapter One included details of the revised roads required at the north end of the station to enable a single level crossing to deal with traffic from Aston Road leading into Aston Street. The original level crossing gates were replaced by lifting barriers in the 1980s.

The signalbox controlling the crossing, the down loop and all station movements was sited at the north end of the up platform, directly overlooking the crossing. This was latterly a standard brick LMS structure, with wood and glass cabin measuring 21 feet 6 inches by 12 feet, and containing a 35 lever LMS pattern frame that had been installed when the nearby military connection was made in 1943 (see below). This box replaced an earlier structure in 1883, which had dated from the opening of the line.

The station became unstaffed as from 19 September, 1966 and so the buildings were entirely demolished, and replaced on the up platform by a steel and glass 'bus shelter'. The site of the station buildings was converted into a car park. The down platform was treated to a more substantial red brick building, including toilets, but this was subjected to abuse by the less desirable elements of society, and was later converted into a secure store. Consequently, another 'bus shelter' was provided for the benefit of passengers. Now lacking a footbridge, passengers wishing to change platforms must use the level crossing. During the early 1970s the goods yard was reduced to just two sidings, and goods traffic withdrawn as from 5 April, 1971. During the 1980s the goods shed was demolished and the goods yard was redeveloped for housing and commercial uses.

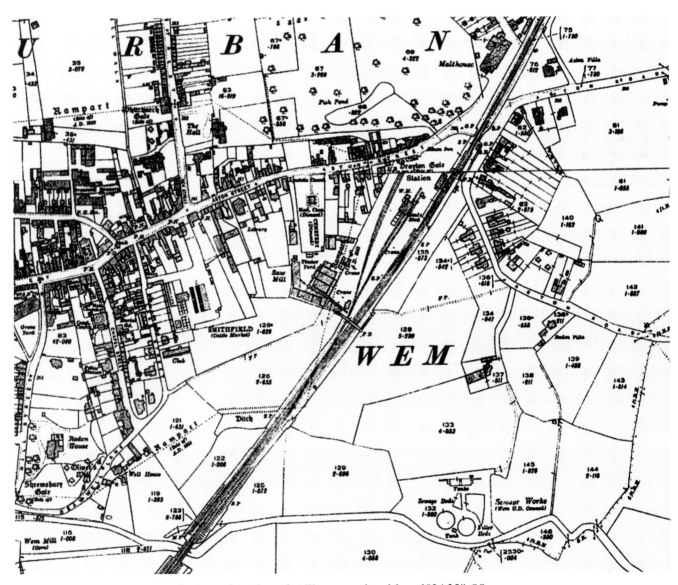

Station and goods yard at Wem, reproduced from 1924 25" OS map

A maltings stood for many years on the far side of the level crossing, on the down side, as a reminder of the town's famous brewing industry. This was Kynaston's Maltings, which replaced seven smaller maltings that were once scattered along High Street and Noble Street, and was worked in conjunction with Drawwell's Brewery. After the rather hectic brewery mergers of the 1980s, Wem Brewery closed in 1988, although it is remembered by the name "Wem Ales" often used for present day beers now brewed elsewhere.

Continuing northwards on a level stretch of track, we arrive at the site of Aston Park signal box. This was a standard LMS all wooden design, and was installed in 1942/43 to control movements into a large military base from two lengthy loops of around 1000 yards on the up side that continued into a slightly shorter headshunt running south. These were linked to a facing crossover on the down line, positioned opposite the box at the southern end of the double loop. A trailing crossover at the northern end of these loops gave further access from the down line. Thus traffic from either direction could lead into the up loops. These loops were connected at the south end to another internal loop, and four north facing terminal sidings. A small engine shed was provided at the throat of the four terminal sidings. At the northern end of the loops, the internal railway then ran as a single line in a northeasterly direction for nearly ¾ mile, terminating just south of Upper Lacon Farm. This single line gave off seven trailing connections on its southern side to terminal sidings that ran between eight groups of buildings, mostly presumably for storage purposes. This history of this base is quite interesting, as it was built by the British government for the benefit of the U.S. Army and immediately leased to them (U.S. Army Depot G-16) for part of the build up to the D-Day invasion in 1944. Construction of the depot began in December, 1942 and was completed by June, 1943 at a cost of U.S. dollars 2.36 million. It provided 450,000 sq.ft. of covered storage and 1.375 million sq. ft. of open storage. It is known that two LMSR locomotives, that had been on loan to War Department, were used to transport materials here during the construction. These were Webb former LNWR 5' 6" 2-4-2T nos. 6632 (LNW 1760) and 6691 (LNW 1143) and were returned to the LMSR at Shrewsbury off loan on 16 and 22 June, 1943 respectively. Several engineering and quartermaster units of the U.S. Army, and companies of the Air Corps Unit were based here. Their first task was to recover equipment that had been shipped into several different U.K ports on different ships. In January 1945 the personnel and their equipment left for Weymouth and formed part of the U.S. 9th Army. During this period six outside cylinder 0-6-0Ts built by H.K. Porter Inc. in the U.S.A. were here, although whether they performed much work, or were simply stored here is not known.

After World War II, the War Department took over the depot, giving it the title "083 Ordnance Supply Depot", although at some time it was used as a Prisoner of War Camp. In its new role, rail traffic continued, at first using the standard "Austerity" type 18" 0-6-0STs. Two Hunslet engines with running numbers 75134 and 75139 (works numbers 3188 and 3190 of 1944) and one with the running number 71509, built by Robert Stephenson & Hawthorns (works number 7163 of 1944) arrived here in January, 1945. The Hunslets stayed here until July, 1946 when they were sold to the LNER as their nos. 8014 and 8015. The RSH left in September, 1946 and became LNER no.8024. All three went to Blaydon shed. To replace these, two new 0-4-0DMs arrived new from Andrew Barclay (running numbers 844 and 845, works numbers 371 and 372 of 1945). No.844 stayed until December 1949 moving to the Sentinel Company in Shrewsbury, then going on to the WD at Old Dalby in Leicestershire. No.845 stayed until 1958 before moving to the Bicester Central Workshops. Sister Barclay 0-4-0DM, No.843 (370 of 1945) arrived in 1958, before going to WD Elstow , Bedfordshire in February 1961. Meanwhile two Drewry / Vulcan Foundry 0-4-0DMs were here : No.830 (works no. DC 2176/ VF 5257 of 1945) had arrived by July, 1952 and left for the WD Central Vehicle Depot at Ashchurch, Gloucestershire by October 1955. No.837 (works no. DC 2183/ VF 5264 of 1945) arrived in June, 1958 and left to the WD depot at Stirling in September, 1960. A Hunslet 0-4-0DM, running no. 850 (works no. 2068 of 1940) was also here by October, 1953 until August 1956 when it moved to Barby, near Rugby.

The depot was closed before 1965, although the exact date is not known. Certainly by that time, the two up loops had been removed, and trackwork simplified so that the facing crossover and trailing connection at the south end was all that remained of the rail connection to the main line. Even this was officially taken out of use on 3 March, 1968, so the depot had presumably closed prior to this date. The signal box was removed in 1967 and taken to Nantwich to replace that at Nantwich station (see below). For the period until the connection was officially taken out, it is presumed that it was rarely used and the pointwork padlocked, with keys being retained at Wem box. The site of the depot is now Wem Industrial Estate, and most of the original storage buildings are intact, being used for a variety of commercial purposes. Only a couple of concrete stop blocks remain today to recall the existence of the internal railway system, although the distinctive style of Army buildings, also visible from the line, gives a clear indication of the history of the site.

Now the line is absolutely dead straight heading northeastwards, and on gently undulating gradients that take us across the typical wide open agricultural countryside of north Shropshire. The next station we reach is **Prees** (14 miles) sited north of a level crossing, but over a mile from the village of that name, and only half that distance from the admittedly much smaller hamlet of Coton. The clock tower of St. Chad's church is visible on the horizon, in the centre of Prees, which has grown around a small hill and has seen a considerable increase in population so that in 2001 this stood at 2,688. The town name means "Brushwood", indicating a possible link for this material as a means of crossing the boggy land hereabouts. An arm of the Llangollen Canal was intended to reach Prees in 1806, but only got as far as Quina Brook, about two miles from the village. Today this arm is only navigable for about half of its length, reaching to a place once known as Waterloo, but now referred to as Whixall Marina.

The main station building is located on the up side, and is of the standard 'secondary' red brick design and construction as at Hadnall. The signal box is located on the down side, south of the level crossing and is of an LNWR brick and wood design

A view from the crossing of Prees station on 23 October, 1969 revealing the original crossing gates and the neat station master's house adjoining the booking hall and waiting room. The goods shed can be glimpsed on the left. [D.P.Rowland]

Another variation on the waiting shelter theme is this brick built structure at Prees, with a backward sloping roof. The LMS nameboard was still in situ at this time – 23 October, 1969. [D.P.Rowland]

A later view of the entire Prees station looking south, revealing the layout of the signal box, level crossing and station buildings and its rural aspect, on 26 May, 1977. The booking office and waiting room on the up side was still extant at this time. [Kidderminster Railway Museum]

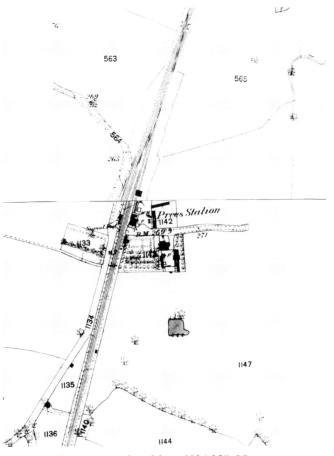

Prees – reproduced from 1924 25" OS map

with 25 levers and a tumbler frame constructed in 1881. Until the 1970s a further two storey, gabled ended house was situated on the up side, next to the level crossing, and opposite the signal box. This is believed to have provided additional staff accommodation. The station became 'unstaffed' as from 19 September, 1966. Today the station building is a private residence, although the flat roofed structure formerly used for the booking office and up side waiting room has been removed, and a smaller gabled ended extension has been built in its place. On the down side, a red brick built waiting shelter of unusual configuration with a tall backward sloping roof was originally provided but demolished in the early 1970s. This building was open towards the platform, so must have been rather draughty for waiting passengers in inclement weather. This was replaced by the usual 'bus shelter', and another installed on the up platform.

North of the station, an up goods loop gave access to the goods yard, which originally contained just a headshunt and two sidings that terminated behind the platforms. One of these passed through a single road goods shed built of red brick, which was demolished during the late 1970s, following withdrawal of goods facilities as from 6 October, 1969. The yard was furnished with a small, 1 ½ ton crane. A further siding was installed around 1920 on the down side, opposite the up goods loop, and accessed by a trailing connection. This is believed to have been mainly used for the unloading of agricultural machinery. Opening this connection was by a key, retained at the signal box. A trailing crossover in the immediate vicinity also gave down trains access to the goods yard. A further trailing connection was also located at the north end of the platforms, although this seems likely to have been installed more for emergency rather than operational reasons. Prees had quite a large staff for its size, for example in the period between 1958 and 1963 there were two porters (whose duties also included issuing tickets), a yard foreman, a crane driver, two motor drivers, two goods clerks and three signalmen.

Continuing in the dead straight northerly direction, the line takes a slight curve to run directly north as we approach the village of Tilstock to the west. After leaving Prees, there is a climb of almost a mile at 1 in 264, but thereafter although the gradient is still generally upward it is not at any great inclination, and with a few level patches of level track. Today, on the right can be seen five large aircraft hangars, which during the 1960-1980 period were used to store part of Europe's "Grain Mountain", rented by the Intervention Board for Agricultural Produce. These hangars are now in commercial use, but originally belonged to RAF, Tilstock whose story we shall examine next.

Three miles after leaving Prees, we arrive at **Heath Lane Crossing**, which had been the site of a crossing for a minor lane running from the main road to Dearnford Hall. At the outbreak of the Great War, it was decided to erect an Army camp to the south, which as already referred to, eventually became known as RAF Tilstock. But in 1915 this was known as Prees Heath Camp, and opened as a base for trench warfare training, with troops housed in tents having a capacity for 30,000 men. In 1916, the camp became the responsibility of Western Command and it was decided to erect wooden hutments, for which a railway connection was required. At some stage the camp was converted into a stores unit, and then into a hospital. On the up side at Heath Lane, two south facing sidings and a north facing headshunt (each of around 200 yards long) were put in, connected to both the up and down lines by a double crossover, so that trains could enter the sidings from either direction. Access was controlled from a small signal box "Prees Camp Signal Cabin" sited opposite the junction on the down side of the main line. From the point where the sidings and headshunt met, a single line ran off in a southeasterly direction across the fields. After about 1/3 of a mile, the line crossed the main Shrewsbury to Whitchurch road (now A49) just on the north side of the Raven Hotel. This road was, of course, a single carriageway at that time and so a single gate was used to control traffic when the line was in use. The line carried on for another ½ mile across further fields to reach the site of the camp, which was on the eastern side of the Wolverhampton road (now A41). It is unlikely that troop trains used this line, especially as there are reports of troops marching from Whitchurch station (two miles to the north) to the camp. After the construction materials had been moved to the site, it is more likely that the line was used for incoming stores such as coal, food and equipment, and outgoing empty wagons.

It is known that one locomotive was used on this site, having been purchased from the Cambrian Railways for £700 on

22nd May 1916 by Armytage & Jones Ltd of Sheffield, who are believed to have been dealers, sourcing the engine on behalf of the Army. This was an 0-4-0ST with 12" x 18" outside cylinders built by Manning Wardle (works number 1523) of their Class "H" and supplied new to the Cambrian Railways at the end of July,1901. When delivered and inspected by the Commandant, Railways and Road Training Centre (Longmoor, Hampshire), it was declared to be in "abominable" condition. This is not surprising as it had been in use on the Cambrian's Van branch, later being laid aside and relegated to the status of 'spare' engine, but in fact had seen no use for some time. Nevertheless, it appears to have worked here, probably for the life of the camp, as it seems unlikely that other locomotives would have been permitted over this lightly laid line. The layout at the camp appears to have been just a single line, although it is not known where the locomotive was kept at this time. It eventually moved to the Air Ministry at the Cardington base (site of the airship development) in Bedfordshire, and was last recorded as being sold to the White Moss Coal Co. Ltd., at Holland Colliery, Upholland, Lancashire in 1933.

Construction of the Prees Heath Army Camp was underway in this 1915 view of the site. Only one line of railway is believed to have been constructed, and that would appear to be this one. Wagons of sawn timber are being unloaded, whilst to the left, a number of the hutments seem to have already been completed. A steam traction engine meanders down the muddy roadway, probably moving the materials to their desired positions. The Great Central coal wagon on the right indicates the inward movement of coal, a necessity at that time for many reasons. [Whitchurch Archaeological & Historical Group]

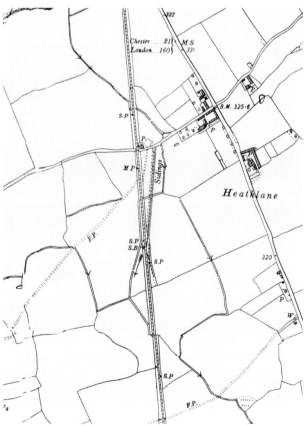

Heath Lane sidings – reproduced from 1924 25" OS map

After the Great War, the camp seems to have been left to return to nature, although as with many other such locations, it is almost certain that some if not all of the huts would have been sold off. The railway had been removed by 1925, leaving the two sidings, the headshunt and the crossover next to the main line. By this time, the small Prees Camp signal box was normally switched out, but in 1934 a decision was taken by the LMSR to introduce an Intermediate Block Section here. This involved altering the control of the Heath Lane Crossing ground frame, hitherto released electrically from the Prees Camp box, to being controlled from the Whitchurch Cambrian Junction signal box. The crossing keeper at Heath Lane lived in a cottage on the up side of the line, immediately north of the crossing, and operated the ground frame that controlled the approach signals either side of the crossing. These alterations enabled the removal of the small Prees Camp signal box, and were completed by 24 October 1935.

Moving forward to World War II, the site was initially used in 1939 as an internment camp for screening German and Austrian refugees, who were housed in tents that could accommodate 2,000 persons. It then became a Prisoner of War camp, until that closed on 4 October 1941. In 1942 it was handed over to the RAF, who built the airfield, extending it across the Wolverhampton road to reach the Shrewsbury road and initially designated it "Whitchurch Heath". The site, with its several runaways and hangars, then covered an area almost four times greater than the Great War camp. But the railway was not reinstated. In

1943 it was redesignated "RAF Tilstock" and became part of "38 Group". Although it had become a glider pilot training school from 1 September 1942 until 21 January 1946, it is also believed to have based Spitfires and Hurricanes. It was also used by RAF No.1665 Heavy Conversion Unit to train crews on Whitley, Stirling and Halifax bombers. On at least one occasion a Stirling overshot the runway and ended up across the Shrewsbury road. After the War, it became part of No.663 Squadron and was used during the 1950s by Auster AOP6 'spotter' aircraft. However, it was soon declared as redundant, and during the 1950s the runways became a popular venue for motorcycle racing. The hangars were used during the 1950s and 1960s for storing 'green goddesses' and other Civil Defence motor vehicles. The remainder of the site was left to general decay, but the hangars were rejuvenated during the 1970s for the storage of grain, as mentioned above. The outlying areas have since returned to agricultural use, but some of the other buildings have been put into commercial use, and today it is a well-known site for parachuting and skydiving.

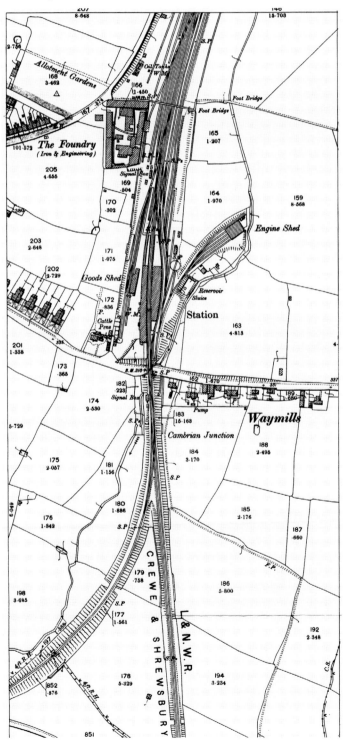

Whitchurch – reproduced from 1899 25" OS map

It is unclear whether the sidings at Heath Lane were used during World War II, but one suggestion is that aviation fuel amongst other stores items was delivered here. Subsequently, the sidings may have been kept in situ in case the base was returned to an operational level, as they were apparently still extant in 1954. The crossover and the headshunt had been removed, leaving just the two sidings connected to the up line. Apart from the RAF, there does not appear to be any other use for these sidings. However, as we have seen in Chapter 4, the crossing keeper here was still being supplied with fresh water until at least 1965. The arrangement here was dispensed with as from 10 October 1988 along with the sidings and signalling in the vicinity. The lane was terminated at each side of the crossing, which was reduced to the status of a pedestrian crossing only, and remained so in 2013. There are no earthworks, remains or other indications of the sidings and other activity here, other than two short isolated pieces of wall.

As the line continues northwards, it passes on the left an area known as Whixall Moss, now graded as a Site of Special Scientific Interest, famous for being the UK's third largest lowland raised bog and for its rare wildlife habitat. Now on a gradual climb at 1 in 290 for a further half mile, it passes beneath the Shrewsbury to Warrington trunk road, carried on a brick built skew bridge. In 1992 a new road providing a by-pass around the town was opened, and the line passes beneath this road, carried on a modern stressed concrete structure shortly before it reaches the original trunk road. Changing to a very gradual descent, at 1 in 1353, the line reaches **Whitchurch** (19¾ miles).

The Roman name for this settlement was Mediolanum ("The place in the middle of the plain"), and it grew from its position on the Roman road from Wroxeter (Viroconium) near Telford to Chester (Deva Victrix). The present town name derives from "White Church", which recognises the parish church of St. Alkmund's built by the Normans of near white stone here. As mentioned earlier in this chapter, Sir Henry Percy was initially buried here after being killed at the Battle of Shrewsbury in 1403. A local hero, Sir John Talbot, 1st Earl of Shrewsbury had his heart buried here after being killed at the Battle of Castillon in 1453 during the "Hundred Years' War". The present church of St. Alkmund's was built in 1712 using local red sandstone on the same site as the original.

An early view from Whitchurch station, looking north between 1905 and 1910. Although of poor quality this image oozes atmosphere, with train disappearing in the distance, possibly to Chester, judging from the signal in the 'off' position on the left. An up train is signalled to arrive shortly at the main up platform, whilst LNWR carriages of four, six and eight wheels are in evidence at the far side of the island platform and in the up yard. [Whitchurch Library]

The view at the north end of Whitchurch station in the mid 1950s, as two Stanier 'Black Fives' (the nearest is no. 45352), return to Crewe on a Test Run. In the distance can be seen the lengthy suspension footbridge that crossed both up and down goods yards. Porter's sack trucks and platform gas lamps complete the period scene. [Derek J. Lowe Archives]

The RCTS "Cheshire Rambler" railtour of 27 April ,1963 ran from Warrington to Chester, then via the Tattenhall branch to Whitchurch, and back via Crewe to Warrington. At Whitchurch, Thompson LNER "B1" Class 4-6-0 No.61039 STEINBOK took the train on its final leg back to Warrington. It is seen here, with the participants, in front of Whitchurch Goods Yard signal box and the foundry of W.H. Smith behind. [Mr. Brough / RCTS]

Whitchurch was granted town status in 1284, and a market charter given in the 14th century. The Llangollen Canal opened in 1808 but passed to the north of the town, and so a short branch was opened in 1811 to link to the town. Traffic on this branch ceased in 1939. Being at the hub of routes to Stafford, Shrewsbury, Wolverhampton, Birmingham, Chester, Wrexham, Liverpool, Manchester, and Warrington the town provided horse drawn coach services for many centuries. Despite being in Shropshire, Whitchurch has long been one of the acknowledged homes of Cheshire Cheese, with many such manufacturers in the town. Today, only one exists in the town, that of Belton Farm Cheese alongside the by-pass. Another famous manufacturer of Whitchurch is that of J.B. Joyce & Co. Ltd., established in 1690, and now the oldest turret clock company in the World. The name crops up several times in this book. Originally located at premises at 40 High Street, they moved to their present premises in Station Road in 1904. The major employer in the town for many years was that of W.H. Smith & Co. Ltd. (absolutely nothing to do with the more famous booksellers) who at its centenary in 1937 employed 250 men. William Smith began his career with the founding of Whitchurch gas works in 1826, then opened a foundry at Dodington in 1837, but by 1879 had established a foundry in Black Park Road adjacent to the station, with its own private siding. This firm of ironfounders and engineers produced a wide range of agricultural equipment, Dutch barns, hydraulic rams, pumps, cheese vats and presses and dairy equipment. Concluding this brief description of the town and its attributes, the composer Sir Edward German was born and lived in the town. To give some idea of the town's size, its population in 2008 was 8,944.

The line first reached Cambrian Junction, which swung in from the west, and for which a signal box ("Whitchurch No.1") was provided at the opening of that line in 1864. As described in Chapter 6, this box was sited in the fork of the lines until 1886 when it was replaced by a standard wooden LNWR box, situated on the down side just a few yards north of the junction. This was equipped with 45 levers and an LNWR tumbler frame. Although the line to Ellesmere and Oswestry was completely closed in March, 1965 this box did not officially close until 8 June 1969. It was retained because it also controlled the junctions at the south end of the station leading to the up goods loop, the former engine shed yard as well as signals and pointwork at the south end of the station.

The station is situated some distance from the town centre, a good walk of around ½ mile, in the district of Waymills. The main station buildings were on the down side, and again based on the standard blue brick design for principal stations, as at Wem, except that there was an extra two storey gabled ended portion at right angles to the line. This was linked by a further single storey section parallel to the line, making the whole ensemble nearly some 50% longer than at Wem. The two storey portions each had single storey bay windows on the road side, and the main entrance, into the booking hall was between the two southernmost portions. The northern two storey section had a separate entrance for the receipt and despatch of parcels. On the platform side, a cantilevered canopy with partial glass panelling and decorative pierced edging ran for the length of the station building, and was further extended over the bay platform for another 10 yards or so, supported by four cast iron pillars. As it extended over the bay platform so the canopy was affixed to a large retaining wall reaching up to the level of the second storey of the main station building. The main station building also contained the usual waiting rooms, toilets and staff offices, plus a refreshment room, run latterly by a Mrs. Burgess. Slightly unusually, the entrance to the footbridge was incorporated in the north end of the range of buildings. The footbridge was of girder construction with steel panelling, glazed from shoulder height and covered by a flat roof. A lift was sited at each end of the footbridge, its position being prominent by towers at each end that were surmounted with hipped pointed roofs. Interestingly, the station clock, which had been supplied by J.B. Joyce (of course!) was suspended over the down platform but the mechanism was not mounted inside the clock. Instead, a rotating shaft connected the clock to the mechanism which was located behind

A view northwards along a deserted Whitchurch station on 31 August 1973 reveals the replaced canopies over the island platform and that the roof over the footbridge has been removed. The station furniture and porters' handcarts hark back to days of steam traction, but would soon be gone. In the distance, the footpath suspension bridge can be just seen.
[J. Maden Collection]

B.R. finally replaced the famous wooden running-in board at Whitchurch with one of enamelled steel, with a much abbreviated message. This wintry scene from 28 December, 1964 records also the replacement upper quadrant signals, but the retention of gas lighting on the platforms. [J. Maden Collection]

an adjoining wall. At its height, Whitchurch employed over 100 persons in the station, goods yard, signal boxes and including 23 in the engine shed.

The original station of 1858 comprised simply an up and down platform. However, although the Cambrian line had opened in 1863, it was not until around 1865 that a second face was added to the up platform converting it into an island. Clearly additional trackwork was required to serve this new platform face, and so the opportunity was taken to lay in a new goods loop on the up side, west of the platform face. Whilst this work was taking place, the existing engine shed and servicing facilities were also rearranged – the subject of this engine shed will be discussed in Chapter 10.

The new island platform (locally referred to as "the back platform") was furnished with toilets, and waiting rooms (1st class and 2nd class ladies, and gentlemen). The footbridge was also installed at this time. This work was performed by Messrs. Collins & Son of Warrington. A cantilevered canopy with decorative pierced edges ran over both of the platform faces, and extended to the north by about 10 yards again supported by cast iron pillars. At the southern end of the island platform a water column with a 'parachute' type water tank was provided for the locomotives on both sides of the platform. As a result, it unusually featured two swivelling outlets, one at each side. At the northern end of the island platform was a wooden running-in board that until about 1960 proudly proclaimed "WHITCHURCH – Junction for Ellesmere, Oswestry, Welshpool, Newtown, Llanidloes, Builth Wells, Brecon, Machynlleth, Aberystwyth, Barmouth and Pwllheli." This was replaced by BR with a metal enamelled sign simply stating "WHITCHURCH – Change for Oswestry and Aberystwyth". Probably the original was rotten by that time, but the replacement was more of an instruction than an invitation, and not nearly so intriguing. During most of the BR days, the refreshment room was managed by a Miss Downes, and was well regarded for the quality of its food and drink.

In the early 1960s the island platform was reroofed with new cantilevered cladding that was pitched higher at the platform edge than in the centre, and the roof over the footbridge was removed. At that time the stationmaster's office was situated at the southern end of the building on the island platform. The canopy over the down platform was also renewed, with the decorative edging replaced by plain edging. On 17 August, 1970 the station was designated to be 'unstaffed' and major remodelling took place, which saw the removal of the buildings on both platforms. The northern section of the canopy on the down platform, from the footbridge alongside the erstwhile bay platform was retained, and although this has subsequently been reclad, it is still supported by the original decorative cast iron pillars. 'Bus shelters' were added on the exposed up and

The roadside exterior of Whitchurch station on 31 August, 1973, showing the fine three gabled construction. The main entrance was between the first and second gables into the booking hall, whilst the third gable acted as a parcels reception, being provided with a short canopy. The tower beyond the third gable marks the position of the lift incorporated into footbridge. Period touches include the red telephone box and the Mark I Ford Escort and Austin Cambridge Estate. [Author's Collection]

down platforms, and the platform edging of the bay platform and the outer face of the former island platform was securely fenced. The original footbridge lasted until June, 2013 when it was dismantled. A new structure, featuring wider stairs was installed, a few yards further south, so that the up (southbound) platform was also slightly extended. However, it seems unfortunate that the opportunity was not taken to provide access to the up platform for disabled passengers and those with prams, wheeled luggage and so on.

North of the station a complex arrangement of sidings and loops was developed over the years. On the up side, the initial layout is believed to have simply consisted of the mainline, with access via a crossover to the goods yard on the down side. This was revised considerably with the opening of the Cambrian line in 1863 as mentioned above, for which transfer sidings were needed. In 1865 the LNWR acquired several strips of land on the eastern side of the line, totalling an area of around 55 yards in width and 800 feet in length. This land was used to create the two up loops that led around the island platform and five south facing terminal sidings north of the station. This layout remained basically unchanged then until the 1970s when the terminal sidings were taken out, and then in the early 1980s the loops were removed.

On the down side, there was a much more extensive layout of sidings. Originally, the goods yard was situated behind, or to the west of the station, with three north facing sidings of which one (known as the 'Warehouse Road') ran through a substantial blue brick built goods shed. The westernmost siding, known as the 'Outside Road' terminated at a side and end loading platform, adjacent to which were several cattle pens. After the opening of the Cambrian line these were supplemented with three more loop lines and several more terminal sidings. This period also saw the expansion of Smith's foundry on the western side of the goods yard, for which a single siding was laid into their works, doubtless for the supply of pig iron, coal, coke and other bulk supplies. Just beyond the northern end of the station platforms, a public right of way had existed across the running lines, marked by a boarded crossing. The direction of this footpath continued across land earmarked for the extension of the foundry, and anyway was by then considered unsafe for pedestrian use. Consequently, it was diverted to a site about 150 yards further north, just beyond the boundary of the foundry land, and a suspension type footbridge erected, very similar to the one at Wem. This footbridge remains today, having been refurbished around 2010. The coal sidings were originally opposite the foundry, but by 1881 the location for these two sidings was just to the north of the foundry, beyond the footbridge. The opening of the Tattenhall branch in 1872 gave an impetus for further development in this area, as another group of four loops were extended alongside this branch. This was not intended for a significant increase in traffic off that branch, although these new loops could be used for that purpose. Rather, it gave additional room for remarshalling and sorting of mostly northbound traffic. In this area, to the east, was a large space for the unloading and storage of timber, served by two north facing terminal sidings. A 5 ton crane was provided in the yard. Some of the sidings were removed during the 1970s, with goods facilities being withdrawn from 1 November 1976, but several remained until the early 1990s when the whole area was cleared. The goods shed remains intact today, now used as a motor vehicle repair business.

The up and down goods yards and running lines north of the station were controlled by a substantial LNWR signal box with the usual gable ended wooden cabin generously glazed. It was mounted on a tall red brick base, contained a 55 lever LNW tumbler frame and was located just north of the station on the down side, in what was the throat of the original goods yard. In his 1872 report on the Tattenhall Branch, the Board of Trade's Inspector, Colonel Rich commented on the seemingly random distribution of uninterlocked point levers in this area, and added that "The LNWR propose to rearrange these and to work them from a Raised Cabin. The sooner this is done the better." However, from maps of this period it would seem that there was already a signal box in this area, and that this much larger replacement dating from 1897, was constructed to cater for the additional levers. It was originally designated "Whitchurch No.2" but became "Whitchurch Goods Yard" for most of its life, and after the withdrawal of goods facilities in 1976, it was simply designated "Whitchurch", as by that time it was the only signal box there. For many years from the 1980s onwards it was rarely used, being 'switched out' for most of the time, but survived as a single crossover from the up to down lines remained in the station area. Finally it was demolished in August 2012. The signal box controlling the junction for the Tattenhall branch was a standard LNWR box with red brick base and wood and glass cabin, standing on the down side in the fork of the junction. Originally, "Whitchurch No.3" it was later renamed "Whitchurch Chester Junction", and contained a 45 lever LNW tappet frame. It closed on 15 June 1969, and was demolished soon after.

Leaving Whitchurch the line curves to a northeasterly direction and climbs, first at 1 in 331, passing on the eastern side Blake Mere (sometimes known as "Black Mere", as nearby to the east is the Black Park estate). The gradient steepens to 1 in 136 to reach the site of **Brick Kiln Lane Crossing** about ½ mile from the Chester Junction box. This level crossing was originally known as "Brick Hill Crossing", and was worked by a resident crossing keeper, being protected by distant and home signals for each direction. The crossing is now user operated, but the keeper's cottage remains, converted into an attractive private dwelling.

Continuing its climb to the highest point of the line, the line passes through a short cutting, and through a wood can be glimpsed Oss Mere, whilst another mile east is the substantial estate and dairy farm of Combermere Park, although the house is not visible from the line. This is the site of a Cistercian Abbey founded in 1138, which after the Dissolution was largely demolished, leaving just the Abbot's House, which remains today. The property was given by Henry VIII to the Cotton family, in whose hands it remained until 1919. Just before arriving at **Poole's Siding** (21 miles) we cross the boundary from Shropshire into Cheshire. This rather remote location consisted of one siding accessed from a trailing junction on the up line only, with a trap point at the exit, and a ground frame adjacent, for operation of the access point.

The siding measured 275 feet from the junction with the main line, and 235 feet from the trap point. Road access was from Ossmere Lane, which passes beneath the line. The exact date that this was put in is not known, but it was fairly early in the life of the line, as it was shown on the LNWR plan of 1865 and in the Working Timetable for 1872. In March 1881 signalling improvements here were approved at a cost of £80, and the completed works approved by the LNWR Signalling Department on 14 July of that year. The purpose of the siding was to supply local farms with basic materials such as coal, lime and fertilizer, sold for cash by the private owner of this siding. A certain Mr. Mitchell is known to have delivered coal to local farms from here. To facilitate this trade a weighing machine was installed here. It is not clear when this siding was taken out of use, but it was certainly before 1967. Today the site is overgrown, but is still securely fenced off and apparently still owned by the BR Property Board. There are indications that it may have been used as a storage area for permanent way materials after removal of the siding.

In the distance to the east can also be seen an obelisk, standing on a small hill. This was erected in 1890 in the memory of Sir Stapleton Stapleton-Cotton, the 6th Baronet, 1st Baron, and 1st Viscount of Combermere. He had a distinguished military career, with notable successful campaigns in India, in Spain and Portugal during the Peninsular Wars, and during the Napoleonic Wars at Waterloo. This monument is a Grade II listed structure.

We are now travelling in an almost easterly direction, on a downhill stretch lasting some 3½ miles from the summit, firstly at 1 in 115, then successively at 1 in 107, 1 in 110, and 1 in 230. In the middle of the third inclination we reach **Marley Green Crossing** where a minor lane crossed the line and was controlled by a resident crossing keeper. A ground frame contained a 6 lever LNW tumbler frame for the approach signals, interlocked to the manually operated gates. This was converted to an "on call" lifting barrier on 21 November 1965 and the signals and ground frame removed. Subsequently, this was converted to user operation. Once again, the crossing keeper's cottage has been tastefully converted into a private residence.

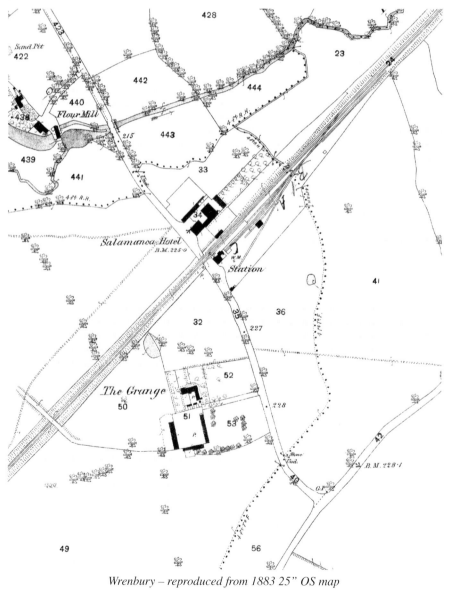

Wrenbury – reproduced from 1883 25" OS map

Continuing downhill there is a fine view eastwards towards the Staffordshire Moorlands, and then after just over another mile we reach **Wrenbury** (23¼ miles). The village of that name is less than ½ mile to the west, whilst a mile to the east is the community of Aston. Entering the station, we first pass the signal box on the up side, then over the level crossing, and into the station. The station buildings here are replicas of the other 'second class' stations seen earlier, and still quite complete although converted to a private residence. The signal box is of the standard LNWR Type 5 brick and wood design (as other medium sized boxes on the line) dating from 1882, with a 20 lever LNW tumbler frame and measured 16 feet 2½ inches x 12 feet. A trailing crossover was sited at the north end of the platforms, which may have been used by trains terminating here on Cattle Auction days. For there had been a huge business in the sale of cattle in this vicinity, starting in 1862 at the Bhutpore Inn, about a mile away in Aston. Coincidentally, this inn was built in 1720 but was named after the Battle of Bhurtpore in 1825-6 at which Sir Stapleton-Cotton took the fort of this name. However, the cattle auctions soon moved to the Salamanca Inn, as this was located on the west side of the station, next

The view at Wrenbury looking south in the 1960s, with yet another variation on the waiting shelter on the down platform. Although primarily constructed of wood, this building was of a substantial size, and also featured toilets. [Kidderminster Railway Museum]

The up side station buildings at Wrenbury were absolutely identical to those at Prees, including their siting and the stationmaster's house. This view, taken on 23 October 1969, shows all to be in excellent condition. The waiting rooms must have been particularly welcoming on a wintry day in this rather exposed location. [D.P.Rowland]

Wrenbury's goods shed, also on 23 October, 1969. By this time the goods yard was long out of use, but the connection to the baby food factory, seen in the background remained in use. [D.P.Rowland]

to the level crossing. Thus the movement of cattle was made much easier. This inn was named after the victorious Battle of Salamanca during the Spanish Peninsular War (1808-1814), and still exists, but is now also a private residence. On the down platform, Wrenbury passengers had been provided with a sizeable gable ended building, running parallel to the platform. Although executed entirely in wood, it featured ladies and gentlemen's waiting rooms and toilets. An open vestibule led on to the platform, and judging from the two brick chimneys the waiting rooms were adequately heated. Wrenbury was designated as 'unstaffed' as from 19 September, 1966 and this waiting shelter was subsequently removed in and replaced by the usual 'bus shelter'; another is sited on the up platform.

The goods yard lay on the up side of the line, almost behind the up platform, and was accessed by a trailing crossover which also connected the up an down running lines.

A lengthy refuge siding on the up side with a capacity for 39 wagons ran back northwards, thus also acting as a headshunt for the goods yard, which was furnished with a small 2 ton crane. The first goods yard siding ran parallel to the up line, and terminated immediately behind the up platform at a side and end loading bay with a large number of adjacent cattle pens. The second siding, also parallel, terminated in front of a small red brick goods shed, whilst the third ran through this shed. The fourth was a mileage siding added in 1877 and running to the perimeter of the yard, being used for coal traffic. Sometime before 1963 a further siding was added, which ran from the lengthy headshunt, north of the goods yard into a factory manufacturing "Truefood" baby foods. This rail connection was taken out when the goods yard closed, and subsequently the factory closed, lying empty for some years, although now part of the site has been converted into making concrete building products. Despite withdrawal of its goods facilities as from 6 July, 1964 the small goods shed survives today and in 2013 sported a "for sale" looking somewhat incongruous as this building stood in the derelict former goods yard.

Wrenbury suffered from two unfortunate accidents in 1869, when firstly three passenger coaches were derailed there, and then three weeks later, a goods train suffered a similar problem there. This 36 wagon train loaded with coal, iron and tin was en route from Newport to Liverpool, and after passing through Whitchurch, an axle on one of the wagons broke whilst descending towards Wrenbury. This derailed 19 wagons, three or four of which were completely wrecked.

Now the line heads in a straight line northeastward, crossing the River Weaver, which at this point is in its infancy, on a blue brick single arched bridge. Then there is a rise at 1 in 384 for ½ mile, before reaching falling for nearly 2½ miles, mostly at 1 in 184 and certainly nothing steeper. Passing beneath numerous overline bridges, most of which only carry minor roads or lanes, the line finally reaches the Shropshire Union's main line canal that runs from the outskirts of Wolverhampton to Ellesmere Port on the River Dee estuary and opened in 1832. This is crossed on a skew bridge, supported by massive blue brick abutments with a girder decking.

Half a mile later, the line reaches the site of **Market Drayton Junction** (27½ miles) at the start of a 60 chain radius curve

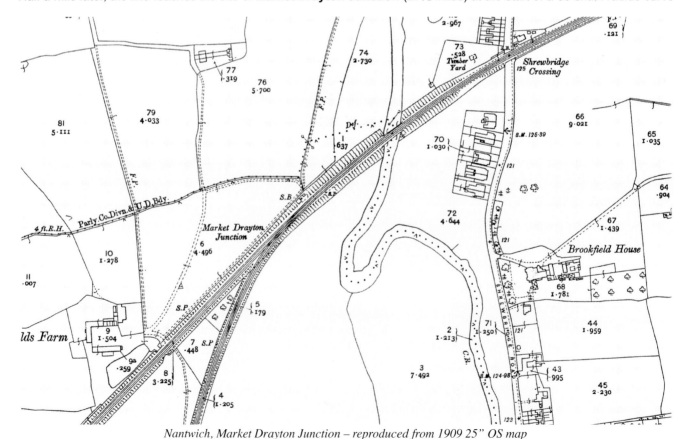

Nantwich, Market Drayton Junction – reproduced from 1909 25" OS map

to the right. The Market Drayton line joined from the south at a north east facing double track junction controlled by the LNWR signal box sited opposite on the down side, near to Fields Farm. The original box had been replaced in 1884 by a typical LNWR gable ended wooden box with red brick base and a 22 lever frame contained in the usual glazed wooden cabin, and this continued in use until destroyed by fire during the evening of 16 /17 January, 1967. Traffic on the branch did not officially cease until 8 May, 1967 so some temporary form of control must have been established for the period in between. Whatever control had been established was removed when the box itself was officially closed as from 23 July that year. The trackbed of the Market Drayton line can be easily discerned across the fields as it approaches the junction site, although nothing now remains at the actual former junction.

Almost immediately after, the line is carried on an embankment across the flood plain of the River Weaver, which it then crosses on an attractive skew bridge of underslung plate girders of 62 ½ feet span, built on piles sunk into the ground alongside the river. The river has grown in width since first crossed just north of Wrenbury, but has still not reached full maturity. At 305 yards from the site of Maket Drayton Junction signal box, the Shrewbridge level crossing is negotiated, which was controlled by "Shrewbridge Crossing" signal box on the down side. This small wooden box was not a block post and did not operate its own signals. Instead, the crossing was protected by means of slots operated from the box on the appropriate stop signals worked by the signal boxes either side.

The next box, at 314 yards "Nantwich Station" is within sight, and is a busy signal box, as it also controls the major level crossing of Wellington Road immediately at the western end of the station. The original "Nantwich Station" signal box was of the standard LNWR brick and wood design, and contained 30 levers with an LMS frame. In 1967 it was replaced with the more modern wooden one (dating from 1943!) formerly at Aston Park, Wem and the three level crossings in the town were converted to automatic lifting barriers, to be controlled from this new box. Consequently, the boxes at "Shrewbridge Crossing" and "Newcastle Road Crossing" were closed.

Nantwich station (28 miles) was situated on an almost level piece of track, and for once, well placed to serve the town. The Domesday Book records the ancient name for this town as "Wych Malbeng". The earliest market recorded here was in 1283 when King Edward I granted a right of fair on the feast of St. Bartholomew. Cheese, grain and salt were traded here from early days, and tanning became an established local industry from medieval days. As a result, glovemaking became an ancient cottage industry practised by "the poor incapable of following any other employ." Later, cotton spinning, and

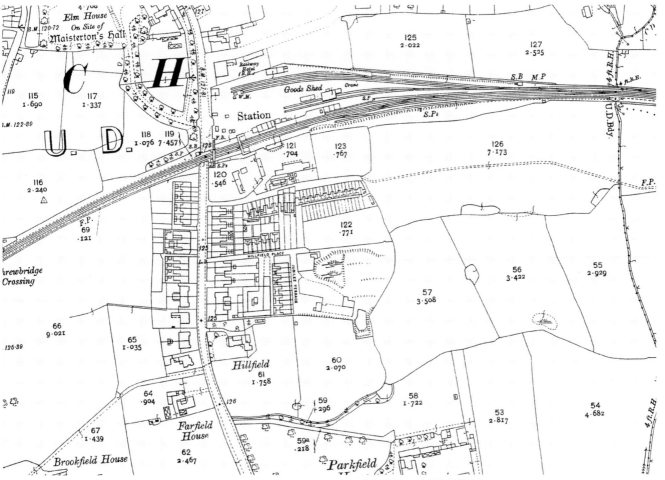

Nantwich station and goods yard – reproduced from 1909 25" OS map

Stanier 8F 2-8-0 no.48151 crosses the substantial steel girder bridge over the River Weaver slightly to the west of Shrewbridge Road level crossing, Nantwich on 1 April, 2013 whilst working the return leg of the "Welsh Borders Steam Special" from Shrewsbury to Crewe. [Author]

Stanier Class 5 4-6-0 No.45060 runs into Nantwich with a down local stopping train on 24 June 1956. It is passing the LNWR Nantwich Station signal box, and is just about to run over the level crossing at the west end of the station. [H. Townley / J.M. Bentley Collection]

This picture dates from around 1910, and it would appear that the entire station staff have turned out for the occasion. The large nameboard on the down platform proclaims this to be "Nantwich Junction" and advises passengers to "change here for Great Western Trains to Market Drayton, Wellington, Wolverhampton, Birmingham, Oxford and London". The footbridge and steps are completely enclosed in a wood and glass surround. [Author's Collection]

On 20 May, 1951 Nantwich station, looking towards Crewe, was still totally unaltered and in good order. The LMSR nameboard was still in place, and would remain so for a few years yet. The extent of the full canopy on the up platform can be seen to good advantage. [Lens of Sutton Association – R.G. Nelson]

A view of Nantwich station looking west on 10 April 1957 shows the level crossing and the signal box at the far end of the platforms. [H.C.Casserley]

The roadside of Nantwich station main station building on the down side on 31 August 1973.The entrance to the booking hall was between the two gables, and the basic layout followed that at Whitchurch, except that the structure was smaller, with only two gables being provided. [Author's Collection]

Also on 31 August 1973, the details of the up side brick built waiting rooms are visible. By this time, the canopy had been removed, as well as the footbridge. Passengers from that time then using the public pedestrian footbridge located adjacent to the level crossing, a few yards to the west. [Author's Collection]

boot and shoe manufacture took over as major industries. The Great Fire of 1583 destroyed nearly 600 timber houses in the town, the fire lasting for 20 days. This was followed by a plague in 1586 during which 140 were buried, and again in 1604 over 400 died in the six months that it lasted. In the Civil War, the Parliamentarians took the town, and garrisoned over 2,000 soldiers here, holding out against Royalist attacks. After the industrial revolution, the town became even more annexed by Crewe, with whom it had always been considered as a twin, and finally in 1973 the Borough of Nantwich and Crewe was formed.

The main station building was sited on the down side built to the standard design for 'first class' stations with the two gabled end two storey portions linked by a single story section, as at Wem. Further single storey extensions at each end of this block contained lavatories and other staff offices. A substantial cantilevered canopy over the platform for the length of the main building was supported by cast iron bracketry attached to the building. A smaller canopy was provided at the northern end of the range of buildings. On the up side a lengthy single storey building, also in blue brick, contained waiting rooms and toilets. This was also furnished with a substantial wooden canopy, but was slightly smaller than that on the opposite platform, and was supported by seven cast iron pillars on the platform. A fully enclosed iron framed footbridge, with wood enclosures and glazing from shoulder height, was sited mid way along the two platforms so that it connected the waiting areas on each platform. Adjacent to the level crossing an open metal lattice footbridge was available for pedestrians to use when the level crossing was closed against the road traffic, and this remains in use today. Beyond the station, six sidings served the goods yard and single road goods shed on the down side, with a crossover from the up running line. A standard 5 ton crane was situated in the down yard. Special instructions at Crewe covered the handling of locomotive coal for the

Nantwich Newcastle Crossing signal box was situated on the up side of the line, on the western side of the Newcastle Road, right at the town boundary (the sign for which can be seen to the right of the crossing). Stanier 'Black Five' 4-6-0 No.44681 is approaching with a down relief express on 4 July, 1953. The halt provided here from 1911 to 1918 was located behind the photographer, whose vantage point is the public pedestrian footbridge, since removed. [H. Townley / J.M. Bentley Collection]

two main sheds, but even so there were frequently occasions when the volume was too great to be handled immediately at Crewe, and so wagon loads of this coal was stored in Nantwich Yard. A single refuge siding was located on the up side, with a capacity for 33 wagons plus engine and brake van. "Nantwich Goods Yard" signal box sited on the down side at the throat of the goods yard, controlled the movements here, but was downgraded to a ground frame sometime in the 1950s. Goods traffic was withdrawn here as from 4 September 1972, but by the late 1970s two sidings remained, on the down side. These had both been removed by the 1990s and the site cleared for housing development and an Aldi supermarket. The station buildings on the up side were removed and replaced with a 'bus shelter', with a further one now provided on the down platform. The main building was retained but let out to commercial uses, and for some years now has traded as an Indian restaurant, having been painted all over in a matt black finish. Due to the enterprise of the local council, and volunteers, substantial hanging baskets and flower beds enliven both platforms today and have won awards from 2008 to 2011.

Now heading almost due east, the line continues around the south side of the town, climbing at 1 in 172 for over a mile and crosses the Newcastle to Nantwich road (now A52) on the level. This was originally controlled by "Newcastle Crossing"

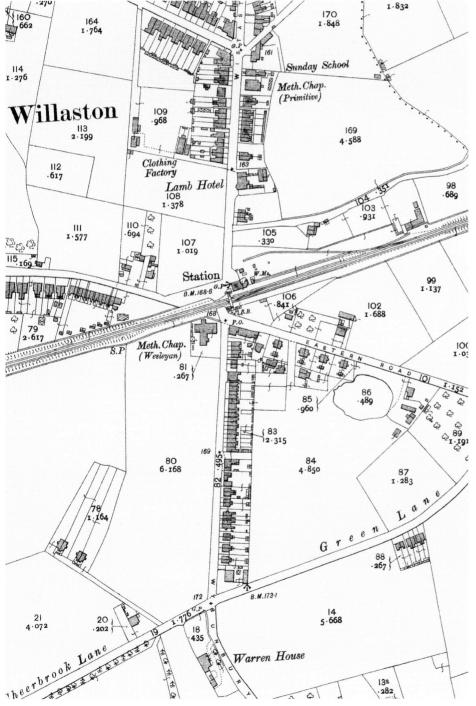

signal box, sited on the up side, west of the crossing. This contained just 5 levers and an LNW tumbler frame in a standard LNW small structure, and closed on 16 April 1967 with the introduction of lifting barriers. A public footbridge was sited on the eastern side of the crossing for the benefit of pedestrians whilst the gates were closed to road traffic, but was removed probably around 1985. The original gates were particularly long, as the road crossed the railway at an oblique angle, so much that it was locally claimed to be the longest level crossing in the country – a claim not believed to be true. A halt was opened here as **Nantwich Newcastle Crossing** on 2 January, 1911 and closed on 1 April, 1918. This was opened by the LNWR as part of their scheme to introduce steam railmotors in response to competition from road omnibuses, and was discussed in Chapter 3. Such halts were usually primitive affairs, normally featuring low platforms constructed mainly of timber, possibly with ash infill, and any shelters for passengers likely to be similarly rudimentary. However, no photographs of this halt have been traced.

Passing now back into fairly flat rural countryside, the line turns almost due east and just over a mile further on, enters **Willaston** (29¾ miles) on level track, immediately beyond the level crossing over Wybunbury Road. This was controlled by

Willaston – reproduced from 1883 25" OS map

The arrangement at Willaston is apparent in this view from 17 April, 1954 with the station master's house on the left, the public footbridge, and the original signal box nestling beneath the far steps. The up side waiting shelter was a rather small, basic design and can be glimpsed on the far platform. [H. Townley / J.M. Bentley Collection]

By 1 November 1958 a new signal box had been erected, on the far side of the level crossing at Willaston, although the original had not yet been demolished. As the station had been closed to passengers for some four years by then, considerable neglect is evident. However, details of the standard station construction are evident on the right. [H. Townley / J.M. Bentley Collection]

its own signal box, sited at the western end of the up platform, adjacent to the road. This box was of a hipped roof design, entirely of brick construction, and dated from the opening of the line. It measured 20 feet 10 inches x 11 feet 4 inches and contained 20 levers, latterly with a standard LMS frame. However, it was replaced on 10th December 1958 by a standard BR flat roofed box of mainly brick construction with composite cabin panels. The roof projected outward slightly to give protection from sun glare as well as rain. It was also sited on the up side, but just immediately west of the crossing, and initially contained manual operation of the level crossing gates. However, it was closed on 28 October, 1984 when operation of the lifting barriers and signalling in the area passed to Crewe Power Box.

The station building was the usual two storey brick built affair for 'secondary stations', located on the down side. Passengers using the up platform had the benefit of a rather uninviting gabled ended wooden shelter, with two windows and a central door that opened on to the platform. However, this station closed on 6 December, 1954 and all traces except for the main station building were swept away. This has since been converted into a private residence. An iron lattice footbridge at the western end of the platforms provided access between the platforms, but was also a public footbridge for pedestrian use when the gates were closed. This has since been removed.

A trailing crossover was positioned in the centre of the platforms, as provided elsewhere, although in this case no other crossover was situated to give an easier access to the goods yard. Consequently, most goods trains tended to shunt the yard when travelling towards Crewe, to avoid a lengthy line occupation. The goods yard was on the down side, east of the station and initially contained two single ended sidings and a short headshunt. Over the years two further sidings were added, including a mileage siding by 1898. In the usual arrangement, this passed around the perimeter of the yard on its northern side. No goods shed was ever provided here, nor a yard crane, although a weighbridge was positioned near to the road entrance to the yard along with its small office, and one for a local coal merchant. Goods traffic was withdrawn here as from 2 November, 1964. The former goods yard has now been covered by a housing development.

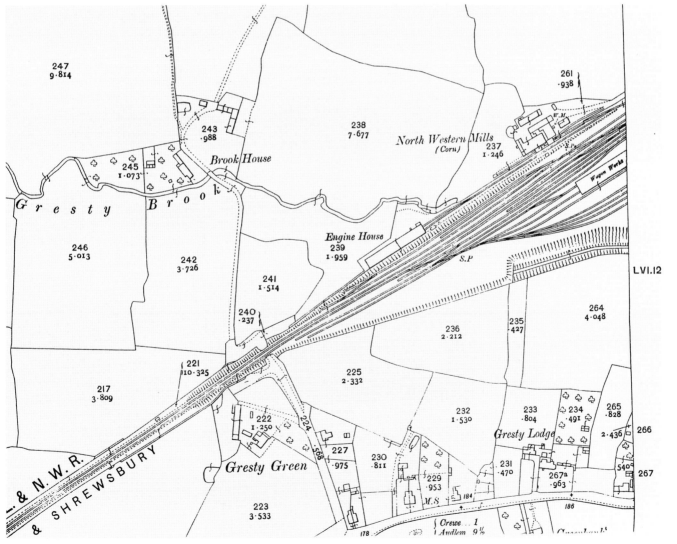

Crewe Gresty Bridge, including engine shed – reproduced from 1910 25" OS map

The station was situated more or less centrally in this somewhat sprawling community, which has now developed into a suburb of Crewe, and Willaston's current claim to fame is that the World Worming Championships have been held here since 1980.

Leaving Willaston the line climbs at 1 in 369 for a mile, passing what was originally agricultural land which has now seen considerable residential and commercial development, and beneath Ropegreen (or Rope) Bridge to arrive at **Gresty** (32 miles). Here, alongside the continuation of Gresty Lane as it runs close and parallel to the line another halt was provided, as at Nantwich Newcastle Crossing. It was in use for the same period, i.e. from 2 January, 1911 until 1 April 1918 primarily served by railmotors operating from Northwich to Nantwich.

Almost immediately we come to the new marshalling yards at Gresty Green created as part of a major reorganisation that started in September 1927, and was completed one year later. The down side yard comprised 19 east facing terminal roads and two arrival loops. Each of the sidings were allocated specific destinations for the goods, and had a total capacity of 1,227 wagons. The up yard was much smaller, comprising just one loop and two west facing terminal sidings that each had a capacity for 25 wagons. This up yard was later expanded into five reception loops and four terminal sidings. Both up and down yards remain in use today, although the down yard is primarily used by the Engineer's Department for stabling its fleet of special rail vehicles and associated equipment and wagons. A large goods depot was also erected here, and a separate depot for cold storage sited at the southern extremity of the site. Three more sorting sidings were added during 1940. A further siding ran from the southernmost loop eastwards into a Ministry of Food "Buffer Depot", also erected during World War II. Both yards were controlled by a new signalbox, "Gresty Lane No.2", of standard LMS design containing 18 levers and sited on the down side at the entrance to the reception loops. This closed on 28 October 1984 with the opening of the Crewe Power Signalling Centre. The intention for these yards was to avoid running goods trains into Basford Hall yard for sorting, as at that time the approach lines were at full capacity. Whilst this certainly achieved a relief to running line traffic in Crewe, it was still necessary for trip workings to be run between the two yards, and some workings from the Shrewsbury line still had to run into, or depart from Basford Hall.

It is worthy of note that today we meet electrification catenary at Gresty Lane sidings, as during the electrification works between 1960 and 1963, this was erected from Crewe South Junction for around one mile to this point. Initially, this was to facilitate electrically worked freight traffic onwards to Manchester.

Just beyond was the Gresty Lane locomotive shed on the down side, which will be covered in Chapter 10. This was accessed from a trailing connection from the down line just west of the road bridge over Gresty Lane, which ran for some distance west as a single line, giving off connections to the private sidings of the North Western Corn Mills. These were later to become the mills for production of the famous Mornflake Oats.

Passing this engine shed, this the area was developed in the 1880s with two loops on the down side, but more substantially on the up side with the creation of a yard of four loops and five terminal sidings facing west. In between a red brick wagon repair shop was built, served by three lines entering the shops.

As we pass over Gresty Lane bridge, lines diverge off to the south and to the north. When the line opened, there was no direct link to the south and to what later became known as Basford Hall Yard. But eventually, in the 1880s a single line was put in running south also from this junction, and so creating a triangle towards what would become site of Crewe South locomotive shed (opened 1897). This area was then developed to the west and south of Crewe South depot to become Basford Hall sidings, and by 1910 four running lines ran from the Shrewsbury line to Basford Hall. Just to the southeast of

As the line approached the environs of Crewe it crossed Gresty Lane, at which point we see Stanier "Princess Coronation" Class 4-6-2 No.46248 CITY OF LEEDS heading an up North and West express service in July, 1961. The overhead catenary (as far as Gresty Lane sidings) is already in place. This was taken from Crewe South shed yard, with the edging of the turntable just in the lower right corner. [Author]

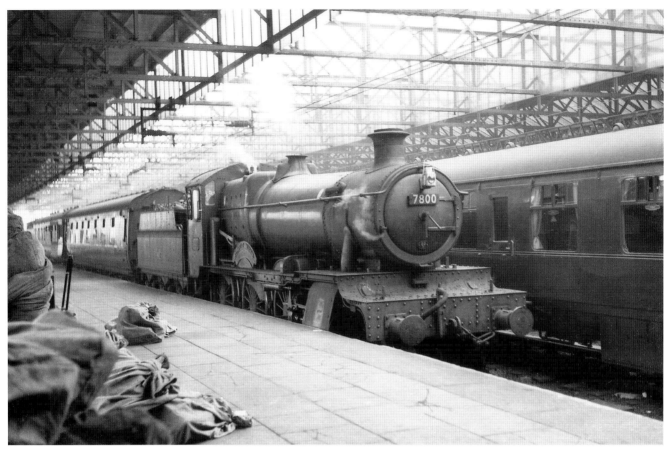

Hawksworth "Manor" class 4-6-0 No.7800 TORQUAYMANOR has just arrived at Crewe with the 12.45pm from Aberystwyth on 17 October, 1962. Despite the lengthy nature of the journey, this was evidently only considered to be a stopping train, judging from the headlampcode. All terminating trains used the south bays in Crewe station, which at that time were numbered 4B (this one) and 3B. [Lens of Sutton Association – R.G. Nelson]

this connection with the Shrewsbury line, a new large goods depot was erected, served by six roads which passed through the building. Due to the large amount of cattle traffic passing through, facilities were installed in the adjacent sidings here for the very necessary task of feeding and watering livestock. Slightly west of this depot and the junction, also on the south side of the line, the GWR erected its own goods yard of five sidings and a depot, which was a more modest affair served by just one terminal road. Both of these depots were to the east of Gresty Lane, which gave road access.

The line to the north ran to what was originally the only sorting sidings and goods depots for traffic from the Shrewsbury line. This yard was sited alongside Crewe station, on the west (or down) side, and was separated by the goods avoiding lines. Just after the junction at Gresty Lane, and west of where the line ran north, a further line ran from here curving directly north to a cattle market (opened 1883) immediately south of the later Crewe Alexandra football ground. By 1896 a Permanent Way Works was erected near to the junction at Gresty Lane, served by a yard accessed from a backshunt from the cattle yard lines. The creation of the Independent Lines (1899-1906) resulted in the disappearance of the original surface goods avoiding lines and the associated sorting sidings and goods depots mentioned above. For the Shrewsbury line, a double track spur was installed, connecting to the Independent Lines at Salop Goods Junction, thereby facilitating through traffic for North England, Scotland and North Wales.

This series of junctions was initially controlled by a single signal box sited on the down side of the line east of Gresty Lane bridge. However, as the area became more complex this was replaced in 1899 by a new box (LNWR Type 4) sited at the junction in the centre of the running lines, and was to be the first electrically powered signal box in the country. During the 1927/8 remodelling this became "Gresty Lane No.1", and was subsequently been renamed simply "Gresty" after the closure of the No.2 box. It remains in use to control movements on the running lines and yards to the west, and was modernised in 1976 with the replacement of the lever frame by a mini Individual Function Switch (IFS) panel. At this point our line continues almost straight ahead, crossing the Independent Lines, then curving northwards and joining the West Coast Main Line directly opposite Crewe South signal box. This 'art-deco' style structure was opened in 1940 to a reinforced 'bomb-proof' ARP design, and was decommissioned on 6 June 1985, when its functions were taken over by the new Power Signalling Centre at Crewe. However, this imposing structure remains intact. We now finally run into **Crewe** station (32 ¾ miles).

A full history of the development of Crewe station is really outside the scope of this work, but a brief summary follows, to assist with understanding of the way Shrewsbury traffic was dealt with. When opened in 1837 by the Grand Junction Railway, Crewe station comprised two platforms (one northbound and one southbound) and was designated a "First Class station", indicating that all passenger services stopped there. The station building was described at the time as being 'a very handsome building in the Elizabethan style, with extensive waiting and refreshment rooms with every convenience for the accommodation of passengers'. The platforms were extended in 1840 with the opening of the Chester line, and by 1849 two additional running lines through the centre of the station had been added. Widened platforms and new bays followed in 1867, and in 1878 extensive enlargements were made. These included moving the main entrance from a low level site adjacent to the Crewe Arms Hotel, modifications to the road overbridge, and additional platforms. Construction of the Independent Lines started in 1896, and this massive and complex project was probably not truly completed until 1906. These lines ran on the west side of the line, from just north of Basford Hall Yard avoiding the station altogether to the Chester line, whilst further tracks burrowed beneath the main lines to the north of the station, serving both the Manchester and North lines. Around this time, a further island platform was added on the west side of the station, virtually doubling its size. This arrangement remained until 1985, when the westernmost face of the later island platform was taken out of normal use, but was retained for Post Office sorting duties and emergency use. Otherwise, although some changes were made to allow faster through running, and platform numbers were altered, the general layout remained the same.

Passenger trains terminating at Crewe were generally the stopping trains from Shrewsbury, as well as those from Wellington and Market Drayton, and eventually in BR days, some from the Cambrian lines. These used the two platform bays at the south end of the station, which in 1985 were changed from 3B and 4B to 8 and 7. Through trains would use any of the main platforms, as appropriate to their origins or destinations.

CHAPTER TEN

LOCOMOTIVE SHEDS

Shrewsbury

The first LNWR locomotive shed in Shrewsbury was a single road affair in the SUR goods yard at Abbey Foregate on the north side of the joint line to Wellington. Directly opposite on the south side of the line, the S&BR also had a single road engine shed. However, a locomotive shed was built in 1855/6 at Coleham, about 5/8 mile south of the station for the independent Shrewsbury & Hereford Railway, which had opened in 1852. This was a five road straight shed, brick built with a slated, hipped roof. After acquisition by the GWR and LNWR in 1862, LNWR occupied three roads, and the GWR the northernmost two. In their usual spirit of cooperation, a dividing wall was installed!

Possibly the shed at Abbey Foregate remained in use by goods engines working in from Stafford, but by 1862 it had become a wagon repair shop. In 1866 the LNWR had 51 locomotives allocated to Coleham, so that the accommodation was becoming too cramped (the usual, familiar story). Eventually, the LNWR erected a new ten road straight shed in 1877 just to the south, as well as providing its own coaling stage and turntable. The new shed was built in the familiar Webb 'northlight' pattern, and was to retain its original roof until closure.

Meanwhile, the GWR soldiered on with the original five – road shed until 1883, when it constructed a roundhouse to the rear of this shed, roofed in the 'northlight' pattern and supported on iron lattice frames and columns. This shed abutted to the side of the 1877 LNWR straight shed. A new, standard GWR coaling stage was added in the yard also at this time. The two erstwhile GWR roads in the original shed were converted into a repair shop, and the original three LNWR roads became part of the GWR running shed, also giving access to the roundhouse. Further locomotive accommodation was provided by the GWR in 1932, when their former wagon repair shop was demolished. A new three-road shed of steel framing and corrugated sheeting was erected on the northern side of the original 1855 shed.

To summarise the position at nationalisation, BR inherited a very rambling arrangement that comprised three straight sheds totalling 19 roads (of which two were for locomotive repair shops), plus a roundhouse for which access could only be made through one of the straight sheds. No further modernisation was carried out, so it was in a particularly decrepit state by the time of its official closure on 6 November, 1967. The cleared site remained unused for many years, but has now been redeveloped for commercial purposes.

During LNWR days the shed was coded 30, which it retained until 1935 when it became 4A under the LMS. Together with the former GWR shed, it was assigned 84G under BR Western Region authority in 1950, and 89A on 1 January, 1961. From 9 September, 1963 it was returned to the LMR and recoded 6D, which it retained until closure to steam as from 5 March,

A fine view of the LNWR shed yard at Shrewsbury, some time shortly after 1903, with Webb Class "A" 3-cylinder compound 0-8-0 no.1843 taking centre stage. An unrecorded 'Jumbo' is behind it, and a 'Cauliflower' 0-6-0 stands in front of the far road of the northlight pattern shed. The later turntable was installed in the vacant plot above the 0-6-0s tender. Coal has been very neatly stacked, and whitewashed to prevent unauthorised use. [LNWR Society]

The interior of Shrewsbury LNWR shed in LMS days showing "Prince of Wales" Class 4-6-0 No. 25845 at its home shed. This was only one of the class to be built with outside Walschaerts valve gear (although four others were converted accordingly), which because its seemingly ungraceful action became known as 'Tishys' after a famous racehorse of the period which had a habit of crossing its legs. The wooden smoke hoods inside the shed appear to be in very good order, something that did not usually last for very long. [W.Potter]

This hipped roof portion of the GWR depot at Shrewsbury, known as "No.2 shed" was originally built in 1855 by the Shrewsbury and Hereford Railway. However, towards the end of steam, this shed seems to have become even more derelict than the LNWR shed. This view shows gaping holes in the hipped roof of the shed and increasing clutter as the shed staff struggle to service Collett "5101" Class 2-6-2T No.4147. [P. Ward]

An atmospheric view of the GWR coal stage around 1956, with two pannier tanks (the one on the left is Hawksworth "16XX" Class No.1642) in the former GWR shed yard. This general scene of decay and untidiness emphasises the difficulties of servicing steam locomotives at that time. [R. Mulford]

This view from 28 August 1949 shows almost all of Shrewsbury shed (sometimes known as 'Coleham'). On the extreme left is the GWR straight shed dating from around 1877, through which access was gained to their 1881 roundhouse situated behind. To the right of the GWR coal stage is the two-storey office block, then next, further back is the LNWR nine road straight shed. Finally, on the extreme right is the LNWR coaling stage. [B.Brooksbank]

It was not until the final years of steam that locomotives of both former companies, and B.R. regions, actually began to mix at Shrewsbury shed. On 25 August 1963, we see here "Castle" Class 4-6-0 No. 7032 DENBIGH CASTLE in the company of another "Castle", a B.R. Standard Class 4 4-6-0, a Stanier 'Black Five' and a "County" 4-6-0 all in the former LNWR shed yard. [P.Ward]

From the road overbridge south of Shrewsbury shed, the evening sunlight glints on the side of the LNWR building in 1963, with locomotives by Stanier and Ivatt visible. [P.Ward]

B.R. Standard Class 5 4-6-0 No.73095 is turned on the turntable at the side of the LNWR Shewsbury shed in 1963. Evidently the turntable pit drains had not been functioning too well. The Shrewsbury breakdown crane and attendant vehicles are stabled alongside the shed. [P.Ward]

1967. Diesel locomotives continued to be serviced here until June, 1970 and the whole site was cleared by 1975. Visiting locomotives along with the odd remaining Class "08" retained for shunting the yards were thereafter refuelled and given basic servicing, just south of the station, at the new area alongside the Wellington line that had been developed for the servicing of DMUs.

Whitchurch

As we have seen in Chapter 6, the OEWR line only initially reached Ellesmere in 1863, and that company had no locomotives or rolling stock. So the LNWR operated the line until it reached Oswestry in 1864, at which coincidental time the Cambrian (formed in July of that year) were expected to be in a position to take over. However, the situation regarding ownership of locomotives inherited by the new Cambrian Railways was far from clear, and it may be that the LNWR continued to operate

In its final years the LNWR coal stage (or 'coal hole') was an unlovely place. A Stanier 8F 2-8-0 is refuelled amongst the debris and desolation in 1963. [P.Ward]

at least some of the services to Oswestry for some time. Locomotive facilities were therefore required at Whitchurch, and whilst watering and coaling was provided in 1863, plans from that year reveal that no locomotive shed had been erected at that time. Certainly a single road shed to hold one locomotive had been completed by 1865, seemingly capable of holding just one locomotive, and presumably for the benefit of an LNWR locomotive used for marshalling exchange traffic to and from the OEWR line. This shed was located on the eastern side of the station, alongside a water tank mounted above a large brick built "engine house", that had served to pump water from a nearby brook to the tank, which also supplied water columns at the platform ends.

By the early 1870s there were three LNWR locomotives stationed here, as the Tattenhall branch had opened in 1872 for which services further engines were then based at Whitchurch. Although Cambrian locomotives (and their GWR successors) visited for servicing, none were ever based here. In fact, even their overnight presence was actively discouraged, although it frequently became necessary. Consequently, Cambrian engines in particular spent much of their time running light to and from Oswestry shed as the result of unbalanced workings.

Towards the end of the 1870s, the desire to improve the layout of the up loops and sidings was incorporated with the need

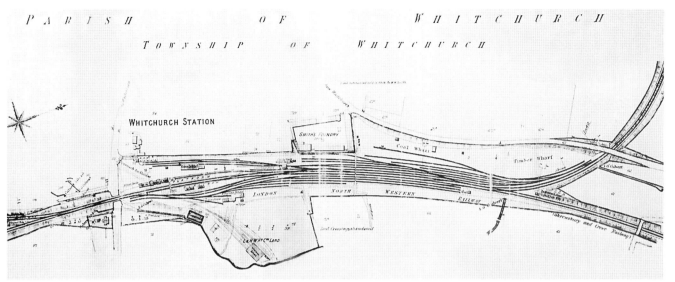

L.N.W.A. plan of proposed changes at Whitchurch dated 1883, showing existing locomotive shed and planned new shed. [Whitchurch Library]

to improve locomotive accommodation. As a result a field and a brook northeast of the station and belonging to one, Henry Williams was acquired in 1879 by the LNWR. Eventually, a four road shed of the standard Webb pattern was authorised, and constructed in 1883. The design featured red brick walls, a 'northlight' pattern of transverse ridged wooden roof and individual smoke vents for each road. Offices, stores and a small workshop ran along the back of the building, which was almost uniquely situated in a delightfully rural setting, with open fields on three sides. The shed was located further east than the original, and at almost 90 degrees to the island platform, thus giving waiting passengers good (and on occasions, possibly tantalising) views of its interior. A sizeable reservoir to the south of the shed was fed from the brook running nearby and pumped to the original water tank, which was retained. This was necessary because back in 1858 a trial borehole had found that water from the local water table contained brine, unacceptable for locomotive use. Coaling of locomotives remained primitive during the life of the shed, being directly from wagons parked on a slightly raised siding on the north side of the shed yard. Meanwhile the original single road shed had been demolished.

Although the Board of Trade recommendations at the opening of the OEWR Ellesmere line in 1863 required the installation of a turntable, no such equipment is recorded on plans for that year. However, by 1865 a 42 foot turntable was in position, adjacent to the original single road shed. However, this was replaced by a 60 foot turntable in LMS days, sited slightly further to the east.

Whitchurch was always a sub-shed of Crewe North, in LNWR days being given the code of 15W, which their locomotives carried on a small white plate with black lettering attached to the rearward facing edge of the cab roof in typical LNWR fashion. Crewe North was designated as the District Depot with the code of "15", whilst Crewe South was "15B". LMS policy dictated that the shed lost its permanent allocation, its status as a subshed of Crewe North meaning that locomotives from there were simply 'out-stationed' there. However, in practical terms Whitchurch still retained an unofficial allocation, which continued into BR days. The BR shed code for Crewe North became 5A, under which Whitchurch remained as a sub-shed.

Dean GWR "Duke" or "3252" Class 4-4-0 no. 3277 ISLE OF TRESCOWE alongside the water tower in Whitchurch shed yard in the 1930s. The original single road locomotive shed, dating from around 1862 was positioned on the line that the engine is occupying, slightly to the left of it. [J.M. Bentley Collection]

Whitchurch shed in 1936 with some of the regular occupants at that time . From the left ; aFowler 2P 4-4-0, a Stanier 'Black Five', a Bowen-Cooke "George the Fifth" 4-4-0, and Fowler Compound 4-4-0 No. 1136. [S.V. Blencowe Collection]

Another example of the muscle required to turn a locomotive, as "Dukedog" 4-4-0 No. 9027 is moved on Whitchurch's 60 foot turntable on 2 September, 1950. [J.F.Ward / J. Maden Collection]

On 6 December, 1953 Whitchurch shed played host to Stanier class 4 2-6-4T No. 42566, Fairburn Class 4 2-6-4T No.42263, and Hawksworth "Manor" 4-6-0 No. 7820 DINMORE MANOR. The neat four road shed was rather short, as evidenced by the interior rear wall being clearly visible. [Kidderminster Railway Museum]

Apart from one wagon, the shed at Whitchurch is deserted as "Dukedog" No. 9020 moves on to the turntable in the yard in 1953, some 70 years after the construction of the shed. [Whitchurch Archaeological & Historical Group]

In April 1958, Collett "43XX" Class 2-6-0 No.6358 has evidently arrived on the Cambrian line, and needed turning before working back in the Oswestry direction. However, the 60 foot turntable was only manually operated, as can be seen from the efforts being made by the locomotive crew. [Kidderminster Railway Museum]

In LNWR days enginemen based here were booked to work several through goods trains between Birkenhead and Stafford via Crewe, but such workings ceased soon after the Grouping of 1923. Thereafter, the shed provided crews mostly for the local passenger services, but they were also required to sign for the roads from Crewe to Chester, Whitchurch to Oswestry (normally the responsibility of Oswestry crews), and Shrewsbury to Stafford via Wellington. In 1951 there were seven enginemen's turns from Monday to Friday with eight on Saturdays, but no regular work for Sundays. But crews from both Crewe North and Crewe South also signed the road to Shrewsbury and regularly appeared on duties over the line.

The shed closed in September, 1957 with the withdrawal of passenger services on the Tattenhall branch, but remained in an operational condition. This was because the "Trial Runs" from Crewe Works were still a regular feature, and apart from these locomotives needing to use the turntable, there was still a need for covered accommodation should any of the locomotives involved need the attention of a fitter. Of course, locomotives from the Cambrian lines also still used the turntable, and occasionally the shelter of the shed for servicing, but no staff were employed thereafter. Subsequently, various locomotives were occasionally stored or 'garaged' here, as described in Chapter 5, plus the English Electric gas turbine locomotive, already mentioned in Chapter 8.

Eventually however, the shed building and water tower were demolished – probably around 1965. The site has since returned to nature with a large copse now occupying it. The turntable was taken out, and has since found a new use at the Severn Valley Railway.

Crewe Gresty Lane

This two road shed was sited in a hollow on the north side of the down Shrewsbury line, adjacent to Gresty Brook. Consequently, the shed did not receive a great deal of direct sunshine, and with its proximity to the brook, was frequently a damp and rather unpleasant place. It was actually owned by the LNWR and leased to the GWR, but was of a very clear GWR design. It was of a brick construction with a slated roof and individual roof ventilators, and is believed to have been erected around 1870, to hold four engines. Presumably, GWR locos visiting from Wellington prior to this time were serviced at Crewe North shed (which in fact was the only shed in Crewe at that time). No reason has been established why the LNWR would wish to own this shed, as it certainly never made use of it. The only possible reason is that, as the GWR were only in Crewe by virtue of running powers over the LNWR, they did not wish the GWR to feel too much "right" to be there.

Notwithstanding the logic of their action, the LNWR shared the cost of an enlargement in 1899 with the GWR. This entailed doubling the amount of engine accommodation to eight locomotives, by extending the length of the building to the rear, such that the final dimensions of the shed were 220 feet by 30 feet, with offices measuring 60 feet by 10 feet. A single line ran from the down running line, after serving the sidings of the North Western Corn Mills, and divided in front of the shed. Ash pits were placed on both shed roads, and a typical GWR "parachute" type combined water tank and column was positioned alongside the southernmost track, adjacent to a small coaling stage, which involved manual coaling of locomotives.

No turntable was ever provided. Although Crewe South shed did not open until 1897, a turntable was available there beforehand, so locomotives could use that, or travel to Crewe North for turning. Indeed, this practice continued even after 1897, for passenger tender locomotives that had run into the through platforms at Crewe station. Generally, the tender locomotives arriving at Crewe from the GWR Market Drayton line were working on freight turns, and did not always use the turntable at Crewe South, instead using the triangle arranged as part of the reorganised running lines in the area between Salop Goods Junction and Basford Hall yard.

The allocation varied from a maximum of seven in the 1930s to two just before absorption as a subshed. During 1921 the

Collett 5101 class 2-6-2T no. 4120 standing at the entrance of the two-road shed at Gresty Lane, as viewed from the embankment carrying the Shrewsbury line. The front part of the shed appears to be in terminal decline at this time. [J. Maden Collection]

only locomotives allocated here were Gooch double framed "131" class 0-6-0 no. 312 and Armstrong "360" class 0-6-0 no.366 – both considerable veterans at that time. From the 1930s onwards the allocation generally consisted of two of Collett's "5101" class 2-6-2T and one of the ubiquitous "57XX" class 0-6-0PT, although some of the 4-4-0 classes still lingered. Into the BR days, the use of GWR types continued. The allocation had consisted of one pannier tank (for shunting duties) and one Prairie tank (for the local passenger turns). The pannier tank was then changed every two weeks when it went to Wellington for its washout, and the Prairie tank alternated every day. But following the shed's transfer to the LMR in 1953, these were gradually replaced on passenger duties by the Ivatt Class 2 2-6-2Ts from Crewe North's allocation.

Locomotive crews based here worked the passenger turns to Wellington, but they also worked further afield on freight turns which obviously involved a variety of locomotives from other sheds. Such work took them regularly to Oxley Sidings, Wolverhampton and prior to nationalisation as far as Banbury and Oxford.

The shed was listed as GWR shed number 74, and although a sub-shed of Wellington was coded independently as CEW, retaining this coding after nationalisation until 10 February, 1950 when it officially lost its own allocation of locomotives, which had in any case dwindled by then. In July, 1951 the shed was placed into the London Midland Region of BR for administrative purposes, and from 19 April 1953 the shed became part of the Crewe Motive Power District, and was officially classed as a sub-shed to Crewe North, but for the most part there was little change to the workings. The one effect was that shunting of the former GWR Gresty Lane sidings became an LMR duty for Crewe South shed, and was generally performed by one of their diesel shunters. The shed was officially closed on 17 June, 1963 but for some time prior to this date, visiting locomotives had increasingly gone to Crewe South for servicing, and the shed building had become rather dilapidated by this time. It remained empty for some time, but was demolished by 1990, and the site is now covered by industrial development.

Crewe Gresty Lane shed on 29 May 1960, with Ivatt 2-6-2T no. 41231 being watered. An unidentified GWR 4-6-0 stands in the adjacent shed road. The cramped nature of the site is apparent, with the embankment to the left and Gresty Brook to the right. [R.S.Carpenter Collection]

CHAPTER ELEVEN

MODERN TIMES

In this chapter the services and structures for the period from 1966 to the present will be examined.

Passenger services

In Chapter 3 we left the line in 1966, with diesel locomotives having almost entirely replaced steam as the means of traction, as locomotives on the "North & West" services, and DMUs on the local stopping trains. At that time there was a fairly generous level of service for both the through expresses and the stopping trains, as follows :

		Mon	Tues	Wed	Thurs	Fri	Sat	Sun
Through express workings :								
1966 Summer	Up	7	7	7	7	10	18	7
	Down	10	11	11	11	11	22	7
Local services:								
1966 Summer	Up	7	7	7	7	6	6	0
	Down	10	10	10	10	9	9	0

Into the 1970s a change was made in the way services were operated, with many of the former through trains then making stops along the line, notably at Nantwich, Whitchurch and Wem. Although local stopping services still called at all intermediate stations, the distinction between through expresses and local trains started to become blurred. For example, the up expresses in 1973/74 totalled 4 Saturdays excepted, 5 on Saturdays, and none on Sundays. But the local services totalled 8 for Monday – Saturday, although 4 of these were Crewe – Cardiff through trains; Sundays saw two locals, both Crewe – Cardiff, although one of these stopped at Whitchurch only. It is notable that by this time, the through trains to destinations in the South West, such as Bristol, Plymouth and Penzance, had been withdrawn from this route, being instead concentrated on the former MR route north of Bristol. In the down direction there was just one express Saturdays excepted, three on Saturdays and one on Sunday; the stopping weekday services were 11, with four working Cardiff – Crewe and one the Shrewsbury – York mail train. Sundays saw two locals, both of which were Cardiff – Crewe and both stopped only at Whitchurch. Most of the intermediate stations had been downgraded to unstaffed stations by this time, and today Yorton, Prees and Wrenbury are designated as "request stops". This situation is summarised below, together with the following periods, and not making any distinction between express and stopping services :

		Monday - Friday	Saturday	Sunday
May 1973 –				
May 1974	Up	12	13	2
	Down	12	14	3
September 1992 –				
May 1993	Up	25	24	5
	Down	22	21	5
December 2013 –				
May 2014	Up	28	25	13
	Down	28	26	14

It will be seen that the level of service increased measurably from the 1970s to the 1990s, which can be attributed to the decision to route more through trains to different destinations in South Wales. These still mostly originated initially at Crewe, but were eventually almost all extended to Manchester (Piccadilly), with some also running from Chester and / or Holyhead.

Those services heading south of Shrewsbury for Pembroke Dock, Milford Haven, Carmarthen Llanelli and Tenby went forward via Hereford, Newport and Cardiff. All intermediate stations on our line are now unstaffed, but the scheduled 'stopping services' still make mandatory stops at Wem, Whitchurch and Nantwich : Yorton, Prees and Wrenbury are 'request stops'.

An immaculately turned out Brush Class 47 (identity unfortunately not recorded) passes through Wem station in 1972 with a down express. The waiting room on this platform appears to only recently been opened. [Shropshire Railway Society]

For a while in the 1970s the Manchester – Cardiff services were the province of the useful Sulzer Class 25 Bo-Bo diesel locomotives. Here No.25056 passes the closed Hadnall station in June 1978 with such a service. [G. Cryer]

The down platform at Wem on 2 April 1976 as seen from a southbound train. A "Peak" diesel locomotive is occupying the down line just beyond the level crossing, probably at the rear of a permanent way train. The modern, brick built waiting room on that platform was still in use for that purpose– before the attention of vandals, but otherwise the station looks rather neglected, especially as the station car park has been taken over by Isherwood's timber merchants for storage purposes. The grain dryers, prominent in the background, have now long gone. [Author's Collection]

At Wem, an unidentified 'Sulzer' Class Bo-Bo passes through the station with a Cardiff to Manchester express in the late 1970s. The new 'bus shelter' waiting room on the up platform can be seen on the left. [M.H.C. Baker]

A Metropolitan Cammell 2-car diesel multiple unit pulls into Prees station with an up train around 1982. The crossing gates have been replaced by lifting barriers , whilst the original booking and station offices on the up platform have been demolished, and were later replaced by an extension to the former station master's house that reached to the rear of the platform. [Shropshire Railway Society]

A solitary passenger awaits the arrival of Arriva Trains Wales DMU No. 150259 with the 11.20 Crewe – Shrewsbury on 26 May 2012 at the now rather featureless Prees station. [Author]

A single car Arriva Class 153 No. 153327 pulls into Wem station on 20 June 2012 with the 11.20 Crewe – Shrewsbury service. These single cars are used on stopping services during off-peak times. A colour light signal has been adopted for the down starter, whilst the up signal protecting the level crossing remained as a semaphore at this time. [Author]

Another view of a North and West service on the reverse curves south of Yorton in July, 1989 headed by a Class 37 Co-Co diesel. Eventually, these four-car locomotive hauled services were replaced by the new generation of diesel multiple units. [M.H.C. Baker]

An impressive view in July, 1989 as an English Electric Class 37 Co-Co heads the four carriage 1715 Liverpool Lime Street to Cardiff near to Yorton. [M.H.C. Baker]

Nantwich station on 27 July 2012, with Arriva Trains Wales Class 150 No. 150236 forming the 11.30 Manchester Piccadilly – Carmarthen service. These units were used on the bulk of the services over the lines to Wales. [Author]

The long shadows of an autumn afternoon are cast across the track as Brush Co-Co No.47500 runs through Wrenbury station with chartered special from returning from Shrewsbury to Skegness on 6 October 2012. Sister engine No. 47760 was attached at the rear. This working should have been steam hauled form Crewe, but due to the unavailability of any steam locomotives, the diesel traction was substituted. [Author]

The change in style of services offered has resulted from the almost exclusive use of DMUs, Back in 1966 all of the through services were locomotive hauled, earlier often by the WR diesel hydraulics of both "Warship" (on West Country trains) and "Western" (on South Wales trains) classes. At first the diesels were changed at Shrewsbury for steam haulage to Crewe in the dying days of that era. As electrification was completed there, it was clear that rather than have to change again to electric haulage at Crewe, it was more efficient to change just once. So the diesel hydraulics worked through from Cardiff into Crewe. An example was no. D1049 WESTERN MONARCH that arrived in Crewe on 27 March, 1966 with the 11.50am Plymouth to Manchester, and returned southwards on a troop train around 5.00pm. At the same time, the English Electric Type 4s (Class 40) also often appeared, as did the occasional "Peak" 1-Co-Co-1 (Classes 45 and 46). Less frequently, the 'Hymek' diesel hydraulic locos turned up on these workings. For example, no. D7088 turned up at Crewe on the 8.45am Cardiff to Manchester on 22 January 1966, returning on the 12.55pm Manchester to Plymouth. Eventually, these locomotives were superseded by the almost ubiquitous Brush Class 47s on these trains, although some still managed to appear into the 1980s. However, as we have seen the services were reduced somewhat during the 1970s, and most of the Cardiff services were worked by 3-car DMUs, albeit allegedly with buffet facilities. However, these did not last long, and the service reverted to locomotive hauled trains,although "Inter City" DMUs, displaced from elsewhere were tried. At first, the familiar, but rather aging and underpowered Class 25s were used, but eventually the SR released the 'Crompton' Class 33 locomotives, made redundant with the complete electrification of the Kent and Bournemouth routes. These became well known on this route, to the extent that they achieved something of a 'cult' status. Subsequently, the Class 158s were introduced on the through services, since mostly replaced by the excellent Class 175 "Coradia" units. However, one locomotive hauled service remained until 15 September 2012. This was the "Gerallt Gymro" (locally known as "The Wag"), which ran as the 05.33 from Holyhead via Chester, Crewe and Shrewsbury to Cardiff and 05.10 return unbalanced working, and was regularly hauled by a Class 67. In order to save an annual subsidy of around £ ½ million this service has been rerouted from Chester via Wrexham to Shrewsbury.

In the meantime, the stopping services had been the province of those DMU classes first introduced in 1958 (Class 101 and the many derivatives), but by this time becoming rather tired. During the second half of the1980s the Class 150 'Sprinters' were introduced and achieved immediate success, giving a much smoother ride and being quicker on acceleration and top speed. The single car Class 153 'Sprinters' are often used on non peak time services, often in combination with diagrams taking them separately southwards from Shrewsbury over the Central Wales line.

Locomotive hauled trains continue to appear, although mostly on special workings such as excursions. These have tended to rely on the ubiquitous Class 47s, although other types have made appearances such as Classes 20, 37, 57,and 67. Steam specials also traverse the line from time to time, as Shrewsbury is a popular destination, albeit mostly from the south. Nevertheless, some specials from northern origins make use of the line, usually attaching the steam loco at Crewe and travelling outward via Chester to Shrewsbury, returning via Whitchurch. A selection of these is given in the attached illustrations.

An unusual excursion started from Whitchurch on 16 June, 2012 when Class 20 Bo-Bo nos. 20309 and 20312 were used. It picked up passengers at Wem, Shrewsbury, Wellington, Telford Central, Codsall, Wolverhampton, Tame Bridge Parkway, Birmingham International and Coventry on its way to Canterbury.

Concluding this section, it is interesting to note that in 1867 the time for stopping passenger trains between Crewe and Shrewsbury was around 1½ hours and for expresses around one hour. The comparable journey times today are around half of that : 50 minutes for stopping trains and 30 minutes for expresses. Even more recently, in the early 1970s the service between Manchester and Cardiff took around 4 ½ hours, which compares with 3 hours 10 minutes today.

Freight workings

Comparing 1966/67 to where we left off in 1965/67, there was a notable increase in freight traffic, with about double the number of up workings and a 50% rise in the number of down workings. It is believed that at least some of this can be attributed to BR having realised that much of this traffic could be routed away from the increasingly congested former MR route to the Midlands and the North, on to this rather under utilised route, with its generally more favourable gradients.

A comparison of workings over the next four decades follows :

	Mon	Tues	Wed	Thurs	Fri	Sat	Sun
October 1966 – March 1967							
Up	10	14	15	15	14	16	3
Down	13	18	18	18	18	18	2
May 1970 – October 1970							
Up	10	13	12	12	13	9	1
Down	11	16	18	21	15	17	2
May 1994 – September 1994							
Up	7	6	6	5	7	1	1
Down	6	8	7	9	8	2	2
December 2012 – May 2013							
Up	7	17	17	17	12	4	3
Down	5	12	12	12	9	10	2

In 1966/67, Nantwich was still served by a single SO working from Crewe Basford Hall at 06.56 that worked to Whitchurch arriving at 08.35. This returned at 10.25 calling at Nantwich briefly from 10.56 to 11.09 on its way. This timetable also marked the final time the water cans were collected and delivered to the crossing keeper at Heath Lane. They were collected by the daily 06.40 Coleham to Whitchurch pick up goods (arrive 11.35), which continued on to Crewe at 13.14. As no return working was scheduled, it is presumed that water cans were actually exchanged at Heath Lane, rather than collected by one train and deposited by another as previously. The two local freight workings represented the only workings to visit the intermediate stations at this time, other than through goods workings that spent time in Whitchurch.

The major change over these years has been the complete elimination of 'wagon load' workings and its replacement by 'block' workings, especially those sponsored by individual companies. Many of these workings are run on specific days only, and so there is less of a general daily pattern of freight workings. Also many more are run on an 'as required' basis, in order to fit in with the requirements for production materials of the companies involved. So it is encouraging to see that the overall level of traffic has been maintained.

The origins and destinations for freight workings has changed considerably, but the main traffic still consists of steel from South Wales, imported coal from the Bristol docks and general merchandise from anywhere in the country to the docks of Bristol and South Wales, or vice versa. Then the corresponding empties have to be worked in the opposite direction.

Company block trains include bulk cement, minerals, oil products, car components and complete vehicles.

The diesel locomotives involved in these workings have been extremely varied over the years, starting with some of the earliest of the "Modernisation Plan" classes such as the Classes 20, 24 and 25 Bo-Bos, and the Class 40 Co-Cos. Inevitably, the Brush Class 47s took over many of the duties, and were supplemented by the English Electric Class 37. Making frequent subsequent appearances were the Romanian, Crewe and Doncaster built Class 56, the Doncaster built Class 58, the Mirlees Class 60, and today almost universally the General Motors Class 66, and their successors the Class 70.

Accidents on the entire line were relatively rare, and some are mentioned in other chapters. Here, it is appropriate to briefly mention a more recent occurrence, which happened on Saturday 7 July, 2012. The 16th wagon of a northbound coal train, travelling at just 14 mph, was derailed at Crewe Junction, Shrewsbury at 4.13pm causing slight damage to that wagon, as well as damage to the pointwork, crossings and plain track. There was disruption to passenger services, with trains from Crewe being terminated at Wem, and buses substituted between there and Shrewsbury. The line was reopened within 24 hours.

A new signalling system, to be operated from the Wales Railway Operating Centre in Cardiff was due to open in November, 2012. This work was carried out under a £22 million contract awarded to the contractor Invensys. In fact, testing of the operation of the level crossings en route did not take place until late November that year. Technical problems further delayed the implementation of the new system, which was finally commissioned over the weekend of 12 to 14 October, 2013. The effect was that all of the intermediate signal boxes between Shrewsbury Crewe Junction and Crewe Gresty Lane (exclusive) were closed from that date. Somewhat surprisingly the manual box at Crewe Gresty Lane is expected to continue in operation until 2019, whilst those around Shrewsbury will survive until 2050 ! The new system also provides for bidirectional running on both lines between Wem and Nantwich, where there are appropriate crossovers. The remaining semaphore signals have now been replaced by colour light signals, and notably the gantry at the north end of Shrewsbury station, which featured in many photographs over the years, now has only one semaphore signal. Interestingly, the local residents in Wem have expressed a desire to retain the box adjacent to the level crossing, to be used for some sort of community function.

Significant passenger levels along with this latest investment therefore indicate that the line has a bright and permanent future.

English Electric Type 4 (later Class 50) Co-Co diesel electric No. D416 rattles haul of wooden bodied mineral wagons through Nantwich station on 25 May 1969. The locomotive is displaying reporting code 8Z91, indicating that this was a special working. The down waiting room was still extant, although it had lost its ornate glass canopy. [Kidderminster Railway Museum]

General Electric Co-Co no. 66846 wearing Colas livery speeds through Yorton station on 26 May 2012 with the 6F52, 13.15 Donnington RFT to Arpley Sidings working. The steps for passengers to board or alight here, due to the low platform height, are still in use here. [Author]

General Electric Co-Co No. 66606 runs through Nantwich station powering the 4V22, 09.30 Fiddlers Ferry Power Station – Stoke Gifford coal empties on 27 July, 2012. The efforts to enliven the station with flower beds and hanging baskets really pays off. [Author]

Modern main line steam workings

The line has proved to be useful for many main line steam tours visiting or passing through Shrewsbury. The following is a small selection of those from recent years.

Gresley "A4" Pacific" No. 60007 SIR NIGEL GRESLEY in B.R. blue lined livery, runs out of Whitchurch southbound with its support coach on 5 April 1997. This was due to have hauled the "Blue Venturer" railtour from Carnforth to the Mid-Hants railway, but that was cancelled, so the Pacific ran in the programmed path as a light engine move instead. [Author]

Stanier Class 5 4-6-0 No.45110 approaches Wem with the northbound "Yuletide Chuffer" on 19 December 1998, which it hauled from Bescot via Wolverhampton and Shrewsbury to Crewe and Chester. It returned via Wrexham to Shrewsbury and Bescot. [Author]

Bulleid "Battle of Britain" Light Pacific no. 34067 TANGMERE has just passed beneath the A49 Whitchurch by-pass on its way north with the "Great Britain II" railtour that it hauled from Bristol to Preston on 8 April 2009. [Author]

Whitchurch station on 4 September 2011, as Stanier Class 5 4-6-0 No.44932 passes through with the "Lune Rivers Special" that it worked from Carnforth to Shrewsbury and return. [Author]

A Last Look Along the Line

The fine architectural values of Shrewsbury station can also be appreciated from within the station, as this view illustrates. The Gothic structure is surmounted by an impressive array of ornamental chimneys, surviving today. On the right, an Arriva single car unit, no. 153212, is preparing to leave platform 4B with the 14.42 stopping service to Crewe on 25 November 2013. [Author]

At Hadnall, two Class 158 DMUs pass the remaining station buildings on 3 September, 2012 whilst forming a late running 0705 Milford Haven – Manchester Picccadilly. These buildings had been used as offices for many years. [Author]

The immaculately maintained substantial down side waiting room at Yorton on 26 May 2012. Due to the low platform height, steps are necessary for any passengers joining or alighting at this 'request stop' station. [Author]

The up side station building now forms part of a private residence at Yorton, and is a credit to the owners. In this view of 26 May 2012, the facilities for waiting passengers can be seen to consist of the usual 'bus stop' shelter. [Author]

A view at Wem on 26 May 2012, where as following misuse by the general public, the brick built waiting room had been converted into a store room and staff quarters. A new 'bus stop' shelter had been erected, in an effort to quell the activities of the local vandals, and passenger information screens installed. At this time the signal box still controlled the busy level crossing at the north end of the station. [Author]

Prees station looking south on 26 May 2012 looking south, showing the rather spartan passenger facilities, and the manual signal box, then still in use. [Author]

The level crossing and former Prees station building on 26 May 2012. The latter is now an attractive private residence, with a gabled ended extension replacing the original flat roofed booking office and waiting room [Author]

A southbound local service formed by two-car DMU No.150260 calls at Whitchurch on 4 September 2011 and attracts a good number of passengers. Passenger waiting facilities consist of the usual steel and glass shelters, and to the right of Platform 1 is the outer edge of this once island platform, now fenced off. Although refurbished the foot bridge is still the original. [Author]

On 11 August, 2013 Arriva Trains Wales "Coradia" 3-car unit no. 175113 calls at Whitchurch with the 13.48 Cardiff Central – Manchester Piccadilly. The truncated remains of the 1960s rebuilt downside platform canopy are still in evidence, as is the wall forming the western boundary of the erstwhile Tattenhall branch bay platform. Just two months earlier the original footbridge was removed, and the replacement shown here was installed, slightly further south. This entailed a small extension of the up platform, and repositioning of the waiting shelter on the down platform. However, whilst the new footbridge incorporates wider stairs, there is still no provision for disabled persons or passengers with child wheelchairs to cross the line. [Author]

On 4 September 2011, the station at Wrenbury looked quite smarter, although the 'bus stop' shelters represent only the basic comfort for waiting passengers. The former station buildings alongside the up platform are in use as a private residence. [Author]

The down platform at Nantwich on 27 July 2012, showing its reuse as an Indian restaurant, and painted a most unattractive all over matt black. Fortunately, the floral display on this platform relieves the dullness of the paint scheme. [Author]

Willaston station building and level crossing on 27 July 2012. The former station building and waiting room on the down side are now a private residence, while nothing remains of the up side platform structures. The signal box has also been removed, control of the crossing over Wybunbury Road now being performed by the Crewe Signalling Centre. [Author]

CHRONOLOGICAL LIST OF IMPORTANT EVENTS

1848 Shrewsbury & Chester Railway opened to Shrewsbury (16 October)
1849 Shropshire Union Railway opened to Shrewsbury (1 June)
1852 Shrewsbury & Hereford Railway opened for goods to Shrewsbury (30 July)
1853 LNWR (Crewe & Shrewsbury Extension) Act authorised line (20 August) Shrewsbury & Hereford Railway
opened for passengers to Shrewsbury (6 December)
1855 LNWR / GWR joint locomotive shed opened at Coleham, Shrewsbury
1856 LNWR Act passed, extending time for construction of line (21 July) Brassey awarded contract for construction of line (7 August)
1857 Plans for goods avoidance line at Shrewsbury deposited (30 November)
1858 Colonel Yolland inspected line for Board of Trade (17 August) Line opened to passengers & goods (1 September)
1861 Conversion of line to double track commenced (completed 1862)
OEWR Act authorised construction of Oswestry – Whitchurch railway (1 August)
1863 Whitchurch single road locomotive shed opened OEWR opened from Ellesmere to Whitchurch (4 May)
Nantwich & Market Drayton Railway opened (19 October)
1864 Cambrian Railways formed (25 July) OEWR opened from Oswestry to Ellesmere (27 July)
Remodelling of Whitchurch station completed
1865 Plans deposited for Tattenhall branch (30 November) Second face on Whitchurch island platform installed
1866 LNWR (New Lines) Act authorised Tattenhall branch (16 July)
1867 Doubling of NMDR completed (July) Wellington – Market Drayton line opened (16 October)
1869 LNWR (New Works & Additional Powers) Act extends time for Tattenhall branch (12 July)
1870 Crewe Gresty Lane locomotive shed opened
1872 Colonel Rich inspected Tattenhall branch for Board of Trade (21 September) Tattenhall branch opened (1 October)
1877 New LNWR locomotive shed opened at Coleham, Shrewsbury
1883 New Whitchurch locomotive shed opened
1886 Severn Tunnel opened (1 December)
1888 Crewe – Bristol expresses commenced (1 July)
1891 York – Shrewsbury TPO introduced
1899 Crewe Gresty Lane locomotive shed enlarged
1902 Shrewsbury station and track remodelling completed
1907 Major accident at Crewe Junction Shrewsbury (15 October)
1911 Nantwich Newcastle Crossing and Gresty halts opened (1 January)
1915 Alley & MacLellan open Sentinel Works, Shrewsbury
1916 Heath Lane sidings & line to Prees Heath military camp installed
1918 Nantwich Newcastle Crossing and Gresty halts closed (1 April)
1922 Cambrian Railways absorbed into GWR (25 March)
1923 LNWR absorbed into the new LMSR (1 January)
1924 Shrewsbury station northern overall roof replaced by canopies
1928 New No.1 signal box, and up and down yards at Gresty Lane opened
1938 Grindley Brook Halt opened (4 July)
1942 Aston Park signal box (Wem) and Army depot opened *(approximate)*
1948 LMSR nationalised, BR formed (1 January)
1954 Willaston closed to passengers (6 December)
1957 Tattenhall branch passenger services withdrawn (16 September)
Whitchurch locomotive shed closed (September)
1958 Diesel multiple units introduced for stopping trains, Crewe to Shrewsbury Willaston new signal box opened (10 December)
1960 Hadnall closed to passengers (2 May)
1962 "Pines Express" routed from Crewe to Nantwich and Wellington (10 September)
1963 Crewe Gresty Lane locomotive shed closed (17 June) "Pines Express" routed from Crewe to Shrewsbury (9 September)
Nantwich – Wellington line closed to passengers (9 September) Tattenhall branch closed completely (4 November)
Shrewsbury station remaining overall roof removed
1964 Yorton goods facilites withdrawn (6 April) Wrenbury goods facilities withdrawn (6 July) Hadnall and Willaston goods facilities
withdrawn (2 November)
1965 Oswestry – Whitchurch passenger services withdrawn (18 January) Ellesmere – Whitchurch goods services withdrawn (27 March)
Marley Green Crossing ground frame removed (21 November)
1966 Yorton station designated unstaffed (15 August) Wem, Prees and Wrenbury stations designated unstaffed (19 September)
1967 "Pines Express" route transferred away from Crewe – Shrewsbury line Aston Park signal box moved to Nantwich Station
New Nantwich Station box also replaces Shrewbridge and Newcastle Road Crossings signal boxes Market Drayton Junction signal
box, Nantwich, destroyed by fire (17 January) Nantwich – Wellington line closed completely (8 May) Market Drayton Junction
signal box, Nantwich, closed (23 July) Shrewsbury locomotive shed closed to steam (9 September)
1968 Prees goods facilities withdrawn (6 October)
1969 Whitchurch Chester Junction signal box closed (15 June)
1970 Shrewsbury locomotive shed closed completely (June) Whitchurch station designated unstaffed (17 August)
1971 Tilley Road Crossing ground frame and signals removed (17 January) Wem goods facilities withdrawn (5 April)
1972 Nantwich goods facilities withdrawn (4 September)
1973 Yorton signal box closed (15 April)
1976 Whitchurch goods facilities withdrawn (1 November) Shrewsbury station trackwork rationalised
1984 Willaston, and Gresty Lane No 2 signal boxes closed, No 1 box renamed "Gresty" (28 October)
1998 Sentinel Works, Shrewsbury closed
2013 Intermediate signal boxes closed (12/13 October), level crossings controlled from
Wales Railway Operating Centre, Cardiff

INDEX